THE MODE IN
Hats and
Headdress

A Historical Survey with 198 Plates

R. TURNER WILCOX

DOVER PUBLICATIONS, INC.
Mineola, New York

Bibliographical Note

This Dover edition, first published in 2008, is a republication of the 1959 revised and updated edition of *The Mode in Hats and Headdress including Hair Styles, Cosmetics, and Jewelry,* first published by Charles Scribner's Sons, New York, in 1945.

DOVER *Pictorial Archive* SERIES

Library of Congress Cataloging-in-Publication Data

Wilcox, R. Turner (Ruth Turner), 1888–
    The mode in hats and headdress : a historical survey with 190 plates / R. Turner Wilcox.
        p. cm.
    "This Dover edition, first published in 2008, is a republication of The Mode in Hats and Headdress Including Hair Styles, Cosmetics, and Jewelry, first published by Charles Scribner's Sons, New York, in 1945"—T.p. verso.
    ISBN-13: 978-0-486-46762-7
    ISBN-10: 0-486-46762-7
    1. Hats. 2. Hats—Pictorial works. I. Title.

GT2110.W55 2008
391.4'3—dc22

2008020645

Manufactured in the United States by LSC Communications
46762706   2020
www.doverpublications.com

To
RAY WILCOX
AND
RUTH WILCOX

FOREWORD

AFTER THE PUBLICATION and gratifying reception accorded *The Mode in Costume*, I decided to bring to all those who may be further interested, a close-up, as it were, of headdress and hair arrangement practiced since earliest times. *The Mode in Hats and Headdress* is the result of this decision.

There is no doubt that hair arrangement and head ornament in fulfilling the desire for personal adornment antedates the wearing of clothing. No part of costume is so universally important as the headdress, which is worn even when body garments are dispensed with, as the appearance of the aborigines abundantly proves. Coiffure and headtire in both sexes have from prehistoric times served to establish the individual's rank or position in society, to impress the lowly and to challenge the enemy.

Today, when fashion is available to all classes, the choice of attire betrays not only the person's pecuniary and social status but the temperament, taste and even the emotions of the wearer.

Mode, like history, repeats itself in a never-ending cycle. As the wheel of fashion turns, we have simplicity, ornamentation, over-elaboration, the fantastic and then around again to simplicity. The recurrence, however, of each distinct style is influenced and colored by a new period and environment and this fact contributes not only to its freshness and novelty but often to its charm.

For a century and a half the male with his cropped head and simple hat has held rigidly to a scheme of utter simplicity. Periodically, the basic unadorned hat, except for sports, is adopted by women but never for long. From the modish angle, a woman's hat and hairdo must be regarded as purely an ornamental aid in enhancing her allure. And since the differences in the body structure are the first and principal attractions between the sexes, it cannot be denied that a change in the feminine head contour becomes an added difference and contributes greatly to that end.

It has been my aim to record for the artist, the hairdresser, the hatmaker, the stage designer, the teacher and the student, all the available head designs of history. And so it is that if this work proves a valuable source and a practical assistance to the professional and student alike, I shall feel amply repaid for the study and not inconsiderable effort expended in its preparation.

Bringing *The Mode in Hats and Headdress* up to date has been a pleasurable task in view of the interesting new developments arriving in the years it covers. I am sure the student will find the additions both informing and valuable.

R. T. W.

Tenafly, New Jersey
June 1959

CONTENTS

CONTENTS

CHAPTER TEN

THE SEVENTEENTH CENTURY   108

Cavalier costume · dress in American Colonies · lovelock · mustache, a curl ·
cadenette · single pearl earring · rules at Harvard · the Van Dyck · mustache
grooming · lip-beard · Roundhead · full-bottomed wig · wigmaking · short
bob · campaign wig · soldiers' hair · powder · combs · perfume · beaver hat ·
Puritan, Pilgrim, Quaker · tricorne · Monmouth cock · military headgear ·
church dress · removing the hat · montero · Monmouth cap · lace · sumptuary
edicts · ribbon · wigs or "heads" · English ringlets · sheep headdress · heartbreakers · favorites · veils · wire frames · set-out combs · hurluberlu · cabbage
head · boss or bundle · fontange · wig for riding · Spanish coiffure · Champagne · Beau Fielding · Dutch coif · biggin · French hood · Little Red Riding
Hood or cardinal · headkerchief · huke · conch · traveling hat · witch's garb ·
straw · mask · patch · cosmetics · pearls · Temple stones · pins
17 PLATES—pages 123–139

CHAPTER ELEVEN

THE EIGHTEENTH CENTURY   140

French and English modes · fashion babies · Namby Pamby · Beau Nash ·
full-bottomed wig · corners · knotted wig · tie wig · bagwig · solitaire · pigtail wig · Ramillies wig · cadogan · Macaronies · pigeon's wings ·
Greek toupet · Adonis wig · white powder · Meissen porcelain · colored powder · decline of the wig · black silk bag · the flash · the wig
in America · papillotes · bewigged stage characters · hedgehog style ·
cocked hat · carrying of the hat · Kevenhuller · Ramillies cock · Nivernois ·
bicorne · Holland or Pennsylvania hat · jockey hat · tall beaver hat · hatmaking · Phrygian cap · muscadin · men's earrings · Scotch bonnet · military
headgear · the boater · salute of the hand · cockade · pompadour · patted
coiffure · feminine wig · powder · extravagant heads · coiffure bottles · tulle ·
feathers · ingénue coiffure · hedgehog · baby coiffure · hairdressers · Princess
de Lamballe · decline of high powdered heads · chapeau-bonnet · Ranelagh
mob · dormeuse · Charlotte Corday · gypsy hat · straws · Gainsborough hat ·
doll hats · turbans · riding hats · Venetian tricorne · lace · French hood ·
calash · thérèse · veils · mask · patches · cosmetics · toilet water · pearls ·
eyeglasses · jewelry · Rose Bertin · fashion journal · silhouette
26 PLATES—pages 161–186

CHAPTER TWELVE

DIRECTOIRE, 1795–1799   187

Incroyable · dog's ears · hoop earrings · Brutus haircut · blond wig and black
collar · stovepipe · chapeau bras · bicorne · return of wigs and false hair ·
classic style · antique oil · Titus cut · dog's ears · à la victime · merveilleuse ·

xi

THE MODE IN
Hats and
Headdress

ANCIENT EGYPTIAN

CHAPTER ONE

THE EGYPTIANS in the protodynastic period wore their natural hair which was thick, wavy and dark brown. The ostrich plume was a masculine ornament for the head. Women dressed the hair into many tight braids and added ivory combs and hairpins.

Much attention and time was devoted to the care of the hair and elaborate hairdressing to which false hair was added. This led to the fashion of the wig in ancient Egypt. Both sexes, replacing natural hair with a ventilated wig, cut their hair very short or plucked or shaved their heads. Excessive heat and reasons of cleanliness as well as religion, had to do with the custom. Priests, the governor and the chief judge adopted the uncovered shaved head.

The Greek historian, Herodotus (484–425 B.C.) made the statement that the Egyptian whose head was shaved early in life, acquired a much harder skull than the Persian whose head was covered with a thick growth of hair. The hair was left to grow during a period of mourning.

Wigs were made of human hair, black sheep's wool or palm leaf fibre dyed black and attached to a woven porous foundation which afforded ventilation and protection against the sun's hot rays. Though black was the chosen color, it is known that there were blonds among the Egyptians. In the highly sophisticated period after about 1150 B.C., wigs worn by men and women were often of brilliant color, having been dyed red, green or blue. For pure creative and artistic decoration, the Egyptian headdress has never been surpassed. It is interesting to note the conventionalizing of ornamentation over the centuries, of the ribbon headband, flowers and feathers into stylized motifs of metal and jewels.

Wigs were worn by nobility, officers of rank and the wealthy, the lesser man wearing a skullcap of felt or no covering at all. The early Egyptians who were skilled in the dressing of animal skins, wore caps of leather.

The very short bob-like wig first worn by royalty, was later taken up by the commoner, but wigs of shoulder length or longer were confined to the upper class. Very often, the natural hair of the laborer was cut in a short bob. The klaft, Coptic for hood, was a national headdress worn by both sexes, an apron-shaped headcloth of linen worn tight round the forehead and falling loosely at the sides and back.

The crowns of the pharaohs were of several styles fashioned of metal, felt, straw, cotton, linen and wool, striped and embroidered. There was the tall pointed atef crown, another high flat-top shape wider at the top than at the head and the fillet of ribbon or metal with lappets hanging in back. A skullcap of fine linen was sometimes worn under the heavy crown. The high unadorned bonnet-like crown was worn by the early kings of Upper Egypt. About 3000 B.C. when the victorious King Narmer united the two kingdoms, he added the red wicker-work crown of Lower Egypt to that of Upper Egypt.

The Egyptian soldier of the New Kingdom wore a small round bronze helmet, from the center of which rose an apex or spike upon which was wound a ball of wool. Another decoration was a pair of buffalo horns, often woolen balls and the horns combined on the helmet. Contemporary with the Greco-Roman period, the same round helmet had metal horns. Although iron was known in antiquity, bronze appears to have been the oldest metal employed, dating back to about 3700 B.C. in Egypt.

In feminine headdress, the wig served the same purpose as the modern hat and a lady owned several in different styles and for different occasions. Some women retained their own hair to which they added false hair to simulate the size of the wig, the whole dressed in many tight braids, the fashion varying with the period. In the late period of foreign domination, the use of the wig over the cropped or shaven head gave way to long natural hair worn in Greco-Roman fashion.

Women wore interlaced flowers in their hair, the favorite blossom being the lotus, emblem of abundance. Works of art were the circlets of fine gold wire ornamented with small flowers of carnelian, lapis lazuli and turquoise glass. Both men and women wore the fillet or ribbon headband finished in back with the symbolic bowknot and short hanging ends, later simulated in metal, silver or gold and encrusted with semi-precious stones and glass.

Here is a description of such a crown or fillet of the Old Kingdom, 2680–2280 B.C. Of copper covered with gold leaf on a plaster coating, the circlet, a museum art treasure of today, is further enhanced with lotus flowers, birds and large rosettes formed of papyrus colored with paint and gilded gesso. Carnelian inlays also decorate the lovely piece.

Crowns and wigs changed with the dynasties and sometimes queens are portrayed with the tall bonnet-like crown and no wig. Both kings and queens can be seen wearing the crown over the striped fabric apron-shaped headdress. Especially handsome was the crown of vulture or hawk design, the head of the bird protruding from the forehead. It surmounted a wig and supposedly was worn only by an unmarried queen or princess.

The vulture signified the goddess of Upper Egypt and the cobra or sacred asp, the goddess of Lower Egypt, and, after the joining of the two kingdoms, both insignia were placed on the royal headdress. They were removable and fitted the different crowns that the ruler might wear to the various ceremonials. The sun disk sign of Uraeus, the sacred feather of truth, the cow's horns, emblem of Hathor, goddess of love, all were ornaments of princely insignia.

Another sign of sovereignty was the postiche or false beard of metal, an adaptation of the genuine beard originally worn by the early kings. Sometimes gold threads were braided into the trim-kept, often dyed, beard. The plaited beard became the design of the later gold postiche, an ornament worn also by queens. It was held in place by a ribbon tied in back under wig or crown or attached to a gold chinstrap.

Both men and women made use of cosmetics. The eyes were accented with two colors, black and green, collyrite or kohl (the latter its Oriental name) and powdered green malachite. A black line was drawn round the eye with a small ivory or ebony stick dipped in kohl. The cheeks were colored with an ointment made of red clay mixed with a touch of saffron. Carmine was applied to the lips, the eyelashes were tipped with black pomade and the veins of the bosom accented with blue. That age-old artist's pigment, white lead, was known both to the Egyptians and the Chinese and, though surely harmful to the skin, was used by their ladies to paint the face. Creams, oils and ointments were lavishly indulged in, men employing perfumed oils even for shaving.

In early times, the aromatics were only for religious ceremony and embalming but gradually Egyptians carried the use of them into their daily life. The precious perfumed oils were purchased from the priests who prepared them in the laboratories of the temples. Frankincense, saffron and myrrh were popular perfumes and still in use today. That the Egyptians were skilled in making perfumes was evident when after thirty-two hundred years, the tomb of Tutankhamen was opened and the perfumes used were still fragrant.

A strange custom indulged in when banqueting, was the wearing of an ornamental ritual cone of perfumed fat on top of the head or wig. When the party "waxed high" as we express it, the cone melted and ran down over the person.

Combs for dressing the hair were fashioned of metal, bone, ivory, boxwood and ebony. There were beautifully designed containers for the many cosmetics: small dishes, bottles and flagons of alabaster and finely polished stone and glass.

Small boys had their heads shaved, leaving a braided "lock of youth" on either side, while the long natural hair of little girls was plaited into several tight pigtails.

Ancient Egyptian

King in white felt or wool atef crown or bonnet of Upper Egypt - 3000 B.C.

King in red wicker work crown of Lower Egypt - fine feather - 3000 B.C.

King - the two crowns in one - white, red and gold - gold postiche - late period

Queen - wig - gold circlet with jewels - ribbons at back - 2656 - 2633 B.C.

King in wig with striped linen cover - blue and yellow - false beard - 2780 - 2762 B.C.

boy with shaven head - lock of youth - 1500 - 1200 B.C.

boy with shaven head - braided lock of youth - 2160 - 1788 B.C.

lady in wig - gold circlet with colored stones - white papyrus lotus - orange ribbons - 2656 - 2633 B.C.

girl with own hair in pigtails - 2160 - 1788 B.C.

King - blue and yellow striped linen headdress - gold postiche and insignia - 1590 B.C.

Princess in wig strung with gold beads - gold circlet - gold and enameled uraeus and rosettes - gold lappets - 1890 - 1840 B.C.

sacred serpent - goddess of Lower Egypt

wig of short spiral curls - 2560 - 2420 B.C.

vulture - goddess of Upper Egypt

RTW

Ancient Egyptian

Princess-wig with silver cords-silver circlet with green enameled red and white enameled disks- white papyrus flowers-1887 1850 B.C.

King in blue crown or royal war helmet of metal or wicker- uraeus insignia- 1580- 1085 B.C.

Queen in vulture headdress of metal over wig of tiny curls- 1580 B.C. through Ptolemaic Period

Lady in headdress of beads, gold disks, colored stones and glass-gold headplate-over wig of small tight braids- 1501-1447 B.C.

high official- wig of spiral curls- white ribbon- flexible gold feather- late B.C.

Queen in helmet crown of green-blue fabric- enameled band-yellow headband-red ribbons- uraeus insignia-1375-1358 B.C.

court lady- wig of braids ending in curls-ribbon band- 1580-1300 B.C.

Queen in vulture headdress- gold body- blue feathers-wig of tight curls- 1580 B.C.

King- fillet crown of inlaid silver over curled wig- 1590 B.C.

King- gold fillet crown over curled wig- vulture and serpent-sun disk in back- carnelian, lapis lazuli and turquoise glass- 1352-1340 B.C.

Lady-wig of braids ending in curls- heavy braids in back- 1375 B.C.

RTW

Ancient Egyptian

Queen-banqueting headdress-circlet of ribbon and colored glass-lotus flower topped by perfumed cone of fat-striped ribbon on wig- 1318-1298-B.C.

King in banqueting headdress-ribbon band-perfumed cone of fat-wig of spiral curls- 1318-1298 B.C.

Warrior-bronze helmet-embossed-apex with ball of wool-wig of spiral curls-late period

Queen-gold crown-insignia sun disk, cow's horns, double plumes, two uraei-wig of small curls- 670 B.C.

Lady with natural hair-inlaid gold circlet with lotus motif-ribbon-jeweled earrings-late period

King-wig of spiral curls- 1198-1166 B.C.

metal crown and circlet over wig of spiral curls-insignia sun disk, cow's horns and uraeus- 1580-1085 B.C.

Lady with striped linen headdress over natural hair edged with fringe-enameled silver circlet-jeweled earrings-late period

conventionalized silver and enamel uraeus- 2065-1785 B.C.

Queen-gold circlet with uraeus, disks and tail worn over striped linen cloth-natural hair braided with pearl strings-gold earrings-late period

Cleopatra in coiffure of Graeco-Roman fashion- 69-30 B.C.

RTW

MESOPOTAMIAN

CHAPTER TWO

THIS TERM COMPRISES Chaldean, Babylonian, Assyrian, Median and ancient Persian civilization. Chaldean, Babylonian and Assyrian will be considered as one since they shared in common the distinctive characteristics of dress. The Babylonian Empire boasted a culture nearly as old as that of Egypt. It consisted in 1917 B.C. of Elam, Assyria and Syria. Babylonia was conquered 1250 B.C. by the Assyrians who in turn were subjugated by the Medes, to be in turn conquered by the Persians in 640 B.C.

Our information on the costume of these empires is to be had from coins and sculpture, principally low-relief decorations which ornamented the walls of their palaces and temples. Colors are furnished us by the well-preserved wall paintings of the Egyptian tombs.

Both men and women who were most fastidious and painstaking in the dressing of the elaborate coiffures, wore natural hair or wigs falling in length to the shoulders, waved, frizzed and in tight ringlets. In fact from ancient Phrygia in Asia Minor comes a word in our language, Phrygianize, which signifies "to frizzle or curl up." Curling irons or tongs were used for the

8

spiral curls. Upon festive occasions the hair was powdered with gold dust or scented with pulverized yellow starch. The masculine beard was given the same attention. Ointments were applied to the hair and it is known that the Assyrians resorted to a black dye for eyebrows, beard and hair. Persian men stained their hair and beards with henna dye of an orange-red color. To enhance the brilliancy of the eyes, the lids were edged with kohl. Heavy eyebrows were a sign of beauty especially if they met over the nose, and both men and women drew in the line with kohl. Women also used rouge.

The hats of ancient Mesopotamia were truly modern and with the exception of the beret and the sailor, we find all of today's hat styles represented.

Tire, tiara and mitre or miter, all words of Greek origin in general signifying a crown, were the names given alike to the wide jeweled headband, the Asiatic turban and the tall conical hat which were worn by the Babylonians, Assyrians, Medes and Persians. Among the Persians the tall bonnet or crown was the tiara and the ornamented headband with ties or lappets hanging in back, the miter. Miter, which in our day is generally associated with ecclesiastic headgear, signified as late as the fifteenth century, a simple cap or calotte. Apropos the papal tiara of our time, that dates from the ninth century and the bishop's miter from the twelfth century.

According to Xenophon the Greek historian (430–352 B.C.) the royal tiara of ancient Persia was a tall bonnet encircled with a diadem while the man of lesser rank wore a flexible one with lappets at the sides. Despite his statement, wall carvings extant portray kingly individuals attired in bonnets with lappets.

The king's crown, tiara or miter, which varied in shape and height, was usually of white felt or wool around which was tied a band or fillet of linen or wool in blue, white or purple with two ends or lappets hanging at the sides or back. The crown was also enriched with embroidery, gold, pearls and precious stones. Embroidery, in fact, covered the entire costume with motifs based upon the rosette and was called "Babylonian work." The lappets of the royal bonnet were long and had fringed ends while those of inferior rank were short and unadorned.

The crown or diadem, symbol of kingship in modern Europe and fast disappearing, owes its origin to the tied fillet of linen or woolen material of ancient Eastern Europe.

Other masculine headcoverings were the felt toque with or without turned-up band, the felt skullcap or helmet of the soldier and a draped turban of wool or linen with chincloth covering the shoulders. Persian soldiers wore a melon-shaped bonnet, also a hood resembling the Phrygian bonnet. The generally worn bonnet of Phrygia in Asia Minor, was a pointed hood of woolen cloth or felt. Women too are portrayed wearing it.

Women lived in harems and there is little graphic record of feminine dress, but that they also wore the bonnet is attested by one of the few portraits of the sex, a wall carving of the goddess Ishtar, also another, both wearing either the hat or the jeweled headband. A sheer veil of rich fabric bespangled with jewels was often draped over the headdress, the same coiffure worn today by Persian women and those of the Caucasus.

It is interesting to note that the veil, emblem of feminine modesty, submission and respect, originated not in Egypt where woman was practically man's equal and free to come and go, but in the harem of the Mesopotamian Valley, that cradle of civilization.

Especially among the Assyrians, the headdress was a badge of office, there being certain styles for priests, officials and musicians, even for cooks. The king's cook for instance, wore a tiara not unlike his monarch's in shape but, of course, lacking in richness.

The art of felting acquired from the nomadic Asiatic tribes was known to the Egyptians, the peoples of the Mesopotamian Valley, the Greeks and the Romans and then lost during the Dark Ages. Then as today, felt was made by matting or compacting bits of wool or hair together while moist. Why it was thus possible to produce felt, was not understood until recently. As the art of weaving preceded that of spinning, so the art of felting preceded that of weaving.

The Hebraic law forbade the use of the human form in picture or design. Information upon their costume which is to be had from the records of other countries, especially Egypt, reveals that their apparel reflected the mode of their conquerors.

Babylonian and Assyrian

king-white felt tiara - bands of embroidery and pearls-fringed woolen lappets-hair waved and frizzed-earrings-8th century B.C.

lady-metal miter with pearls-earrings and necklace-hair waved and frizzed

queen or princess-white felt tiara-hair waved and frizzed-woolen tassels-earrings-884 B.C.

priest-metal miter-design of ribbon folds, rosettes and lotus-earrings-hair waved and frizzed

warrior-bronze helmet-hair waved and frizzed

king's attendant-hair waved and frizzed-earrings-9th century B.C.

King in white felt tiara-hair waved and frizzed-earrings-9th century B.C.

King-white felt tiara-mitre with embroidery and pearls-fringed woolen lappets-earrings-hair waved and frizzed-9th century B.C.

king-gold tiara-hair waved and frizzed-7th century B.C.

high official-metal miter-rosettes with pearls-fringed lappets-hair waved and frizzed-earrings

truncated tiara of wool or felt-short lappets-hair waved and frizzed

warrior-bronze helmet-hair frizzed and waved

RTW

Median ᵃⁿᵈ Persian

Median king-white felt tiara-blue, gold and pearl embroidery-earrings-frizzed and waved hair

Median soldier-headband with frontal ornament-hair in spiral curls-beard frizzed

Persian-king's guard-rolled fabric headband-hair waved and frizzed-earrings

Median lady-hair wound with pearls-pearl coronet-gold miter-pearl earrings

Persian-king's guard-metal tiara-waved and frizzed hair-earrings

Median nobleman-gold miter with pearls and gems-hair waved ᵃⁿᵈ frizzed

Persian king-white felt tiara-hair waved ᵃⁿᵈ frizzed-earrings

Persian nobleman-draped tiara or turban of white wool or linen

Persian nobleman-draped turban held by miter or headband-frizzed hair

Persian-king's guard-bonnet with short lappets-earrings-hair waved ᵃⁿᵈ frizzed

Persian nobleman-tiara or bonnet of Phrygian style-wool or leather-frizzed hair

Persian-servant-crownless miter-hair waved ᵃⁿᵈ frizzed

RTW

ANCIENT GREEK

CHAPTER THREE

VARIED INDEED was the mode of the Greek coiffure, a constant change in arrangement, seemingly leaving nothing new to be designed. The masculine style, over the centuries made use of spiral curls, ringlets and the short haircut of today. Often, a fillet or headband of fabric or leather was tied round the head, the two ends left to hang in back. As noted in the second chapter, the Greek names "miter" or "tiara" were given it and also applied to hoods and turban-like headtire of the women. The girdle too was called a tiara.

The first tonsorial establishments, of which there were many, existed among the Greeks. Besides the culture of hair and beard, the attendants were skilled in massage, first aid and small surgery. After his morning bath, the Greek citizen strolled to his favorite "tonstrina" where he enjoyed not only bodily attention but social and mental intercourse with his townsmen. The atmosphere of the ancient barber shop was not unlike that of the modern men's club.

Beards were in favor until Alexander's time (356–323 B.C.) when he ordered the clean-shaven face, fearing that the soldier's beard might serve as a handle to the enemy in warfare.

Feminine hair was long and dressed artistically, always preserving the contour of the head. It was cut short as a sign of mourning. Though the classic coiffure, parted in the middle and drawn into a chignon at the back of the head, is the style most commonly known, there were spiral curls, ringlets, braids, fringes, frizzing and waving, the curling iron commonly used even by the opposite sex.

The toupee of Cypriote curls, as its name indicates, hailing from Cyprus, was a mass of ringlets or several rows of spiral curls built up upon a wire frame and worn over the front of the head from ear to ear. It was a clever, flattering piece of adornment to the feminine face, a style especially favored by the Roman ladies and worn also by men in a modified version.

Greek women were naturally blond but often dyed their hair and wore colored wigs, preferably of a reddish hue. We read that Athenian women dyed their hair blue, dusted it with powder in gold, white or red, and painted their eyebrows in Oriental fashion. Men and women applied perfumes and ointments to their hair. Women tinted their cheeks and lips with a paste made of red oxide of lead and blanched their skin with white lead.

From the Greek word *kosmētikos,* meaning skilled in decorating, comes our word, "cosmetic." *Kosmētæ* was the name of the lady's maids, of which she had many.

Not only the women but the men wore wreaths of fresh flowers on their heads. At banquets,.weddings and festivals, the servants of the house placed garlands of flowers or ivy and myrtle on the head and shoulders of the guests. Wreaths of laurel crowned the victors in the Pythian games and later were used to indicate academic honors. Laurel, like the olive branch, was a sign of truce, also a sign of victory. The wreath of olive branches when worn by the ordinary man signified the birth of a son.

Hairpins, also known as bodkins or skewers, were fashioned of bone, ivory or metal, ranging from three to seven or eight inches in length and topped with delicate ornaments in silver, gold, jewels and enamels. A spiral hairpin made of gold wire was in use. Combs in the earlier period were of boxwood, and later, of both boxwood and ivory. Feminine earrings were of gold or silver, small in motif but exquisite in design.

Greek ladies wore cauls of gauze, of reticulated golden cord and tiaras and crowns of gold and silver encrusted with precious stones. They wore the fillet of ribbon or metal and threaded the hair with strings of beads or pearls. They were fond of sheer veils, especially Tyrian veils in wool or linen, either white or colored, either wound through the hair or left floating. A bridal headdress was a long sheer white veil sewn with pearls which hung from the ornamented headpiece in back. Another favorite bridal coiffure was dressed with a wreath of violets and myrtle.

In general both sexes went bareheaded but when Greek men traveled, they wore the *pétasos*, a practical hat of felt or straw with wide brim and held on by a chinstrap which permitted the hat to hang down the back when not in use. The brimmed hat hailed from Thessaly in Greece. The winged cap of Hermes, the Greek Mercury, was called a *pétasos*. Women wore the *pétasos* made of fine straw and having a tallish conical crown. Such hats appear on the charming terra cotta statuettes of Tanagra in Boeotia. When in mourning or performing sacrifices, the feminine head was covered with a scarf.

A close-fitting cap of felt or leather, the *pílos,* was worn by the Greek sailor. Too, he wore the tiara or pointed hood of felt, the Phrygian cap. The Phrygian cap was also of leather and became an emblem of liberty in ancient Rome and again in the eighteenth century during the French Revolution.

The helmets of the Greek warriors were superb pieces of design which, while protective, were also artistic and imposing. The most ancient was the Corinthian helmet also known as the helmet of Minerva. It had eye-shaped openings through which to see when worn down over the face. The Attic helmet had cheekguards, at first of a solid piece, later folding back against the helmet when not in use.

Ancient Greek

curled hair and beard-rolled wool fillet

petasos of felt or straw with strap

the skullcap of felt or wool of the common man

spiral curls-leather fillet

charioteer-leather fillet

priest of Bacchus-yellow fillet-fringed and embroidered lappets-ivy leaves

short feather cut

front and back views-toupee of spiral curls-leather fillet-curled beard and mustache

embossed helmet-bronze and brass-horse's mane and tail-cheek guards

the Phrygian miter of embroidered wool

embossed helmet-bronze and brass-horse's mane and tail

Corinthian helmet of embossed bronze and brass

military leader-wreath of olive leaves-spiral curls

soldier's helmet-felt or leather-wooden or metal apex

RTW

Ancient Greek

Cretan-
ribbon
fillet and
strings of
beads -
2000 B.C.

ribbon fillet
wound over a
sheer cap

bride -
gold or silver
caul - jewels -
ribbon lacings -
earrings -
long white
veil

bodkins or
hairpins -
bone, ivory
or metal

miter - star
embroidered
veil - ribbon
fillet

Boeotian
petasos
of straw
from a
statuette
of
Tanagra

embroidered
pillbox - parted
hair - chignon
and spiral curls

beret shaped
cap - twig of
leaves - parted
hair in high chignon

embossed
diadem
and
veil

Cypriote curls -
toupee of spiral
curls - high
chignon

embossed diadem -
rolled gauze bandeau -
golden net caul
with jewels -
earrings

fringe and
spiral curls

embroidered
and jeweled
headpiece

the classic
coiffure of
Venus de Milo

Cypriote
curls -
toupee of
three rows of spiral
curls and a braid

tasseled cap
with fillet and rolled bandeau

embossed diadem -
spiral curls and
chignon

RTW

ANCIENT ROMAN

CHAPTER FOUR

NORTHERN ITALY was settled by the Etruscans, supposedly a people from Asia Minor, about 1000 B.C. Though their origin is veiled in mystery, they eventually handed on to the Romans a luxurious and sumptuous civilization closely allied to that of the Greeks.

Oriental influence is evident in the headgear of the Etruscans, men and women portrayed in sculpture wearing the round skullcap and the conical hood. Oriental too is the manner of dressing the hair in long heavy curls over the shoulders and tiny ringlets on the brow. Men favored the Asiatic fashion in beards.

The short haircut was the prevailing style among the Roman men and they were most fastidious in their care of hair and beard. The razor, it is recorded, was introduced into Rome by Tarquinius, the fifth king (616–578 B.C.), in his pioneering effort to bring about some hygienic reform in daily life. The Romans did not take to the "effeminate" ways of the Greeks and it was over a century before shaving became general. It became the fashion about 454 B.C. when a group of Greek-Sicilian barbers came over to the mainland from Sicily. Barber shops came into existence and were situated on the main streets but were patronized by men who could not afford to keep slaves.

They tell us that the Roman General Scipio of about 234 to 183 B.C. was the first Roman to shave every day. Like the Greeks and the Asiatics upon gala occasions, the nobles perfumed and powdered their hair with gold dust from the first century to about 268 A.D. Baldness was considered a deformity among Roman men, and in such cases a kind of wig was worn made of hair attached to skin. The dignified beard and long hair was retained by professors of philosophy. Too, a long beard signified mourning.

The masculine coiffure with the ends curled under all around was revived by the fashionable Venetian of the fifteenth century, sometimes in the form of a wig of yellow silk, the style known as the coiffure *á la Zazzera*. The names of Titus, emperor in the first century, and the Consul Brutus of the sixth century were revived in the last decade of the eighteenth century with the fashion of the short haircut of uneven length affected by men and women of the European "beau monde."

The tutulus originally was the headdress of braids worn by the flamen or pagan priest and his wife, the braids built up in conical shape. Eventually, the conical shape evolved into a pointed cap with an olive twig on top tied by a fillet of wool.

The Greek pilos became the Roman pileus, the close-fitting cap of felt or leather of Roman soldiers and sailors, and it was also worn at festivals and public games by athletes for protection. The Greek pétasos, petasus in Latin, was also adopted by the Romans.

The pointed hood or tiara from Phrygia in Asia Minor became in Rome an emblem of liberty worn by manumitted slaves. In the eighteenth century, it was again adopted as such, "le bonnet rouge" of the French Revolutionists.

The helmet of the Roman warrior was a continuation of the beautifully designed Greek piece and often crested with ostrich, other feathers, cropped horse's mane and tail. Iron was the metal usually employed, but bronze, leather and thin brass were also used and the helmet of the general was often entirely of gold. Bronze, that metal of great antiquity, dates back to 2000 B.C. in Northern Europe and its use for arms and armor lasted centuries after the general employment of iron in the period of the Roman Empire.

To flatter Caesar, who became bald, the Senate decreed that he be permitted to always wear the wreath of laurel. It thus became the emperor's crown, though later fashioned of gold and set with precious stones. Because of its association with pagan divinity, it was believed that lightning could not strike laurel, for which reason the Emperor Tiberius always wore the wreath during a thunderstorm.

Men and women made use of the beauty spot or "patch," of Oriental origin. These patches were of soft leather, the Romans being skilled in the preparation of fine leather. It is recorded that orators speaking from the tribune wore patches. Both sexes whitened their skin with chalk or white lead and used a lip rouge of vegetable dye.

Ladies, like men, applied oils and perfumes to the hair and, when fancy moved them, dyed their locks. The dyes originated with the Gauls, who colored their own hair red. The Germans acquired the secret of the formula and made it up into balls of caustic soap which they exported to Rome and the provinces. Red was especially favored but we also read of blond wigs made of hair bought from the northern Gauls.

Women adorned themselves with beautiful and often elaborately dressed coiffures and wigs in which the hair was braided, frizzed, curled and waved by curling irons. Ribbons and strings of beads were threaded through the hair. For some built-up headdresses, false hair was added, also false chignons. The Roman lady of the first century wore the toupee of Cypriote curls, a flattering piece of framework around the face. It was a solid mass of ringlets built up on a wire frame reaching from ear to ear across the front of the head, a fashion from Cyprus as the name implies.

Rome's great contribution to art was her fine portrait busts of marble or bronze for which some vain ladies had several separate wigs fashioned of hair or carved in stone, thus keeping the portrait to date in the mode of the coiffure. The slaves of wealthy women were especially trained in the art of hairdressing by professors of the coiffure.

Valeria Messalina, a wife of the Emperor Claudius in the first century A.D., wore a yellow wig on her visits to places of ill repute, the yellow wig being a sign of the courtesan. The name Messalina has ever since signified a dissolute woman. And Faustina, an empress of the second century A.D. and wife of Marcus Aurelius, a woman also noted for her profligacy, was the possessor of several hundred wigs.

The artistic caul or net was worn fashioned of various materials. Handsome ones were of meshed gold or silver cord interspersed with pearls and gems and there were jeweled diadems. The Vestal Virgins, priestesses of the goddess of the hearth, wore the reticulum, a net headdress of red yarn, the color red believed to ward off evil spirits. The Roman bride wore a like red hairnet on the eve of her wedding.

Men and women wore the chaplet of fresh flowers, and as with the Greeks, wreaths of the various foliages were awarded for military deeds of valor.

About 208 A.D., the Christian Church required women to cover the head upon entering the place of worship and it became traditional thereafter to wear the veil in any religious assembly. Purple was the color of the veil of the early nun. The Christian bride wore a white or purple veil and the flowers of her bridal wreath were picked by herself. A flame colored or yellow veil floated from the head of the Roman bride. On her brow she wore a chaplet of vervain, a plant credited with sacred properties.

Bodkins or hairpins resembled those of the Greeks, and were made in metal, bone, ivory, gold and silver with heads chiseled in tiny delicate figures of Venus, Psyche, Isis or conventional designs. Some pins had holes in the ends through which to pass and tie the fillet. Exquisitely carved combs for combing the hair were, like those of the Greeks, of boxwood and ivory.

The Roman lady of high rank had many personal maids, sometimes as many as two hundred. There was a slave or attendant for each individual operation of the toilette as, for instance, the scrubber of the teeth, the layer-on of white and red and the stainer of the eyebrows. There were perfumes, pomatum, face powder, rouge and white paint, tooth powder and paste. "Pharian varnish," which whitened the skin and caused freckles to disappear, was made from the entrails of the crocodile of which there were many off the Island of Pharos at the mouth of the Nile. Various herbal preparations were also concocted for the same purpose. Costly caskets of ivory and crystal held the beautifiers which were called by the Greek name of *kosmētikos* and the slaves, *kosmētae*, since all things fashionable went by Greek names.

The Empress Poppaea, wife of Nero in the first century A.D., originated the method of keeping the skin white and soft by the use of a plaster formed of bread and asses' milk. It was applied to the lady's face by her maid upon retiring and left to work its wonders till morning. A train of five hundred milch asses was kept in constant attendance to supply her bath. Poppaea was also the first Western lady to wear the mask as a means of protecting the complexion. Theretofore the mask had been used only in the theater. This fashion, as many Roman fashions did, undoubtedly came from the East, Arabian women wearing black masks with dainty clasps.

Etruscan

pileus of felt with rolled edge-hair in round curls

man's coiffure-curls-metal diadem

tutulus headdress of braids-metal fillet and jewels-back hair in rolled curls

parted coiffure with rolled curls hanging in back

young girl in tutulus shaped bonnet of rolled fabric-waved and curled hair

wreath of fresh flowers

man's head-coiffure in curls-felt pileus

warrior's helmet of bronze-horsetail plumes

athlete-pileus of leather or felt

man's head-curls over forehead-rolled hanging curls-tutulus shaped felt hat-rolled brim

curled coiffure and beard with long hanging curls in back

RTW

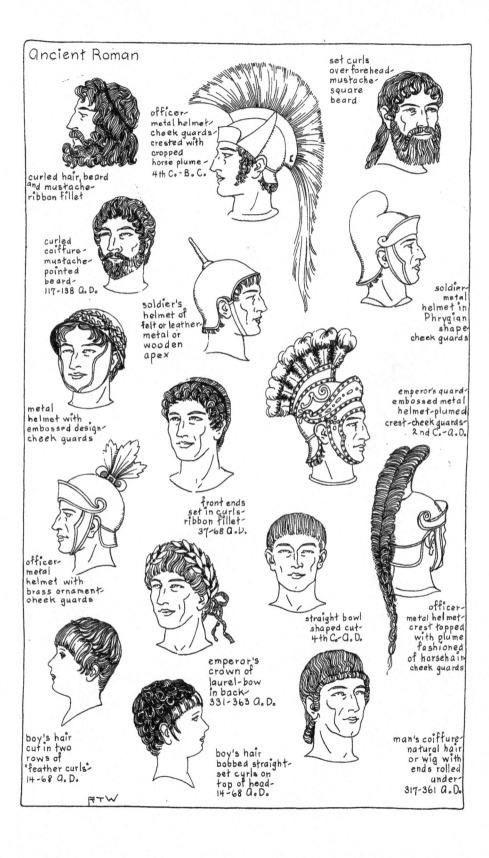

Ancient Roman

curled hair, beard and mustache-ribbon fillet

officer-metal helmet-cheek guards-crested with cropped horse plume- 4th C.-B.C.

set curls over forehead-mustache-square beard

curled coiffure-mustache-pointed beard- 117-138 A.D.

soldier's helmet of felt or leather-metal or wooden apex

soldier-metal helmet in Phrygian shape cheek guards

metal helmet with embossed design-cheek guards

front ends set in curls-ribbon fillet- 37-68 A.D.

emperor's guard-embossed metal helmet-plumed crest-cheek guards- 2nd C.-A.D.

officer-metal helmet with brass ornament-cheek guards

emperor's crown of laurel-bow in back- 331-363 A.D.

straight bowl shaped cut- 4th C.-A.D.

officer-metal helmet-crest topped with plume fashioned of horsehair-cheek guards

boy's hair cut in two rows of "feather curls" 14-68 A.D.

boy's hair bobbed straight-set curls on top of head- 14-68 A.D.

man's coiffure-natural hair or wig with ends rolled under- 317-361 A.D.

RTW

Ancient Roman

dancing girl with fillet

vestal virgin in draped scarf

bodkins or hairpins - 3 to 8 inches long

waved hair - center part - rolled in back - front frizzed - 1st C. - A.D.

center part - spiral curls drawn to nape in chignon - 1st C. - A.D.

waved hair with coronet braid - 2nd C. - A.D.

Cypriote curls - toupee - back view lower left - 1st C. - A.D.

front view above

front and back views of toupee over wire frame - back hair in knotted curls - 1st C. - A.D.

Cypriote curls - toupee of rolls over wire frame - late 1st C. - A.D.

Greco-Roman - hair waved and parted - chignon and curls - jeweled diadem - string of amber beads

Cypriote curls - toupee - 1st C. - A.D.

Cypriote curls - toupee - late 1st C. A.D.

hair parted round head - rolled front carried to back - 3rd C. - A.D.

center part braid carried to top of head - 3rd C. - A.D.

braided coiffure of the 2nd C. - A.D.

parted and braided coiffure - 4th C. - A.D.

RTW

BYZANTINE AND ECCLESIASTIC
CHAPTER FIVE

IN 395 A.D. THEODOSIUS THE GREAT at his death divided the Roman Empire between his two sons. The eastern part styled East Roman, Greek or Lower Empire, took its name from the ancient capital Byzantium or Constantinople and lasted till captured by the Turks in 1453. Constantinople, a Greek Christian city, at its height was the most opulent city in the world, containing vast quantities of priceless works of art including those of the great classical Greek artists. Much was converted into bullion for use against the marauding Crusaders and Venetians and, surprisingly enough, much was carried off into semi-barbaric Europe by the Christian vandals so that little documentary evidence remains of their great culture.

Byzantine costume was a combination design of Oriental and Roman origin which greatly influenced the Medieval and Renaissance periods of Europe. Brilliant mosaics in colored glass set up by the Emperor Justinian and Empress Theodora of the sixth century A.D. in the churches of San Vitale and San Apollinari in Ravenna, Italy, furnish us with the details of the gorgeous Byzantine costume.

Men wore beards and mustaches and their hair moderately short. The long hair of the women was dressed close to the head, retaining the contour, and when not entirely concealed by an elaborately jeweled caul or cap, was intertwined with strings of pearls over which was often placed a heavy jewel-encrusted crown with pendeloques of pearls.

The crowns and fillets worn by both men and women were gorgeous pieces of the jeweler's art, and the turban-like caps, a feminine style, were of sumptuous Oriental fabrics to which jewels, pearls, gold and bits of colored glass were added. Colored glass was an invention of the Byzantines, and they later made use of tiny mirrors as ornaments. Birds in pairs was a favored motif for their long earrings.

The Eastern Empire was in direct communication with the eastern pearl markets and so plentiful was the supply that, not only were the headdresses encrusted and hung with pearls but entire costumes were lavishly embroidered with the lovely iridescent bits. The pearl-sewn costumes of the Middle Ages were a continuation of this Byzantine mode.

The art of felting, which disappeared in the Dark Ages, came to life in the centuries following. Some claim that the good Saint Clément was responsible for its rediscovery. Treading upon rabbit's fur to ease his travel-worn feet, he found that the fur became a solid inner sole of felt. To the hatters of many generations, he was their patron saint, each year honoring him on November 23. Other historians claim that the knowledge of felting returned to the Occident with the Crusaders, who found their enemies in the East using felt for their tents and horse trappings.

It was in these centuries that the ecclesiastic vestments began to emerge as a distinct costume from the dress of the laity. In fact, during the first four centuries there was no difference, but bans by the councils against ecclesiastics following the latest mode gradually made the costume of the period permanent. No change in style was permitted, thereby perpetuating to our day medieval dress in the Church.

An early sign of religious dedication in the Christian church was the tonsure, a manner of shaving the crown of the masculine head and which varied in the different churches.

The evolution of the Oriental miter and tiara is indeed interesting, this headpiece of the ancient Persians being worn by the Christian and Jewish prelates alike. It had no especial religious significance before the eleventh century, being worn by all classes. A sign of rank, however, was the sacred fillet of white wool with lappets or *infulae*. Previous to the twelfth century, popes, priests and bishops appear to have often officiated at their religious duties bareheaded or wearing the coif or cap of white linen.

In the fourth century, the fillet was of metal, gold or silver with a cord passing over the top of the head from front to back and worn over a headcloth of white linen. The fillet widened in the fifth century, the cord becoming a metal band. The sixth century saw the religious headdress ornamented with jewels and enamels, and by the eleventh century the wearing of the miter became obligatory for priests and bishops.

The bishop's miter in the early twelfth century was enclosed in two pointed panels but placed at the sides. Toward the end of the century, the panels were placed front and back where they have since remained. The points grew higher and more pointed till the fifteenth century, when the miter assumed the arch-like shape of today. Planché in his *Encyclopædia of Costume* presumes that the miter increased in height as the wearer acquired greater wisdom. The *infulae* or lappets suspended at the sides or in back continued of white wool but embroidered with gold thread and jewels.

The white linen miter was also worn by the Levitical priest. Popes occasionally bestowed the miter upon laymen or abbots of certain privileged houses or for conspicuous service to the Church. Such a miter was usually of purple silk with ermine lining.

Although the tall conical tiara of Asiatic origin eventually became the papal crown, the miter can also be seen in portraits of popes as late as the fifteenth century. The papal tiara with one crown was first worn by Nicholas I, 858–867. In 1065, Alexander II added the second coronet and the third appeared with Urban V, 1362–1370. In the sixteenth century, a mound with a cross atop instead of a jewel, completed the triple crown of the pope and remains the symbol of his temporal authority. A triple-crowned tiara was worn by the ancient Jewish high-priest.

The coif or zucchetto, the skullcap of Greek origin, was commonly worn by all classes, the quality of the fabric varying according to the wearer's means and position. It was often worn under hood or crown by people of rank and gradually acquired significance in color, especially among churchmen. That of the pope was white and sometimes red, the cardinal's red, the bishop's violet, while black remained a general color for priests. Necessity made the clerical coif custom, occasioned by the tonsure and the icy cold churches.

The origin of the cardinal's red hat is in the black hat with brim, commonly worn by clergy and laity. It was tied under the chin by a cord or slung in back when off the head. In 1245 Pope Innocent IV granted the red hat to cardinals, and with the growth of heraldry, the rank of the wearer came to be designated by the number of tassels which terminated the cords. The color of the brimmed hat of the archbishop and bishop was green, that of the abbot, black.

The flat broad-brimmed hat of the clergy, usually worn over the coif, was replaced in the fifteenth century by the biretta as a headcovering but remained the symbol of rank of religious dignitaries and as such is pictured in their coats-of-arms.

Much latitude was permitted in use, shape, material and color of ecclesiastic vestments, but since the sixteenth century the trend has been toward uniformity. White, even in the earliest times, appears to have been the color of prelates of high rank. That the pope did not always wear white, however, is attested by a miniature in color of the Italian Pope Martin V (1417–1431) wearing a red tiara encircled by three gold crowns. In the Middle Ages, the tall tiara of the pope, because of its resemblance to the ancient Phrygian bonnet, was called a *phrygium*.

Byzantine

emperor's crown-gold with pearls-colored gems and enamel-pearl lappets-6th C.

empress crown-gold with pearls and colored jewels-pearl lappets-hair wound with ribbon-6th C.

nobleman-jeweled crown over purple silk skullcap-early 6th C.

warrior helmet of bronze and brass

nobleman of the 6th C.

veil and coronet of gold and pearls-6th C.

coiffure dressed with ribbon-jeweled bandeau-gold and pearl earrings

empress-gold crown with pearls and gems-enamel-pearl lappets-5th C.

empress-crown of pearls on crimson silk-gold panel with jewels-white silk headdress-pearls and jewels-pearl lappets

turban-shaped coiffure wound with ribbon-earrings-6th C.

emperor-gold crown with pearls-pearl lappets-crimson silk top-9th C.

coiffure wound with ribbon-jewel in front-silk cap-earrings-6th C.

young woman-cap of cord over silk-earrings-6th C.

princess-gold and jeweled crown and hair ornaments-7th C.

young woman-pearl-sewn cap of silk-6th C.

RTW

Byzantine Ecclesiastic

tonsure-
shaved crown
of head-
6th C.

cardinal-
red hat
with cord-
worn over
red hood-
13th C.

cardinal-
red hat with
cord, beads
and tassels
14th C.

cardinal-
red hat
worn over
red cap-
14th C.

papal miter-
white with
gold and
jewels-red
lining-
15th C.

pope wearing
red
coif-
white lining
and edge-
12th C.

papal tiara-
white with
gold and
jewels-
silk
headcloth-
10th C.

soldier-
steel
helmet-
9th C.

bishop-
felt
tiara
11th C.

emperor's
crown-gold
with pearls and
jewel-white
fur-
7th C.

army officer-
bronze helmet-
colored stones-
fur band with
pearls-
9th C.

emperor-
tiara of silk
and gold bands-
hair in
ringlets-
1423-1448

striped fabric
wound round
felt skull cap-
5th C.

emperor-
turban of silk
over velvet cap-
gold bands-jewels-
1449-1453

RTW

Ecclesiastic

bishop's miter-
gold
fillet
with cord
over top-
white linen
headcloth-
4th C.

bishop's miter-
jeweled fillet-
white
linen cap
and lappets-
fringe and
pearls-
8th C.

bishop's miter-
jeweled fillet
over white
linen cap-
pearl sewn
white wool
lappets-
11th C.

bishop's miter-
jeweled fillet-white
headdress and lappets-
10th
C.

bishop's miter-gold
embroidery on
white-red lining-
12th C.

bishop's miter-white
gold embroidery on
red-white lappets-
jewels-
15th C.

bishop's miter-
jewels and
embroidery-
lappets gold
on white-
15th C.

Jewish high-priest-
white turban-
gold fillet-
blue ribbons

papal tiara-
white with
gold fillet
and jewels-
12th C.

papal tiara-
white with
gold and
jeweled fillet-
gold top-
540-604 A.D.

two-crowned
papal tiara-
with fall
around back-
worn over white linen
coif-jeweled crowns-
13th C.

triple-crowned
papal tiara-
interwoven white
folds-jeweled crowns-
white lappets with
gold embroidery-
white linen coif-
14th C.

Jewish high-priest-
white tiara-gold
fillet-white
lappets tied in back

RTW

SARACENIC OR MOORISH—THE TURBAN

CHAPTER SIX

SARACEN IS a general term which derives from two Arabian words meaning "children of the desert" and comprises the Persians, Ottoman Turks, Arabs and the Moors of Spain and Northern Africa. Saracen or Moor is the general name given by the Occidental to the Moslem or Mohammedan of Europe and North Africa.

The representation of the human figure was discouraged by the Mohammedan religion; therefore documentation on their dress is not to be had earlier than the Middle Ages of Europe. It was then that the illustrators of the exquisite Persian manuscripts and a laxity of the old belief produced scenes of their daily life upon gorgeous Persian textiles and ceramics. The magnificence of the Saracenic Empire was inspired by the older and richer culture of Persia and it attained its height in luxury and learning at both ends of the kingdom, in Spain and Persia.

The period of the Moorish occupation in Spain which lasted eight centuries, ending in 1492, is known as Hispano-Moresque.

Men followed the European fashion in beard, mustache and coiffure. The masculine headdress consisted as it does today, of the turban, wound round the head or over a crown or skullcap, the tall bonnet or *tāj*. There is also a draped headcloth with neckcloth.

The turban, of obscure Oriental origin, is noted as a particular style of headtire worn by the men of the Mohammedan faith and is, essentially, a scarf of fine linen, cotton or silk folded round the head. Dulband was its Persian name, meaning a sash. The English name derives from turband, tolibant or tulipant, all variations of the flower tulip, suggested by the design of the folds. An important detail in wrapping the turban is to leave the forehead bare so that when prostrated at prayer the wearer's head touches the ground. It is considered a crime in Mohammedan countries for an unbeliever to wear the turban.

The turban varies in shape, size, folds and color according to degree of rank, race, profession and locale. The single piece of cloth ranges from twenty to thirty inches wide and six to nine yards long to a piece of six to eight inches wide and ten to fifty yards long. Mohammedans have described as many as sixty-six different types. A controversial theological question revolves, especially in hot climates, around how soon after prayers the scarf may be removed. The skullcap is usually worn at work.

Both men and women of the Mohammedan faith wear the *tarboosh,* Arabic for the brimless felt skullcap, a cap of Greek origin. The Egyptian wraps a scarf round his tarboosh and certain Indian races drape it round the *kullah,* the Persian name for the pointed skullcap. Sir Sayyid Ahmad, the Indian-born Mohammedan educator and reformer, introduced the cap into India in the nineteenth century. In Afghanistan, the scarf is swathed round a conical cap and the Hindu winds his scarf round his shaved head. Some Indian races wear a made-up turban.

In the same category as the tarboosh, can be placed the fez and the *chéchia,* varying but slightly in shape. Chéchia is the name for the Berber *tashashit* or skullcap which has a tassel. The Turkish fez, usually red and tufted with a blue or black tassel, got its name from Fez, chief city of Morocco. It was supposed that the dull crimson hue produced by the juice of a berry which grew in the vicinity could not be procured elsewhere, but in recent times the red cap was successfully made in France and Turkey.

When the Turks conquered Constantinople in 1453, they adopted, with modification, the Byzantine costume including the Greek cap. But the headdress of the followers of Mohammed, the turban, was draped in folds round the cap, thus signifying "right of conquest." A picture with caption of the sixteenth century tells us that the Turk "whose turban is always very clean," wore a large umbrella-shaped hat of felt over his turban when going out in the rain.

The reformer Sultan Mahmud of the early nineteenth century decreed the turban no longer obligatory but the crimson skullcap was to be retained. After World War I, in 1923 Turkey under Mustafa Kemal, decided to become a modern nation and proclaimed herself a republic. The Mohammedan code of laws was abolished, and in 1925 the Western form of civilization was adopted. The national dress of men and women was outlawed, taking with it the centuries-old skullcap. Persia followed suit in 1928 by adopting Western dress for men and in 1936 for women.

The *tāj*, Persian and Arabic for crown, traces its origin to the ancient tiara of the Mesopotamian Valley. The tall, brimless cone-shaped cap can be seen today in all Moslem countries, where it remains a headdress of distinction.

Beautiful long hair on the feminine head was a source of great pride and much loving care was given it. Young women wore theirs flowing, and before marriage, painted the face, bosom, arms, fingertips and toes. Kohl and indigo were applied to the eyes, rouge to the lips and cheeks, henna to the fingertips and toes. The veins of the bosom were accentuated with indigo, an ancient Egyptian fashion.

Noble women seldom left the palace, and then usually to attend the mosque. They covered the face up to the eyes with a neckcloth of fine cotton, linen or silk, another over the head or hat and then a shawl over all. The feminine headpiece was always a charming tarboosh or the tall *tāj* of such rich fabrics as gold or silver tissue, silk brocade and later, velvet. Veils were sheer, of plain and striped fabrics, fringed with silk and metal thread. Long earrings were a general adornment and both sexes were fond of ornate jewelry, wearing many lavish pieces.

The weaving of velvet is supposedly of great antiquity, but its definite appearance was in the thirteenth century, when we note its manufacture in Paris and Venice. Velvet, a precious fabric, became the favored material of the nobles and wealthy people.

That delicate tool by which fine handwork is produced, the steel needle, was introduced into Europe by the Moors, but the first European manufacture of the article took place in 1370 in Nuremberg.

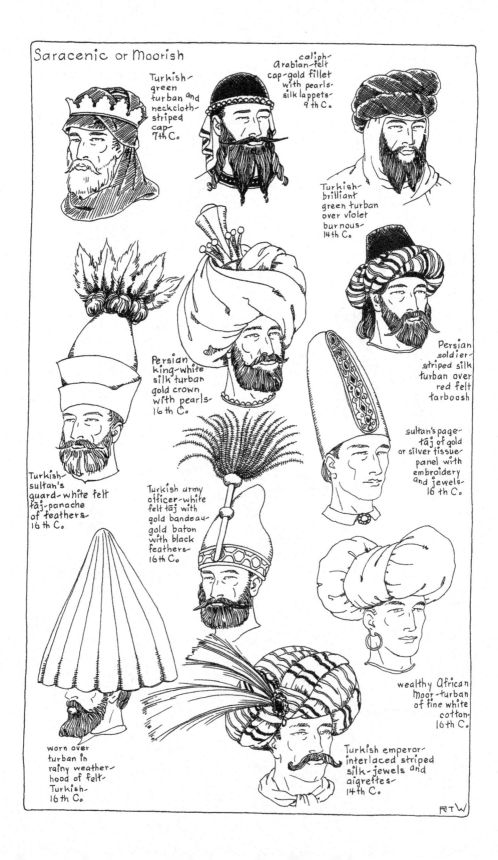

Saracenic or Moorish

Turkish-green turban and neckcloth-striped cap- 7th C.

caliph- Arabian-felt cap-gold fillet with pearls-silk lappets- 9th C.

Turkish- brilliant green turban over violet burnous- 14th C.

Persian king-white silk turban gold crown with pearls- 16th C.

Persian soldier-striped silk turban over red felt tarboosh

Turkish-sultan's guard-white felt tāj-panache of feathers- 16th C.

Turkish army officer-white felt tāj with gold bandeau-gold baton with black feathers- 16th C.

sultan's page-tāj of gold or silver tissue-panel with embroidery and jewels- 16th C.

wealthy African moor-turban of fine white cotton- 16th C.

worn over turban in rainy weather-hood of felt-Turkish- 16th C.

Turkish emperor-interlaced striped silk-jewels and aigrettes- 14th C.

RTW

Saracenic or Moorish

Turkish high ranking official-tāj of folds of white linen, silk or cotton- 16th C.

Turkish official of high rank- turban of folds of white cotton, linen or silk- 16th C.

Arabian noble- turban of fine white linen 16th C.

Persian soldier- turban wound round tall crown of one dozen pleats- 16th C.

Persian prince- white turban wound round tall crown- jewels and feather- 16th C.

Persian noble- turban in set folds- rich jewel- 15th C.

Persian warrior- steel helmet- chain mail cheek guards- 15th C.

Turkish Janizary- white felt helmet- gold ornament- varied precious jewels- 16th C.

bishop of Constantinople- bands in form of cross- lappets at side- 16th C.

RTW

Saracenic or Moorish

Persian-
tāj of gold
brocade-
jeweled gold
disks- fringed
voile scarf-

Turkish-
tarboosh of
velvet or satin-
jewels and
pearls

Turkish-
tarboosh of
turquoise blue
velvet or satin-
gold tissue
bands with
pearls

African Moor-
white shawl
over gold
tissue
tarboosh-
white
chin
cloth

Turkish sultana-
jeweled
cidaris of
silk and
velvet-full
length
veil

Arabian-
tarboosh
of velvet or
silk-rolled
bandeau-
gold leaves
and pearls

Persian-
jeweled bandeau
and earrings-silk
voile turban and
neckcloth-
flowing hair
bound with silk

Turkish-
tarboosh of
velvet with
silk fall-
feathers

Turkish-
fringed shawl
over tarboosh-
silk net screen
with velvet
frame

Turkish-
tāj of velvet,
silk or metal
tissue-silk
turban and fall-
jeweled earrings
and necklace

Persian-
tāj of gold
brocade-
white feathers
and jewels-
earrings

Persian matron-
draped velvet
turban and
crown-
white
head
cloth

RTW

MEDIEVAL OR GOTHIC EUROPE
CHAPTER SEVEN

HISTORIANS GENERALLY place the Middle Ages between the fall of
Rome, 476 A.D. and the fall of Constantinople in 1453, or from about 400 A.D. to
the revival of letters.

The traditions of Greece and Rome in dress had been carried over to the
Medieval Period by the courts of the Byzantine emperors but with a definite
Oriental flavor, the result of their contact with the East by way of the wealthy
city of Constantinople. By the end of the twelfth century that influence tended
to disappear when the flourishing cities of Florence and Venice began to set
the tone for the courts of Europe. Oriental luxuries reached the Continent during the Crusades and through the busy ports of Venice and Genoa.

The Italian mode, more reserved and sophisticated than that of its northern
followers, was the leading influence into the period of the Renaissance. However, though the mode of the French Renaissance was of Venetian inspiration,
we find that as early as the fourteenth century a fashion doll was being sent
yearly from Paris to Venice. A contemporary writer notes that extravagance
in dress was being carried to excess in France and England and that London,
as early as the first half of the twelfth century, was copying Paris.

In the early centuries, the Northern Europeans, following the style of their Roman conquerors, were clean-shaven and wore their hair cut short. Beards and long hair were privileged only to nobility and certain dignitaries. The ruling lasted to the twelfth century. Hair and beard were curled with "crisping irons" and the beard often interlaced with gold thread or dressed into two points.

The king's hair was sometimes long enough to arrange in braids, which lay one over each shoulder, or to curl into long ringlets.

With the invasion of the Normans into England came the fashion of the hair shaved up the back of the head but eventually, long and curled hair returned to favor, even the priests wearing curled locks.

Round the head and holding the hair in place was worn a ribbon or metal fillet usually with short lappets in back, the circlet often enriched with jeweled ornaments. The chaplet, whence derives the French word chapeau for hat, of fresh flowers, as in the Age of Antiquity, was worn by both men and women. There were also flower chaplets fashioned in gold and enamels.

Bobbed hair with a fringe over the forehead appeared in the twelfth century, a trim mustache and cropped beard often accompanying it. The bobbed haircut lasted to the beginning of 1600. Smart Venetian gentlemen either bleached their hair or wore wigs of blond or yellow silk and such a coiffure is to be seen in a portrait by Giovanni Bellini, painted about 1475. It was called "coiffure à la Zazzera" and a like hairdo can be seen in a portrait bust of ancient Rome, Constantius II. Another fashion of the fifteenth century was a fluffy, frizzed shoulder-length bob which looked as if the hair had been braided tightly into tiny plaits at night and then combed out in the morning. The long coiffure was called a wig whether natural or false.

Masculine headcovering in the early Moyen Age varied in style; the Phrygian-shaped hood or chaperon, the cowl which was a hood attached to a mantle, and the coif or cap which tied under the chin. There was also the brimmed hat resembling the ancient Greek pétasos with its chinstrap by which the hat hung in back or was tied to the belt when not on the head. A movable ring on the string pushed up to the chin held the hat secure on the head. In the ninth, tenth and eleventh centuries gentlemen usually went bareheaded, wearing cap, hood or hat only when traveling.

We find the coif worn by all classes in the last years of the twelfth century. At first considered "effeminate" and contemptuously referred to as the "woman's bonnet," it became a fashion which lasted nearly two centuries. It came from Byzantium where it was worn by the clergy, under the crowns of the nobles and of hare felt or leather padding under the metal helmet. The coif worn by men in Medieval Europe was always white, of fine linen for elegant people and of a coarser weave for the less dressy ones. It was a counterpart of the infant's bonnet with the same little strings tied under the chin. It returned in the eighteenth century for wear under the heavy wig and was retained until late in the nineteenth under the wig of the English lawyer.

The finest caps were made of batiste, a closely woven sheer fabric which appeared in the thirteenth century but, unlike the cotton batiste of today, was made of fine linen thread. It bears the name of its originator, the Frenchman Baptiste of Cambrai.

In the fifteenth century, the coif or cap of colored felt or velvet, usually in red, took the place of the white linen cap.

The hood or chaperon, a headcovering of both sexes, took on a new and popular manner of wearing in the masculine world at the end of the thirteenth century. Of Italian origin was the idea of using the face opening as the headband, crushing the whole on top of the head with the point or tail hanging down on one side, the remaining folds on the other, resembling a cock's comb. The hat was known as the chaperon turban or the twisted cockscomb turban, and here we have the origin of the term "cockscomb." In Italian, it was the *cappuccio*.

For many years, the chaperon was arranged into folds each time when placed upon the head but eventually it was fashioned and sewn into a real hat.

In the second half of the fourteenth century with the vogue for petal-scalloping or dagged, jagged or castellated edges, the edges of the turban folds were cut in like manner.

The chaperon was next made up over a stuffed round turban or "roundlet" and the tail or liripipe acquired great length. Besides liripipe, the English called it a tippet, but tippet appears to have been any pendant piece of the costume. Only a noble was permitted to wear a long-tailed hat, a very short one sufficing the commoner.

It became the fashion in the second half of the fifteenth century to sling the chaperon over the shoulder, holding it by the streamer, the wearer often having another hat or cap upon his head. Carrying two hats, one on the head, the other attached to the liripipe, did not appear redundant to the "well-dressed" man of the Gothic Period as it would seem to us. Back of him was the age-old custom of a cap on the head and the practical weather hat or pétasos hanging in back, to be placed upon the head when required.

By the end of the century, the fashion had run its course for smart young men but the arrangement with streamer over one shoulder was retained as a badge of rank by older professional men, as were the flowing robes of the period.

The round stuffed ornament grew smaller and the liripipe shorter but the badge it became can be seen today on the left shoulder of the French magistrate and on the robe of the Knight of the Garter. The cockade too, worn by liveried servants, is reminiscent of the roundlet with the pleated and dagged-edged chaperon.

Some contemporary drawings show dashing young fellows carrying their hat aloft on their swagger stick. Of this period is the cap and bells of the jester or the fool's cap which originated in the universally worn hood of the Middle Ages. The small silver bells were a fashionable trimming, especially on the parti-colored clothes and the baldric in the fourteenth and fifteenth centuries. Parti-colored combinations spread to the bonnets and hoods of both sexes.

Of varied shape were bonnets made of wool, hair or cotton felt, cloth or velvet. That traditionary English hero and outlaw of the twelfth century, Robin Hood, is commonly portrayed wearing the conical hood with self brim pulled down in front and shading the face. The general color of felt was black and not till after 1300 were felts and beavers dyed in colors.

Beaver was called "hair." Just when beaver was first employed for hats is not known but it is recorded that beaver hats were imported from Flanders before the end of the fourteenth century. In 1386, Chaucer wrote of a "Flaundrish bever hat."

Straw hats were also worn and the hat of countryfolk was a brimmed affair fashioned from rushes.

Velvet was a precious fabric especially favored by the nobles and people of wealth in the Medieval Period. It first appeared in Venice and Paris in the twelfth century, the weavers of Venice establishing a guild in 1247. We find black patterned velvets in the fourteenth century, colored velvet not being produced in Venice until the fifteenth century.

The very tall, steeple or sugar-loaf felt bonnet of the fourteenth and fifteenth centuries was often worn over the hood or chaperon. Fine felt, fabric and straw hats were made in the Duchy of Milan in the fifteenth and sixteenth centuries and were known as "Millayne bonnets." Thence comes our English word "milliner," the London maker of feminine caps and bonnets being called a "milainer."

The Anglo-Saxon word for hat, haet or haett appears to have signified a shape resembling the pétasos; that is, with crown, wide brim and easily removed from the head. Otherwise, until the sixteenth century, any hat other than the hood was a "cap" in English or a "bonnet" in French. A coarse, green woolen cloth called "bonet" was popular for men's headgear in the Middle Ages and from that, came the term "bonnet" applied to the masculine hat or cap. The name "bonnet" was not given feminine headgear until the end of the eighteenth century and since the early nineteenth century has designated the small bonnet with strings tied under the chin. And the Scotsman of today still calls his cap a bonnet.

Early in the fourteenth century, the feather appeared for the first time as an ornament on European headgear, at first a single, long, upstanding feather secured in a golden socket or held by a jeweled medal. Feathers were indeed costly and by the end of the fifteenth century, the fashion had assumed the proportions of a craze. The plumage of rare Oriental birds was imported and ostrich and peacock were very elegant.

In the second half of the fifteenth century, feathers were used in profusion on the fashionable masculine hat, each one a different color and its spine ornamented with pearls or other gems. This plumed hat was sometimes worn over a coif of velvet or cloth usually red or crisscrossed with gold braid. It also hung down in back, the head covered with the coif. Very rich were fur-trimmed winter hats and "peacock's hats" with brim and perhaps crown flatly covered with the tail feathers.

An English record of 1369 tells us that caps were of "divers colours," especially red, and had costly linings. Another writing in the time of Edward IV (1461–1483) gives the information that tall black bonnets were "most genteel."

The nobleman often employed his crown or jeweled necklace as a band on his "brimmed bonnet." Though from Byzantine times sovereigns are always pictured wearing jeweled gold crowns, all people of rank and wealth wore crowns in those days. Not until the sixteenth century did the size and shape of a crown or coronet signify definitely the wearer's family status.

The doges of the ancient Republic of Venice in the twelfth century wore the tall, conical, felt tiara of Oriental origin which they called the *corno*. The corno or "ducal bonnet" in 1249 changed from the tall conical shape to a cap with the point rising from the back and from then, was always worn over the white linen coif. The ducal bonnet disappeared from history with the last doge of Venice in 1797 in Napoleon's destruction of the helpless Venetian Republic.

The headcovering of both sexes was an ornamental part of the costume worn indoors and out. Men did not remove their hats when ladies were present. The king always wore his headpiece but his courtiers remained uncovered in his presence. Only royal permission, a special honor, permitted a noble to wear his hat before the sovereign. The custom was to remove the hat in deference to a superior with the words "your servant." The significance of the gesture passed into oblivion with the centuries but the act remained as a common greeting in "tipping the hat."

The Church required that the feminine head be covered when present in any religious assembly and so we find in the early centuries of the Middle Ages, women used the palla or mantle as headcovering or a white headcloth of linen or silk draped over the head and round the neck. This piece was the *couvre-chef*, coverchief, headtire, headrail or wimple, which also served as headtire when traveling until the twelfth century.

A law governed the length of the scarf, the noble lady's veil reaching to her feet, that of her sister of lesser rank reaching only to the waist. The loveliest *couvre-chefs*, often handsomely embroidered, of the Moyen Age, were made by the "couvre-chef-makers of Rheims" and worn by the patricians of Italy and the noble women of England. The wimple worn by all classes to the latter part of the thirteenth century survived as headcovering for the lower classes until the fifteenth century.

A bandlette or snood of silk held the wimple in place. Ladies of quality wore a crown or circlet over the veil and the young girls of noble family wore either the gold or silver circlet.

In the twelfth century appeared the arrangement of a chinband and a headband, folds of white linen about one and a half inches wide, to which the wimple was pinned. Sometimes these bands were considered decorative enough, especially by the Italian ladies, to be worn without the wimple.

The lady of the tenth to the twelfth century wore her hair flowing or in two braids. Flowing hair continued to be the coiffure of young unmarried women and brides through the Middle Ages. Queens, for the coronation ceremony wore theirs in that fashion as late as the fifteenth century. The long braids hung in front, often reaching to the hem of the garment. If necessary, false hair was added for length and thickness or the braids of the owner's hair were finished with long silk cases stuffed and of various colors, sometimes finished with tassels or metal ends. The braids were also bound with gold or silver "ribbands" finished with ornamental pendants. A gadget in use through the Middle Ages for parting the hair was a small stiletto of crystal or ivory mounted with gold.

The turret, a crownless white linen toque, was worn in the twelfth century over the chinband or barbette, sometimes over the wimple and with either flowing hair or a coiffure dressed in a chignon at the nape of the neck.

Following the turret and in the thirteenth century came the "mortar toque," resembling its predecessor in being worn over the barbette but covered on top and varied in its use of fabric. Velvet, satin and taffeta were employed, embroidered with pearls and gold thread. The coiffure remained the same.

In the same century, the barbette was replaced by the chincloth or *gorget,* a piece of linen or silk draped over chin, neck and shoulders and pinned to the hair at the sides of the face. The combined wimple and gorget became the headdress for widows and women of religious orders, remaining so until the twentieth century. Women of the Church, however, were forbidden the wimple of silk, wearing then, as now, one of plain white linen.

There were colored wimples in the latter part of the fourteenth century but the preference seems to have been for white and saffron. Veils, nets and gorgets were worn by all classes, the difference being in the quality of the fabric.

The chaplet or circlet by the fourteenth century designated the wearer as an unmarried woman and the cap, the matron. Saint Catherine's Day, observed in France each November 25, carries on this tradition. On that day, the single girl of twenty-five dons Saint Catherine's bonnet, a richly decorated piece. Legend has it that the Saint succeeded in converting the wife of the Roman Emperor Maxentius (305–312 A.D.) to Christianity and crowned her with an angel's crown. Why a fête day for the spinster should commemorate this event, is not clear.

Hairdressing and headcovering became elaborate in the fourteenth century, the white linen toque disappearing in the last quarter of that period. The hair still parted in the middle, had braids turned up and dressed at the sides of the face, forming "bosses" or horns. This fashion often required false hair, the use of which was common. Jewel-headed pins held the gorget and the wimple to the hair.

Then followed, also in the fourteenth century, the headdress of many names, which enjoyed a vogue of nearly three hundred years. It was called the golden net caul, the reticulated headdress, crépine, crestine and crespinette. The hair was concealed in silken cases covered with a heavy net of gold or silver cord, interspersed with pearls, jewels, beads or spangles. The caul was often attached to a jeweled crown or circlet.

The escoffion became the fashion and very popular too, worn over wimple or caul or perhaps both, a stuffed roll of varied shapes, turban-shaped, heart-shaped and two-horned. They were all designated as the escoffion although the two-horned headdress finally acquired the name for its very own. The steeple or sugar-loaf appeared but was uncommon until the fifteenth century.

Such headdresses were worn over or attached to a concealed calotte which had a black velvet or gold loop showing on the forehead. The loop was called a frontlet, sometimes a *bongrace*. Ladies of high rank wore a gold loop and in England, the velvet loop indicated that the fair wearer had an income of ten pounds or more a year.

The richest fabrics were employed, damasks, silks, velvets, brocades, gold and silver fretwork, gold embroidery over brilliant color and sewn with spangles, pearls and jewels to which was added floating drapery of gold or silver tissue, sheer white linen, silk with dagged edges and in all lengths. Gauze, a loosely woven transparent silk came from Gaza, Palestine, whence its name. It was brought back by the knights of the Crusades to their ladies.

There has always been much conjecture over the *hennin,* that Oriental headdress dating back to the tiara of the ancient Persians and before that, to the Etruscans. The tall pointed cap had been worn over the centuries by the Italian popes and an ancient manuscript in the Vatican contains a portrait of the Italian Lady Mathilde, the "great Countess of Tuscany," (1046–1115) wearing a tall steeple hat over her wimple. A bas-relief from the tomb of Marie de Molina (1284-1321) portrays the Spanish queen of Castille in a two-horned headdress worn with the reticulated caul and the wimple. We read that Queen Isabelle of France in 1326, wore a steeple hennin and that Isabelle of Bavaria (1371-1435) introduced the escoffion or two-horned headdress into France. Then, another authority states that it appeared in 1428 in Flanders and in Paris in 1429.

The hennin very likely did reach Paris by way of the Low Countries, as France was an impoverished country at the time and Fashion, in that period, issued many of her decrees from the wealthy cities of Ghent and Bruges. Hennin could be from the Flemish word *hennen* for cock, prompted, no doubt, by the cock's crest or comb.

The hennin acquired its great height after 1430 and the period of its greatest vogue was from 1440 to 1470. Despite the protestations of the opposite sex and the clergy, the fashion of the escoffion and the hennin lasted over a hundred years. The Italian adaptation of the fantastic style was confined to a low hennin and a modified version of the two-horned escoffion with short veil or none at all. By the middle of the fifteenth century in France, the variations became bizarre and in England overstepped all bounds, reaching in some noted cases, a height of three feet. A woman of the French bourgeoisie was permitted a hennin not higher than sixty centimetres or about twenty-four inches.

The wide fold of black velvet which adorned the hennin in the second half of the fifteenth century remained the framework of the gable or diamond-shaped headdress. That style appeared at the end of the century but is more definitely associated with the sixteenth century, especially with the reign of Henry VIII (1509-1547) through the handsome and documentary portraits of his court painter, Hans Holbein, the younger (1497-1543).

The wired or "butterfly headdress," a variation of the hennin, came into fashion about 1470. The embroidered and beaded box-like cap with flat top was perched on the crown of the head and draped with a flaring angular arrangement of sheer lawn held in butterfly shape by fine wire. The cap was of colored silk sometimes embroidered in silk and gilt to which precious stones were also added.

Of the fourteenth century is the cornet, a pointed or horned lingerie cap, origin of today's insignia of the trained nurse. The medieval headdress and costume were retained over the centuries by women of religious orders of which nuns were the first to staff the modern hospital. The cornet was quite generally worn to the eighteenth century.

Cornets and caps of lace are mentioned by a Belgian writer in the fourteenth century although lace-making is placed by authorities in the fifteenth century in Italy and Flanders. France, England and Germany learned the art of lace-making from Flanders. The evolution of lace-making was a process of centuries of needlework and cutwork, culminating in real lace patterns in the sixteenth century.

Stiffened gauze appeared in the second half of the fifteenth century but the invention of starch was nearly a hundred years away, about 1560, so one supposes that a glue sizing must have been employed.

The bride of the Moyen Age wore over her flowing hair, either a chaplet or fillet of fresh flowers or one of enamels and jewels. A favorite bridal piece was an embroidered or jeweled calotte, particularly the tiny mesh cap of pearls.

The chaperon or hood, like that of the men, was a headcovering for outdoors. Women also adopted the liripipe. The black hood was considered a garment of dignity and in the reign of Edward III of England (1312–1377) could not be worn by prostitutes. We read that in 1472 in several English towns, such women were compelled to wear striped hoods. In France, the black hood could be worn only by women of station and the velvet hood by ladies of the court. This hood in the sixteenth century came to be known as the French hood, also the "venerable hood" of poetry and literature.

For hunting on horseback, women copied the masculine style of the large felt hat which they wore over the wimple and gorget.

The headdress of the Middle Ages was fastened with a great number of pins. Ordinary pins were costly gadgets in the thirteenth and fourteenth centuries, whence our expression "pin money." A tax levied on the common people paid for the queen's pins. The use of pins became general in the fourteenth century. They made most acceptable gifts presented by swains to their lady-loves, and in England became a special New Year's gift. Women of all classes saved their pin money to buy the necessary articles yearly, on the first and second days of January. Parliament, in an effort to curtail this feminine extravagance, permitted pin-makers only those two days of the year on which to sell their coveted wares. An entry of 1347 charges twelve thousand pins for the trousseau of the daughter of the English king, Edward III. English ladies received their pins from France and there is note of an act in 1483 prohibiting the importation of the articles. The original model was a shank of wire with wire round one end, forming a head.

Blond or black hair were the desired colors in the Medieval Period and both men and women colored their locks with saffron or an infusion of onion skin. A strong prejudice existed against red hair, which, it was believed, harbored undesirable qualities in the character of the person so unfortunate as to possess it.

The desired complexion of the period was pale and delicate, and powders of harmful pigment were employed to secure it, even to painting the face with white lead. There were epilatory pastes, pomades for the skin and lips and a powdered dentifrice for whitening the teeth. English women used rouge for the first time in the thirteenth century. Soapmaking became an important industry in the thirteenth and fourteenth centuries.

The very naked look of the feminine head in this period of fantastic headdress was acquired by plucking all the hair that showed below the headgear on the forehead and the back of the head. In fact, a lady would in public, with the aid of her small mirror or piece of polished metal, pluck a few hairs in very much the same manner that our women of today casually make use of their powder and lipstick. Her eyebrows, too, were plucked to a thin line. For combing the hair, combs were of bone, boxwood and ivory and late in the period, the artist turned his attention to designing exquisitely carved ones often set with jewels.

It was in the fifteenth century in Bruges that the art of cutting diamonds in facets was developed and Agnes Sorel (1409-1450), the favorite mistress of the French king, Charles VII, was the first woman to wear them.

Medieval Europe

Frankish nobleman-
gold circlet
with
ribbons-
9th C.

Norman
and
English-
9th C.

Italian duke
or doge-
fabric-gold
and jewels-
11th C.

Italian
noblewoman-
fabric-gold
band with
jewels-over
wimple-
11th C.

calotte of
blue fabric
with pearls-
German-
11th C.

gold crown
with jewels-
hair in
braids-
French-
12th C.

Norman and
English-
braids in
silk cases
and ribbon-
12th C.

noble-fabric,
gold and ribbons-
French-
12th
C.

jeweled
crown over
wimple-
ribbon
bound hair-
French-
12th C.

ribbon cases-
metal points
with
ribbon loops-
English-
12th C.

square gold crown-
trefoiled ornaments-
jewels-
Anglo-Saxon king-
10th C.

Venetian noble-
biretta of silk-
pearls-
silk cord
insignia-
12th C.

Venetian doge-
corno of felt
with gold
and jewels-
12th C.

RTW

Medieval Europe

wimple with jeweled circlet- French- 12th C.

felt or woolen calotte-felt hat worn over calotte-cord with bead- curled hair- English- 12th C.

wimple over head band and chinband- white linen- 12th C.

coif of white linen tied under chin- 13th C.

felt hat with pearls- curled hair- English and French- 13th C.

calotte of felt- English- 12th and 13th C.

pinned bands to which wimple was pinned- white linen- 12th C.

jeweled gold crown over white wimple- white gorget- German- 13th C.

gold crown over white linen chinstrap and calotte- German- 12th C.

gold crown with jewels- white linen chinstrap- French noble- 13th C.

gold crown worn over white linen wimple- French- 13th C.

felt hat over woolen chaperon or hood- gold crown- gold ring on wooden spike- French- 13th C.

felt bonnet over white linen coif- French- 13th C.

toque and chinstrap- white linen folds- flowing hair- knotted green silk mantle reaching to ground- Italian- 13th C.

RTW

Medieval Europe

straw hat over white linen coif - French peasant - 13th C.

white linen head and chinbands - embroidery - flowing hair - Spanish - 13th C.

Italian gentleman - red moiré hat - white brim - late 13th and early 14th C.

cornet headdress - white linen gorget pinned to rolled braids - English - early 14th C.

velvet biretta - pearls - white linen coif - French - 14th C.

cornet coiffure - white linen wimple and gorget - white linen fold over jeweled crown - braids in buns - English - 13th C.

white linen crownless turret and and coif pressed creases - net over chignon - French and German - 13th C.

gold circlet - jewels - curled hair - French courtier - 14th C.

red silk toque - white linen border, wimple and chinband - French - 13th C.

red silk toque - white linen wimple and chinband - English - 13th C.

jeweled crown and circlet - white linen wimple and chinband - German - 13th C.

Venetian doge - red silk corno - gold and jeweled crown - white linen coif - 13th C.

curled hair - felt hat - pleated band - white linen coif - Italian - 13th C.

calotte over hood - white cloth striped red and blue silk - white ostrich - young French courtier - 14th C.

calotte over wimple - gold circlet with pearls - French - 14th C.

RTW

Medieval Europe

the hood or chaperon worn by all classes and both sexes—early 13th C.

velvet chaperon turban worn over white linen coif—French—1310

cloth capuchon with liripipe—circa 1360

the jester's hood with additional asses' ears and silver bells—English—early 14th C.

hood or chaperon with liripipe tied round head—English—14th C.

velvet chaperon turban with liripipe—French—circa 1395

cloth chaperon turban—Italian—late 14th C.

chaperon turban of silk worn over white linen coif—German—early 14th C.

chaperon turban with liripipe—petal·scalloped edges—Flemish—early 15th C.

bobbed hair—French—circa 1468

RTW

Medieval Europe

chaperon turban-
silk with
embroidery and
colored spangles-
early 15th C.

roundlet with
chaperon and
liripipe-jeweled
brooch-
French-
mid 15th C.

chaperon with
liripipe-
velvet
with pearls-
French-
circa
1410

roundlet with
chaperon and
liripipe worn
over felt coif-
cloth or silk-
petal-scalloped
points-
French-
early 15th C.

chaperon
turban with
liripipe-
velvet-
Italian-
early 15th C.

roundlet with
liripipe-cloth
or silk-
French-
mid 15th C.

roundlet
draped with
folds of silk-
worn over
felt coif-
Flemish-
1st half 15th C.

roundlet of silk
with pearls and
colored stones-
French-
1st half 15th C.

coiffure à la
Zazzera-
silk wig
usually yellow-
Italian-
circa
1475

RTW

Medieval Europe

velvet chaperon—turned up felt brim—liripipe draped round shoulders—Italian—2nd half 15th C.

chaperon into badge and cockade

modern badge of office of French magistrate—black with ermine

roundlet with liripipe—felt cap—French—1458

sugar-loaf felt bonnet over cloth chaperon—14th and 15th C.—English

bag cap of velvet—jeweled medal—felt coif—French—early 15th C.

chaperon and liripipe into badge of office of French magistrate—felt bonnet—frizzed hair—1464

felt bonnet—petal scalloped edge—metal ornament—long feather—English—early 14th C.

hunting hat of felt—rose colored crown—ribbon stripes—turquoise blue brim—gold crown—pearls—Italian—14th C.

brown felt with jeweled medal—worn over red felt coif—French—15th C.

felt hat with braid design—French—1st half 15th C.

RTW

Medieval Europe

young dandy-
sugar-loaf or steeple
hats of felt-
fur-ostrich
plume-satin
streamer-
French-
3rd quarter
15th C.

red felt hat
over cap-
jeweled crown-
yellow
feathers-
Franco-
Flemish-
1480's

corno
of felt with
jeweled knob-
gold circlet-
Italian nobleman-
15th C.

velvet bonnet-
fur band-
pearls and
silk tassel-
army officer-
French-
1st half
15th C.

felt bonnet-
young nobleman-
French-
circa 1488

steeple
felt hat-
French-
last
quarter
15th C.

crushed satin
crown-velvet
brim-
French-
2nd half
15th C.

satin
turban-
ostrich
feathers-
German-
end of
15th C.

ducal
bonnet or cap-
red felt-
mortar shaped-
Italian-
last quarter
15th C.

RTW

Medieval Europe

sugar·loaf felt bonnet· bobbed hair· French· 1468

felt hat· gold ribbon· pearl ornament· Flemish· 15th C.

black felt bonnet· pearl coronet· French· 2nd half 15th C.

hunting hat of beaver with peacock feathers· cord tied under chin· French and English· 15th C.

beige felt bonnet over red calotte· emerald green feathers· gold rings· French· late 15th C.

sugar·loaf felt bonnet· jeweled medals· cock feather· cord band· French· 15th C.

red felt bonnet over blue calotte· rose and white ostrich feathers· French· late 15th C.

yellow felt striped with brown ribbon· mauve ostrich feather· French· end of 15th C.

white felt hat· red velvet bandeau crossed with gold braid· peacock feathers· French· end of 15th C.

RTW

Medieval Europe

bride with
flowing hair-
colored velvet
calotte-pearl
and gem
embroidery-
Italian-
1360

escoffion-
stuffed roll of white
silk-red ribbon
stripes and embroidery-
white lappets in back-
Italian-
14th C.

escoffion-
sheer voile
shirred over a
stuffed form-
Venetian-
14th C.

ends of braids crossed
above forehead-
chignon-
Italian-
14th C.

hunting hat
over white wimple and
gorget-rose felt crown-
brim faced pea green velvet-
Italian-
14th C.

escoffion-
stuffed roll of
gold cloth-
colored
silk bands-
Italian
14th C.

escoffion-
stuffed roll of blue
velvet-gold
network with pearls-
velvet frontlet-
ribbon bound hair-
Italian noble-
14th C.

hunting
hat over white
wimple and gorget-green under
brim-rose velvet crown and
edge-alternating gold and
pale blue bands-gold
coronet with pearls-
Italian-
14th C.

cornet
headdress of
sheer white
linen-looped
up braids-
Italian-
14th C.

escoffion
of sheer white
voile-red
silk ribbon
stripes-jeweled
brooch-sheer
white wimple-
Venetian-
14th C.

RTW

Medieval Europe

short·tailed chaperon of the bourgeoisie· black cloth· buttons and buttonholes· French· early 14th C.

long·tailed chaperon of the nobles· red cloth· Italian· early 14th C.

chaperon worn over reticulated headdress· hood of velvet or cloth lined with vair· caul of gold cord, pearls and spangles· French· 1330

jeweled gold crown over black velvet chaperon·rows of pearls and diamonds· pleated white linen frill·edged tiny lace points· French queen· 3rd quarter 14th C.

velvet coif with gold bands· hair rolled in buns· 2nd half 14th C.

gold circlet with jewels·sheer white wimple·coiffure gold caul over colored silk· French· 14th C.

golden net caul with jewels over colored silk· jeweled gold crown· sheer wimple wired into horns· Spanish queen· early 14th C.

velvet calotte· coiffure in braids looped at sides of face· French· 1343

escoffion· golden net caul over yellow silk stuffed roll· German· 1st half 14th C.

cornet headdress· golden net caul over gold tissue· French· 14th C.

golden net caul over colored silk· sewn with jewels·jeweled gold crown·back view showing high shaved neck· French queen· 1377

RTW

Medieval Europe

escoffion-
stuffed roll of
silk with
gold
lattice
work and
pearls-
sheer silk
wimple-
German-
14th C.

escoffion-golden net caul
over colored silk-
jeweled gold band-
hair plucked
from neck-
English-
late 14th C.

escoffion with
liripipe-gold
frontlet, fringe
and spangles-
red silk-
noble Italian-
14th C.

escoffion-stuffed
roll of silk over
gauze wimple-
English-late 14th C.

hennin or
steeple hat
of cloth,
felt, silk,
or velvet-
gauze
wimple-
frontlet-
English
noble-
late
14th C.

escoffion-
rose gauze-
gold frontlet
with pearls-
gold ribbon-
Italian noble-
14th C.

escoffion-
stuffed roll of
green velvet-
green and
yellow feathers-
pearls-frontlet-
French noble-
14th C.

escoffion of
brocade-pearl
edging-jeweled
chinband-
Italian-
late 14th C.

escoffion of
brocade-colored
wimple-
Italian-
late 14th C.

escoffion-
golden net caul over
blue silk-gold bands
with colored jewels-
white frill and wimple-
tiny gold coronet with
pearls and red velvet
top-English noble-
late 14th C.

RTW

Medieval Europe

escoffion-stuffed roll-
cloth, silk or velvet-
sheer wimple-dagged
edges-jewel-hair
looped in braids-pearl
edged caul-Flemish-
15th C.

escoffion-
golden net
caul over
colored silk-
sheer wimple
held by
jewel-
English-
late 14th and
early 15th C.

hennin over coif
with velvet frontlet-
silk liripipe-
jewel-hair in
braids-
French noble-
early 15th C.

escoffion
of
velvet
with
jewels-
golden net
caul over
colored silk-
sheer wimple-
French-late 14th C.

the trend
toward the
Renaissance-
of silk and
gauze-
Italian-
15th C.

escoffion with
embroidered stuffed
roll on top-
golden net caul
with pearls-
over colored silk-
sheer wimple with
dagged edge-English-
late 14th and
early 15th C.

escoffion-
gold net over
colored silk-
stuffed roll
of silk with
jewels-sheer
wimple-
French-
1419

escoffion-
golden net caul
with pearls
and embroidery-
gold frontlet-
sheer wimple-
French noble-
15th C.

escoffion-
silk, velvet
or cloth-pearls
and jewels-sheer
chincloth-frontlet-
Flemish noble-
15th C.

RTW

Medieval Europe

escoffion of silk-liripipe-lappets-gold tissue with jewels and pearls-black velvet frontlet-French noble-15th C.

escoffion of velvet-golden net caul over silk-pearl edge-feathers held by brooch-gauze drapery-Flemish-1st half 15th C.

escoffion-stuffed roll with embroidery-caul of gold cord, silk and pearls-dagged-edged wimple-English-late 14th and early 15th C.

cornet-black velvet draped with white linen wimple-frilled-edge-Flemish-1st half 15th C.

escoffion with jeweled crown-stuffed brocaded roll-pearls, jewels and brooch-black velvet calotte and frontlet-sheer wimple pearl edged-French queen-1st half 15th C.

gold crown with pearls and jewels-golden net caul over black velvet with pearl embroidery-black velvet frontlet-Scottish princess-15th C.

cornet headdress-gold tissue and pearls-young woman-Flemish-late 15th C.

escoffion of velvet draped with gauze wimple-gauze headband-Italian-late 15th C.

escoffion-stuffed roll over metal frame-jewels and pearls-French-late 15th C.

jeweled gold diadem-reticulated caul of wire and pearls-German noble-2nd half 15th C.

RTW

Medieval Europe

the "little hennin"
silk or velvet
wimple of
stiffened gauze
black velvet
frontlet
French noble
1st half
15th C.

steeple hennin
white silk with
gold braid black
velvet fall white
gauze drapery
French queen
2nd quarter
15th C.

steeple
hennin of
brocaded silk
velvet frontlet
stiffened gauze
wimple French
noble 1st half
15th C.

triple horned
hennin
brocaded silk
gauze wimple
French
1st half 15th C.

escoffion
brocaded silk stuffed
roll and drapery
bead embroidery
gold braid with
pearls French
1st half 15th C.

RTW

Medieval Europe

hennin-white silk
with jewels and
pearls-white gauze
mounted on wire-
black velvet fall-
jeweled brooch-
French noble-
3rd quarter
15th C.

escoffion-gold
cord with pearls
over white silk
stuffed roll-
sheer gauze
wimple on
wire frame-
English-
15th C.

mortar shaped
hennin of
cloth, silk,
felt or velvet-
stiffened gauze
veil-frontlet-
French noble-
15th C.

béret
style
headdress
without
top-embroidered
silk-
Italian-
15th C.

escoffion-
stuffed roll of
blue velvet-
strings of
beads-frontlet-
hair tied
with ribbon-
young woman-
Flemish-
2nd half
15th C.

gold crown with
pearls and topazes-
black velvet
frontlet-sheer
gauze wimple-
French-
1st half 15th C.

escoffion-stuffed roll
of red velvet-pearl
and jewel embroidery-
white linen chincloth-
German-
2nd half 15th C.

escoffion-gold cord net with pearls-
stuffed roll yellow silk-white linen wimple-
German-2nd half 15th C.

RTW

Medieval Europe

hennin of white silk-
bead embroidery-
brown velvet
band and frontlet-
stiffened white
gauze wimple
pinned in
place-
Flemish-
1st half
15th C.

escoffion-
stuffed roll of
velvet and silk-
gold cord and
pearls-black
velvet frontlet-
gauze chincloth
and streamer-
English-
3rd quarter 15th C.

golden net caul
over colored
silk-gold
crown-pearls
and jewels-
English
queen-
late 15th C.

gold crown
with jewels-
caul of gold
tissue, jewels,
pearls and
embroidery-
Spanish queen-
late 15th C.

hennin of
colored silk-gold
braid and pearls-
wired gauze
wimple-
English-
late
15th C.

hennin of silk
with pearls and
ribbon-black
velvet frontlet-
Flemish noble-
circa 1470

escoffion-
white silk-red
bands-gold cord-
pearls-aigrette-
German-
2nd half
15th C.

black velvet fall-
black velvet frontlet-
white linen lappets-hair
in roll and ribbon-bound-
Flemish-late 15th C.

escoffion-
golden net
caul over
colored silk-
silk crescent
with pearls-
sheer linen
chincloth-
French-
15th C.

RTW

EUROPEAN HELMETS

CHAPTER EIGHT

THESE WERE THE DAYS of archers and crossbowmen employing such implements of warfare as stones, arrows, lances and heavy swords. In the first years of the fifteenth century appeared a primitive handgun for bullets.

The helmet of Europe, following the fall of Rome, was a hat fashioned of boiled leather on a wooden frame reinforced with metal. It was of shell-like design with a serrated comb or crest of iron. The use of boiled leather dates back to antiquity, the leather being boiled in oil, wax or water and then steamed for hardness.

Then followed the conical-shaped helmet known as the *spangenhelm* of boiled leather, with small pieces or bands of iron and topped by a knob of wood or colored glass. Such a helmet the feudal lord of the ninth and tenth centuries wore while his followers went bareheaded or wore skullcaps of felt or hats of straw.

The Bayeux Tapestry, that famous document of the eleventh century, pictures the chevalier with conical helmet or *spangenhelm* of boiled leather but with larger pieces of iron, a nose guard and worn over a hood of mail. This was the common headpiece which Saxons and Normans called respectively helm and *heaume*. Like the woolen hood, the hood of mail could be thrown off and left to lie on the shoulders when not in use.

Mail armor, introduced into Europe from the Orient and worn by the Saxons as early as the eighth century, was composed of metal rings sewn separately to a foundation garment of leather or heavy linen. The Crusaders of the twelfth century adopted the Asiatic fashion of linking the rings, thereby eliminating the foundation garment. An invention of the Crusades was a bonnet of leather or cloth stuffed with wool and quilted, to be worn under the heavy chain mail.

The basinet, really a basin as its name implies, was a lighter helmet of a single piece of steel, the conical point being its distinguishing feature. It was worn over the hood of mail. Next, the camail of chain mail eliminated the hood. It was a cape-like affair sliding upon a rod or string, very much like a curtain attached to the basinet. The camail protected the lower part of the face and the neck. A movable visor succeeded the primitive nose guard and the basinet with camail and visor became the battle headdress of the fourteenth century for nobles, knights and sergeants.

Another armor fashion of the fourteenth century was the hood of mail worn over a coiffette or iron skullcap and still another was a real hat of iron with crown and brim also worn over the mail hood. This iron hat or *chapel-de-fer* was not seen during the next centuries but reappears in the seventeenth as the "Montauban" or again "the iron hat."

With the vogue of tilts and tourneys, the knight found the basinet insufficient protection and wore over it or his hood of mail, when he went into the *melée,* a heavy iron pot covering head and neck. The *heaume* usually rested upon the shoulders, permitting freedom of movement inside, had slits for eyes and perforations for air but even so, must have been frightfully uncomfortable. Knights often collapsed from heat and the weight.

The heaume became the headpiece for jousting and tourneying, the basinet replacing it as a war helmet in the middle of the fourteenth century. The tilting helmet was tied to saddle box or girdle or carried by a page to the moment of donning the piece. It gradually became heavier and more elaborate, assuming in the fifteenth century diversified and eccentric. forms and as a tilting helmet, it lasted two centuries.

The *ventail*, a movable front with perforations, followed the visor. The lower part of the face was next protected by a separate piece of armor covering neck and chin, the *mentonnière, bavière, beaver* or *bever*. Sometimes, beaver and visor were in one. A projecting pin on the right side of the visor enabled the wearer to raise the visor for more air or to be recognized. Today's military salute may be the result of that operation, which was performed with the back of the right hand.

The *barbute* of the fifteenth century was a hood-like helmet sometimes with nose guard, all of one piece. It is the helmet supposedly worn by Jeanne d'Arc.

In the fifteeth century and lasting to the seventeenth, the high crowned basinet was replaced by the *salade* or *sallet,* a word of German origin meaning "shell," with low round crown and a wide projection over the back of the neck. This latter distinctive feature was often gilded, painted or covered with velvet. The salade either had slits for the eyes or a movable visor.

The *armet,* invented by the Italians about 1440, was a helmet incorporating all the advantages of the basinet, heaume and salade with visor and beaver. It was a small rounded shell of iron or steel with plating over the ears, neck and chin and a movable visor. The lower part opened out on hinges. It was connected with the suit by a gorget usually of thin laminated plates and often had a barred face guard. The Italian armet had a rondelle or disc projecting on a short rod at the back of the neck and what was originally a protection against its closing by mistake remained as an ornament. The armet appeared in England about 1500.

The bourguignotte, burgonet or burganet was a bonnet-like casque with crest or comb modeled after the antique, similar to an armet but with cheek pieces and sometimes a nosepiece. Its distinctive feature was the browpiece or umbril to shade the eyes. It was first worn by the Burgundians at the end of the fifteenth century and lasted to the end of the seventeenth. This was the final type of helmet to about 1670 when armor disappeared from the field of battle.

The morion, of crescentic shape, appeared in Europe about 1550, introduced there by the Spaniards who copied it from the Moors. The hat-like piece had crown, brim and eartabs. The cabasset was a style of morion but with straight narrow brim.

The casque or burganet was worn by the Cavalier and the Roundhead of the seventeenth century. The nose guard was simply a bar and the back neck protection was fashioned of several plates, whence its name, the "lobster-tail helmet." Then followed the iron hat, the replica in steel of the civil fashion of the Cavalier, the swaggering felt hat. There was also a socket or plume holder set at the side or back of the crown to hold the sweeping ostrich feathers. The iron hat had a nose guard.

Armor in the fifteenth and sixteenth centuries took on great variety and richness, especially when worn for outdoor ceremonies. All armor in the fifteenth century was a dull blue and for parade, damascened or inlaid with gold, precious stones added and the helmet often topped with a huge emerald. The barbute was often covered with costly velvet and enriched with borders of gilded bronze. Embossed pieces of rare beauty were created by armorers for grand princes and their guards.

The armorers of Milan were famous for their works and the steel casques of Montauban were especially desired. The armor of the Court of Maximilian I in the period 1500 to 1530 was noted for its fine detail. It was essentially German, made by Nuremberg armorers and one of its distinctive features is the beautifully roped edges and flutings.

Armor of iron or polished steel was called white armor and used in battle. Because of the difficulty of keeping polished steel clean, bronze became the favored color in the sixteenth century, especially for jousts and tourneys. Black was tried but it was thought that the gilded and damascened surface with chasing and embossing produced a richer and more artistic effect upon bronze. In the seventeenth century, the period of the decline of the use of armor, the suit and particularly the helmet, was encrusted with enamels, pearls, rubies, emeralds and even diamonds.

And a bit upon heraldry will be fitting here. Symbolical and ornamental figures of birds and animals had decorated the warrior's shield from remote times but the real armorial device or family insignia came into existence in the twelfth century. Distinctive ornamentation became necessary to distinguish the armor-clad individual from his opponent in tournament and battle. At that period, each knight assumed whatever motif he fancied for himself, displaying it upon his shield, banners and pennants and the costumes of his followers, thus the term, "armorial bearings."

Great liberty was taken by the artists in designing heraldic insignia, employing birds, animals, fish, windmills, castles, even the human figure or parts of it. The drawing was fantastic and fabulous.

In the thirteenth century, the heaume with crest became part of the armorial design on the shield and it then became the fashion for the knight to have a replica made of his crest in leather, thin sheet metal, papier-mâché or cloth over a framework of light wood or wire, painted in colors and placed atop his helmet. The arrangement was often so attached that it pivoted in the wind and from it, perhaps, a silken scarf floated in the breeze. The scarf or *cointise* might have been a favor from the knight's lady. The huge and bizarre crest had the peculiar effect of making the wearer appear very small.

Though the heaume was the general headdress for games and pageants, there were various other styles of helmets worn. The heaume was often draped with leather or silk cut with dagged edges, a covering which originated as a protection against the rays of the hot Eastern sun during the Crusades. The decorative quality of the drapery was eagerly seized upon by the heraldic artist and in such drawings is known as the mantling or *lambrequin*.

Added to all this was the owner's jeweled circlet, crown or coronet and perhaps his orle. The orle was a wreath or torse of two colors of silk twisted together representing the principal metal and color of the wearer's crest. Here originated the rank as signified by size and shape of the crown, though in this period crowns were still indiscriminately worn by all who could afford them. The Medieval and modern crown, symbol of sovereignty, is a convergence of the linen or wool fillet or tiara of ancient Eastern origin and the medieval metal crown with foliated upper edge. The circlet or coronet signifies princely or lesser rank.

In England, Germany, Flanders and Italy, knights of all rank wore the crest, which was not so generally worn in France. Bishops too had their armorial bearings and carried a banner and brandished a sword in the tournaments.

In the early fifteenth century, the crest gave way to the rage for ostrich feathers which often streamed in profusion from the top of the helmet, surely a more artistic decoration than the cumbersome crest. Military helmets were made with a tube or socket to hold such adornment. A number of feathers on the apex of the helmet was a *panache* and later, the term "plume of feathers" was applied to several worn at the side or back. A famous panache belonged to Henry VIII, composed of eight plumes four and a half feet long from an Indian bird and deemed worth a proper king's ransom, had he ever been captured.

It was Henry of Navarre, Henry IV of France (1553–1610) who wore the first white plume on his hat and on his helmet. To his leaders before the Battle of Ivry, he commanded "not to lose sight of his white panache, that it would lead them to victory and honor."

Jousting was played with tilting spears by a pair of contestants while the tourney took place among a party of men armed with blunt-edged and silver paper-covered swords. For an opponent to succeed in touching or striking the helmet was considered a master stroke.

Upon the contestant's arrival in the town where the games were to be held, he placed his crest and his banner in the window of his hotel. The day before the performance, all crests and banners were placed on exhibition along a gallery and inspected by the maidens and heralds.

European Helmets

Gallic-Roman soldier leather and iron-painted motif-earliest centuries-a.D.

spangenhelm-leather and small pieces of iron-600 a.D.

spangenhelm-worn over chain mail hood-iron and leather with noseguard-French and English-11th C.

basinet of steel over chain mail hood-13th C.

stitched and padded leather bonnet-covered with steel casque-thin mail hood

coiffette or iron skullcap

mail hood over iron skullcap-steel circlet-buckled fastening-English-13th C.

jeweled crown over mail hood-Spanish seneschal-13th C.

steel basinet with chain mail camail-jeweled circlet-shield with St. George's cross-English-14th C.

basinet with movable ventail over mail hood-French-1386

helm or heaume of iron-1271

orle of rolled silk-two principal colors of wearer's crest-Italian-1385

chapel-de-fer or iron hat over hood of mail-French-late 13th and early 14th C.

ringed mail-no. 1-2-3 rings sewn to leather or heavy linen-no. 4 chain mail

1.

2.

3.

4.

RTW

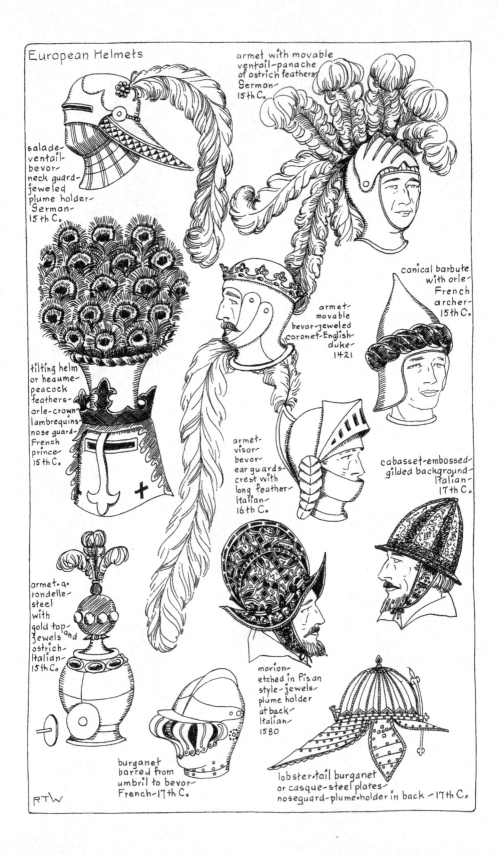

European Helmets

salade-ventail-bevor-neck guard-jeweled plume holder-German-15th C.

armet with movable ventail-panache of ostrich feathers-German-15th C.

tilting helm or heaume-peacock feathers-orle-crown lambrequins-nose guard-French prince-15th C.

armet-movable bevor-jeweled coronet-English-duke-1421

conical barbute with orle-French archer-15th C.

armet-visor-bevor-ear guards-crest with long feather-Italian-16th C.

cabasset-embossed-gilded background-Italian-17th C.

armet-à-rondelle-steel with gold top-and jewels-ostrich-Italian-15th C.

morion-etched in Pisan style-jewels-plume holder at back-Italian-1580

burganet-barred from umbril to bevor-French-17th C.

lobster-tail burganet or casque-steel plates-noseguard-plume-holder in back-17th C.

RTW

RENAISSANCE EUROPE
CHAPTER NINE

AS THE MOYEN AGE and the Renaissance overlap by at least a half century there can be no definite demarcation of dates. The height of the Renaissance is generally placed in the middle of the fifteenth century and its climax about 1500. It originated in Italy and preceded that of its northern neighbors, some authorities say by almost a century.

As in the Medieval Period, the Venetian influence was dominant with its rich and studied elegance and sophisticated coloring but counteracted to some extent by a strong Franco-Flemish feeling. Early in the sixteenth century, costume changed to light and brilliant colors. From the fifteen-thirties, the Spanish silhouette and its flare for black, led the "beau monde" in the "grand manner" until the seventeenth century.

In this, the age of venturing beyond the sea in search of new lands, treasures and commerce, daily life began to acquire new refinements and costume soon revealed the influence of the foreign contacts. Cosmetics and perfumes came from the Orient, pearls and "bever hattes" from the New World, straw and felt hats from Italy, the slashings and puffings from Germany and from Spain came that very elegant headpiece known as the "Spanish toque."

At the beginning of the sixteenth century extending to the fifteen-thirties, the long, straight or crimped bob with deep bangs of natural hair or the wig of yellow or white silk and the clean-shaven face was still popular. Short hair and beards had already been adopted by the Italians and the Swiss when an accident compelled Francois I, French king from 1515 to 1547, to cut his hair. In the fifteen-twenties, on Twelfth-night in a snowball frolic, a firebrand thrown by one of the party, injured his head and necessitated trimming off his long locks. All France copied the new coiffure and Henry VIII of England (1509-1547) ordered his courtiers to follow suit. The style remained in vogue into the early years of the seventeenth century.

Beards varying in shape and length were worn to the middle of the sixteenth century when the Spanish fashion of cropped pointed beard and trim mustache took over entirely. From 1570 to 1590, smart men brushed the front hair up off the forehead. With the invention of starch in the fifteen-sixties, it is said that men starched their beards. In the 'eighties, Frenchmen curled their hair at the temples in the feminine fashion and even dressed it over wire frames.

The well-dressed man did not submit to baldness: he wore a wig. The tilted beret was often attached to a wig in place of a coif. In olden times, a wig did not necessarily signify false hair but was applied to long natural hair.

Henry III of France, king from 1574 to 1589, dusted his hair with a musk-scented powder. He and his courtiers made use of "face-painting," he plucked his eyebrows to an arched line and wore a mask at night to keep his skin soft. Wearing earrings was not a general custom among men but he made it so by insisting that all his courtiers have their ears pierced to hold the baubles. The earring consisted of a jewel on a string which passed through the pierced opening and was tied. The fashion was adopted by other European gentlemen. Ear strings without jewels, tied into the lobe of the ear are to be seen in some men's portraits of the period.

Henry III disliked the masculine style of hat and designed a special one for himself, a diminutive version of the "Spanish toque" with a tiny panache of feathers and a jewel.

That Medieval fashion the chaplet was still to be seen in the first half of the sixteenth century, sometimes of fresh flowers or of small ornaments of gold, enamels and jewels attached to a ribbon fillet. Another masculine vanity was the wearing of a red rose or carnation behind the ear. The Medieval embroidered calotte was worn by men, women and children.

The Renaissance found the smart Venetian wearing the small, round or square, unbrimmed, red or black, felt or velvet cap called a *pileus, biretta* or *bonnet.* It was unadorned and sometimes pinched in at four corners, a very chic piece as it is today. It was eventually worn by all classes and remained with slight variations, the headcovering for church and university with four corners or sign of the cross for a doctor of divinity, three for the university professor. Worn first in the choir, the biretta became the obligatory headcovering of the Roman and the Anglican Churches in the fifteen century. The square trencher or mortarboard university hat of today is an evolution of the fifteenth-century cornered cap.

The use of color in clerical dress was arbitrary prior to 1500, but in 1565 in Milan, black became the accepted color in all Italy. Although certain rules for fabrics were laid down in France in 1561, black was not worn there until 1583. White was to remain the color of the pope's biretta, scarlet for the cardinal's, purple for the bishop's and black for other clerics.

Then followed another version of the biretta, the flat cap or as we know it, the beret. Of Italian origin, it was at first a flat round piece of fabric drawn up by a string to fit the head. Eventually, a band inside the hat was drawn up in like manner and tied in back and there, we have the origin of the tiny bow on the lining of today's masculine hat. It still has its use in designating the back of the hat.

The flat cap or beret was the masculine hat of the first half of the sixteenth century, often worn over a coif of velvet or gold cord net. When a wig was worn, the beret was attached to it. The favorite beret was black but Henri VIII had velvet ones in yellow, orange and green. Later, colors became more general, especially scarlet. During Henry's reign, the Irish were forbidden to wear caps of saffron or "linen color."

The cap for common use was of cloth, while dressier bonnets were of felt, velvet, satin, taffeta, sarcenet (Saracen-net), a thin silk and of straw in the summer. Though often untrimmed, plumes, preferably white in ostrich, marabou, peacock and wool imitation, adorned the hat. A jeweled socket might hold the feather, and spangles and jewels were sewn to the spine. A single ornament was a medal or brooch with a sacred or profane motif. Minute gold ornaments in gold bowknots, rings, and buttons were sewn to the under side of the brim.

As the long beard and long hair in the early Middle Ages denoted aristocracy, so rigid class distinction now evolved a style of headgear for every profession. The hat signified a free citizen and as such, was embodied in coats-of-arms. A piece of attire intended for display more than utility, the hat was worn constantly indoors and out. Townsmen wore black bonnets and if wealthy or men of leisure, they were permitted to add jeweled ornaments.

After 1565, the flat cap became the hat of "city folk," merchants, professional and elderly men, also apprentices and servants. The "city flat-cap" or "statute cap" it became in England where Elizabeth, queen from 1558 to 1603, passed a law compelling every person over seven years of age in the middle classes to wear the cap on Sundays and holidays upon pain of a fine. This for the encouragement of home manufacture, the whole article being made of wool, felt or black knitted woolen yarn. A lord, lady or knight having twenty marks a year was exempt from the decree and anyone less than a knight was prohibited from wearing a cap of velvet by a statute of 1566.

The Reformation in England deprived the ecclesiastic costume of many of the features peculiar to the Church of Rome. So it followed that the flat cap worn by scholars and legal personages was adopted in the sixteenth century by the Protestant Church.

The huntsman cap with the turned-up utility flaps, worn today, appeared late in the fifteenth century. It came to be known as the *monteroe* or *montero* cap, the name of Spanish origin, meaning hunter's cap. But the cap in those times was not only of cloth or felt but of black velvet for the gentleman.

Very popular in the first half of the sixteenth century were wide-brimmed hats with slashed or crenelated brims. Slashings originated in 1477 among the Swiss soldiers who in battle put to flight the Duke of Burgundy and his men. The Swiss mended their ragged clothes with strips of banners, tents and furnishings which the routed Burgundians left behind. All fashionable Europe took up slashings or panes with puffings of contrasting fabric showing through.

The style was carried to most bizarre extremes by the *lansquenets* or German mercenaries who also made most extravagant use of ostrich plumage on their large and jaunty hats. The wide-brimmed hat was also trimmed with points or aglets, tiny metal tags attached to thongs, strings or ribbons which laced all parts of the costume together in this period.

The roundlet or *escoffion,* a stuffed roll in turban fashion, was still worn by Italians in the first half of the sixteenth century by both men and women. It was handsomely embroidered in gold and silk. Such a headdress is worn by the bridegroom in a painting by Lorenzo Lotto (1480–1560).

In the middle of the sixteenth century, the soft crown of the beret took on height over a wire frame, the brim usually narrow. A jeweled necklace encircled the crown and feathers were placed at side or back. This was the very smart "Spanish toque" and was worn by both sexes. It was very popular in Spain, Italy and France.

Equally coveted by dashing gentlemen and their ladies, were Milan bonnets and French bonnets made of costly fabrics, slashed and puffed and finished with jewels, spangles and aglets. A contemporary English writer mentions "Millayne bonnets with holes, pinched and cunningly carved." It was in the reign of Henry VIII that felt hats were first made in England.

A short-lived style of the third quarter of the century was the Albanian hat, a broad-brimmed piece with shallow melon-shaped crown of felt or beaver. The tall crowned hat with wide or narrow brim was better liked. Very swaggering was the wide-brimmed hat cocked up in front and held by jeweled ornament and standing plumes. The "chapeau français" it was called and was of the last years of the sixteenth century. Such a hat was sometimes decorated with a glove which had special significance. The glove worn upon the hat of a gentleman might be a mark of challenge, a favor of his mistress or a memorial of a deceased friend. The Earl of Cumberland wore on his hat a glove given him by Queen Elizabeth. Another such ornament was a lady's laced or tasseled handkerchief shaped into a cockade.

When in mourning, the tall-crowned hat was encircled by a wide crushed band of thin black gauzy stuff called cyprus. Women used cyprus for veiling, also Spanish gauze.

By a government order of Venice in the sixteenth century, Jewish doctors, merchants and other professions were compelled to wear a yellow bonnet to distinguish them from Christian professionals.

The feminine coiffure parted "à la madone," lasted into the sixteenth century and the high forehead was retained throughout the Renaissance Period. The hair was divided into many sections, crimped and braided, with braids, rolls and narrow ribbons wound round the head early in the period. And too, the hair was worn flowing or in long ribbon-bound braids. Unmarried ladies and brides of Italy, Spain, Germany and England followed the style of "disheveled hair" later than the French, the custom disappearing in France by the middle of the sixteenth century.

The bride's flowing hair was topped ·by a coif of silk, either plain or covered with embroidery and jewels, or a chaplet of either real or gold, enameled and jeweled flowers. She was also fond of the calotte of pearl mesh, the Juliet cap we call it. It takes its name from Shakespere's tragedy "Romeo and Juliet," the original story of which was first published in 1476 in Naples. Another bridal headdress was the golden caul, a special recorded one being of gold cord mesh over red satin. Vermillion and scarlet in satin and velvet were favorite bridal colors of the Renaissance.

The *ferronière* coiffure had a jewel suspended in the middle of the forehead from a fine chain or narrow ribbon tied round the head. This headdress of Oriental origin, beloved of painters and periodically revived, was first worn in France by la belle Ferronière, one of the mistresses of François I.

Late in the fifteenth century and long before those of the northern countries, Italian women, influenced no doubt by the great painters of the day, had replaced the concealing caul with a coiffure of arranged tresses. Always charming and artistic, the hair was divided into sections, crimped, rolled and dressed to the head with chignon and often adorned with jewels, pearls, ribbons and filmy bits of gauze. "The pride of hair" or the new fashion of exposing the hair is mentioned in the time of Henry VIII, but in general the English and the Low Countries appear to have had too much liking for the concealing headdress to take up a bareheaded style.

After 1530, the French fashion of frizzing the hair at the temples and dressing up the back prevailed. By the middle of the century, pads and wire frames were being employed at the temples in this "attifet coiffure." In the Venetian version, the temple curls formed upstanding horns. Next, about 1590, the front hair was dressed into a pompadour "under-propped with wire frames" with a chignon in back. Ladies kept their hair in place with a sort of gum or mucilage, the bourgeoise used a paste made of the dust of rotten oak and the peasant used flour.

When necessary, false hair was added and in the second half of the sixteenth century, wigs were worn and dyes extensively resorted to. The word "wig" in those days, often meant a single curl or a set of ringlets, false hair being a periwig or peruke.

Queen Elizabeth, who had as many as eighty wigs at one time, is supposed to have worn them over a shaved head. Her favored colors were red and saffron, though as a young woman she had blond hair. By way of compliment, her ladies dyed their locks red. Wigs were dressed with jewels, pearls and feathers. Mary Queen of Scots, whose wigs came from France, even when in prison changed her wig every other day and it is said, wore one to the executioner's block. Marguerite de Valois, who in 1572 married Henri de Navarre later Henri IV King of France, covered her magnificent black hair with a blond wig.

In fashion also were false cauls, arranged nets of gold cord and satin over coils of hair which were worn over the ears. An old English history of 1572 cites false hair and masks among the articles imported from France. A note of the time informs us that long beautiful hair was in such demand by the ladies that it was not unusual to lure small children into unfrequented places to cut off their hair.

Hair and wigs were dusted with powder, violet for brunettes and iris for blonds and gray hair was whitened with powdered starch. A writer, in 1593, offers the plaint that even the nuns in Paris were curled and powdered. In Italy, blond was the rage and women spent days sitting in the sun bleaching their hair. Ladies sat in their roofless belvedere towers atop their palaces, wearing a wide-brimmed but crownless hat with the hair spread over the brim. Such a straw hat was called a *solana*. When bleaching failed, blond hair was bought from the peasants. The craze for light-colored hair created a vogue for wigs of yellow and white silk.

The cosmetics of the Renaissance were produced in Italy where the first beauty doctors appeared and the first beauty hints, based upon the information brought back by the Crusaders from the Orient, were published. There were powders, creams, salves, lotions, teeth-whiteners and what-not for the skin and hair. To some mixtures concocted of various queer and fearful ingredients, were ascribed magic charm. In "painting the living flesh," the same pigments were employed as for picture painting and the skin treated like any other surface, an art upon which painters gave professional advice.

The Italian Catherine de' Medici (1519–1589) introduced "face-painting" to the French court, red cheeks on a coating of white paint. A delicate pallor was affected for daytime but sublimate was used to color the cheeks in the evening, making pomades and cooling lotions necessary the next morning to counteract the corrosive effects.

The "compact" of that day was "Spanish wool" in red and white, shredded wool impregnated with red or white paint to rub on the face. "Spanish paper" was another compact form, little books containing sheets of paper covered with powdered paint to transfer to the face by rubbing. The idea of a purse-sized book continued in use to the early twentieth century.

Surprising indeed was the practice of Diane de Poitiers (1499–1566), mistress of Henri II, of bathing her face with spring water even in winter. Suffice to say, such harsh treatment of one's complexion did not become general.

The mask, which was to become such a generally worn piece, appeared in the 1540's in the form of a small square of gauze which hung below the eyes, tied round the head by strings. The Venetian mask or loup appeared in the middle of the sixteenth century. It was the half mask of black velvet lined with white silk and its name *loup* (French for wolf) loo mask in English, came about through children being frightened by the disguise. It folded like a book and was carried in the hand when not in use.

Ladies wore the mask outdoors to protect their make-up and the complexion against the sun and cold. It was adopted by men and women for theater and street wear. The black velvet mask was permitted only to the nobles, the bourgeoisie wearing a small curtain of silk or satin with holes for the eyes. Then followed the mask which covered the whole face, of black or green silk, held between the teeth by a silver or glass button. In the 1560's, the use of the mask became general and was seen everywhere.

The patch too, of black velvet had appeared, though it was not to become a general fashion till the next century. It was more often worn to cover a scar or blemish and was so used by both men and women.

The use of perfume was indeed excessive, especially in Italy where all one's possessions were scented. The finest scents came from Venice and among the many kinds, amber, civet and musk are most indicative of the period. Perfume was really a necessity, few persons bathing more than two or three times a year. Small balls of dough or wax were saturated with strong scent and placed in cavities of especially designed brooches, pendants and rings. Pomanders containing such perfumed balls hung from the girdle or were carried in the palm of the hand. In Paris in 1500, an Italian perfumer named René opened the first perfume shop in that city.

The steeple hat and the horned headdress disappeared leaving behind its wide black fold to frame the hood, a fashion to last over half a century. The art of the goldsmith and the hairdresser combined to make a most artistic headtire of the velvet fold set off with gold and jewels and worn over a sheer white coif. It was known as the chaperon-bonnet or French hood. When the back piece fell like a curtain, it was called the fall and when simply a bag which contained the hair, it was called the cale. The side pieces were lappets and often had points or aglets at the sides, these to tie back the hood.

The English version of the hood, because of its outline, had many appellations: the gable, diamond-shaped, kennel or pedimental headdress and was worn to 1550. The under-coif of linen, gold tissue or velvet entirely concealed the hair. The broad fold of silk or velvet and usually black, lined with red or white, was wired to a point in center front. There were satin and damask hoods with coifs of embroidered silk, tied under the chin by narrow white strings. Black velvet hoods over coifs of gold or silver ribbon and ornamented with gold and jewels were only for ladies of rank.

In France, black was for nobility and scarlet for the bourgeoisie. Since velvet was permissible only to ladies of the court, the commoners overcame this decree by entirely concealing the velvet with embroidery in gold, silver, beads and jewels. A sumptuary ruling of Henry VIII compelled the man of means to keep a horse and armor "always ready for the wars" and that ruling described such a man's wife as wearing: "any French hood or bonnet of velvet with any *habillement*, paste or edge of gold, pearl or stone, or any chain of gold about her neck, or upon any of her apparel."

In Elizabeth's time only a gentlewoman "having arms" might wear an "ermyne" cap or one of lattice or lettice, a fur of whitish gray color. The "miniver," a cap of either white fur or white velvet, was also prohibited to any but ladies of rank.

The black hood with wimple and gorget of plain white linen became the headdress of elderly women. They often spent the later years of their lives as abbesses, nuns or sisters in the Church, thus the hood became the headtire of women ecclesiastics.

The barbe, a kind of pleated gorget of white linen attached to the cap under the hood was worn by widows. Ladies below the rank of baroness wore the barbe below the chin and those of inferior position placed it at the neckline. A widow kept her hair covered for two years and if she did not remarry, wore half mourning for the rest of her life. A French fashion for women of rank in mourning for parents or husband, was the wearing of a black veil bordered with white fur or swansdown.

The escoffion or stuffed roll of the Medieval Period survived in turban form and, reminiscent of the hennin, was the tiny Italian corno of silk and jewels perched on the back of the head over the chignon with a floating streamer of Spanish gauze.

The cornet or Dutch coif or cap is outstanding with its two caps of sheer white lawn, linen or cambric stiffly starched or with wired edge. The finest lingerie fabric was of Dutch make, a kind of lawn called "holland."

The process of starching was first perfected in Holland and it is noted that in 1564, a gentlewoman, one Mistress Dinghem Vanden Plasse, excelled in starching and for a goodly fee, taught young English ladies of rank in London to starch. There were many colors, blue and goose-green especially mentioned but the most popular was a creamy yellow and the dainty coifs and the extravagant ruffs and cuffs were stiffened with either English or Dutch starch.

The Dutch coif was also fashioned of embroidered silk, gold and silver tissue. Another form of the Dutch coif was the bavolette of the European bourgeoisie. What looked like a folded towel was pinned to the cap with the folds projecting over the forehead and hanging down the back.

The *Béguines,* an order of nuns in the Low Countries, wore a plain white stitched linen cap, the identical cap worn by all European and later colonial babies and therefore called a *béguin.* Corrupted into English, it became biggen or biggin. Shakespeare mentions "homely biggins" and a phrase of the time was "to Holland for biggins." A cap adorned with embroidery and lace was not a biggin.

With the middle of the century, came the tendency to expose the front hair. A heart-shaped cap supplanted the hood. With its dip over the forehead, it was then called the "attifet" headdress but later came to be known as the widow's cap, in association with Catherine de' Medici and with Mary Stuart, the Tudor cap. The diminutive *"attifet"* headdress followed, really nothing more than a piece of fabric dipping over the forehead, commonly called a "bongrace" or "frontlet."

There were charming feminine versions of the beret attached to the caul and the smart Spanish toque of the men was beloved by the ladies too. A contemporary writer notes it as the "proper hat" for horseback and evening. And to the scandal of the conservatives, ladies dressed for horseback and hunting wore the large "masculine hat" with slashed brim and sweeping plumes.

A most curious mantle covering head and body, was the *huke,* a hooded wrap of black cloth and of Moorish origin worn in Europe from the eleventh century. It became especially modish in the sixteenth and seventeenth centuries particularly in the Netherlands, Flanders, Germany. In this period, it had a cage-like shape held away from the body by means of copper or wooden hoops. The bongrace was the awning-like piece projecting over the forehead, a protection against sunburn. The bongrace took various forms and is mentioned in descriptions of feminine costume in the American Colonies. A form of the huke with the bongrace survives in some French peasant costumes of today.

Fashionable folk of both sexes wore nightcaps of black velvet and other costly fabrics richly ornamented with gold lace and embroidery. Nightcaps worn generally by men, women and children were of lingerie material such as linen, lawn, cambric and holland. Inventories of the period record the individual as possessing eight to a dozen or more of them.

The arrangement of the hood and the Dutch coif required a great many pins and here are some interesting facts about those necessary gadgets. In 1540, pins were imported from France for Queen Catherine Howard, wife of Henry VIII. They were of common brass and cost about two dollars a dozen. Pins of blanched iron wire were manufactured in England in 1543 and needles were first made there in 1545. In the same year, from England to France, came the first bent wire hairpins, fine and flexible wooden pins having been used up to this time. Next, an English act of 1564 prohibited the importation of pins from France. From about 1626, most ordinary pins were of English make.

Hairpins topped with balls of gold, silver, glass or jewels gave the effect of being sprinkled in the hair. There were other hair ornaments such as buckles and clasps designed by the great artists of the Renaissance. These pieces had gold mountings enriched with colored enamels and set with diamonds, rubies, emeralds, sapphires, garnets, beryls, turquoises and pearls. Pearls were so extravagantly used over the whole attire that the period is known as the "pearl age." Pear-shaped pearl earrings were secured to the pierced lobes of the ears by a string drawn through and tied.

Metal combs began to take the place of bone, boxwood and ivory, then followed those of tortoise shell. Combs of lead were believed to preserve and restore the color to faded hair.

Renaissance Europe

béret of red
or black felt-
wig or frizzed
natural hair-
Venetian-1510

pileus,
bonnet or
biretta
of
red felt-
Italian-
late 15th C.

béret of
red or black
felt or velvet-
French-
early 16th C.

béret
of brilliant
colored velvet-
jeweled brooch-
ostrich-
French-
1520

cardinal's
biretta
of red
felt or
cloth-
15th C.

calotte or
zucchetto
of the
clergy-
15th C.

black felt
bonnet
with
jeweled brooch-
French-
late 15th C.

cardinal's
red
biretta-
16th C.

bishop's
violet
biretta-
late
15th C.

biretta-
red or black
cloth, felt
or silk-
gold ornaments-
English-
1496

pope's white
felt coif
pinched into
four creases-
early 16th C.

biretta-
red or black
felt or
velvet-
Italian-
early 16th C.

RTW

Renaissance Europe

red felt bonnet with turned-up brim- Venetian- early 16th C.

velvet bonnet- turned-up flaps- jeweled crown- French king- end of 15th C.

hunting bonnet tied on with silk scarf- felt with brooch- Flemish- late 15th C.

general's biretta in time of war- red velvet- Venetian- 16th C.

felt béret with jeweled brooch- English statesman- early 16th C.

biretta of professors and students- black cloth- English- 16th C.

three cornered black felt biretta- university professor- Venetian- 16th C.

"city flat-cap" of black wool- English- 16th C.

béret of black velvet- Spanish- 1532

two bérets- black over red-tiny gold ornaments at forehead-French- 1530's

black velvet béret-braid edge-cord ties with gold ornaments 1530's

béret over coif- black velvet- gold braid and buttons-French- 16th C.

RTW

Renaissance Europe

light colored felt
bonnet-slashed and
pleated brim-gold medal
French page-
early
16 th C.

felt hat
with gold
ornaments-
caul of gold
cord and beads-
Italian-
early 16th C.

chaplet of
dark red carnations-
and
pink buddleia-
German-
1539

black velvet béret-
gold ornaments and
jeweled medal-gold
braid cap-English-
early
16th C.

corno or
ducal bonnet
of the doge-
brocaded satin
green on ivory-
gold galloon
band-white
linen coif sewn
to corno-linen
strings-
Venetian-
late 15th C.

felt hat-
slashed brim-
jeweled medal-
French-
1520

béret
of black velvet-
notched brim-
German-
1519

béret-
black felt
or velvet-
edged gold braid-
jeweled medal-
gold buttons-
French-
1st half
16 th C.

felt béret-slashed
brim-twisted
rope of pearls
over crown-
jeweled pendant-
German-
1514

felt béret
over coif of
gold cord-
white ostrich-
single small
pearl-
French-
early
16 th C.

felt béret over
cap of silk and
tinsel-gold
cable with
rings-brooch
with pearl
pendant-
German-
1515

RTW

Renaissance Europe

lansquenet-
red felt béret-
folded crown-
large red beaver
hat on ribbon-
white ostrich plumes-
German-
1517

royal herald-
red felt hat-
slashed brim-
white ostrich and
ribbon- German-
1st half 16th C.

black felt
hat with
gold edge-
coif of gold
braid over rose
silk - pearls-
white feathers-
French-
mid 16th C.

satin béret-
embroidered
fleur-de-lis-
edged with
pearls-
Spanish-
early
16th C.

velvet béret-
folded brim-
German-
early 16th C.

felt hat-
notched
brim-
white
ostrich-
jeweled brooch-
English-
early
16th C.

béret-
black velvet-satin
ribbon threaded
through slashings-
German-
1538

soldier's
béret-
cloth with slashings-
Italian-
early 16th C.

lansquenet-
slashed felt
béret over cloth
coif-chinstrap-
German-
early 16th C.

RTW

Renaissance Europe

béret with brim-
black velvet edged
with gold braid-gold
ornaments-white ostrich-
French-1st half
16th C.

felt béret
with rolled brim-
French-
1st half
16th C.

roundlet or
stuffed roll-black
velvet-gold
embroidery-
Italian-
1st half 16th C.

blue
felt béret-
yellow and
blue ostrich-
page-
French-
early
16th C.

béret-
velvet threaded
with gold
braid-
ostrich plume-
Italian-
early 16th C.

small satin
béret with
brim-attached
to calotte-
ostrich plumes-
German-
1538

béret
attached to
wig-velvet-
gold loops-
jeweled brooch-
English-
1536

béret of
cloth with
pearls and
jewels-
French-
mid 16th C.

pileus, bonnet or biretta
worn by all classes-red or
black-felt, cloth, silk or velvet-
Venetian-16th C.

béret
attached to
wig-beaver
with scalloped
brim-white
ostrich-jeweled ornaments-
English-1st half 16th C.

biretta of universities
and professions-
French-1533

RTW

Renaissance Europe

béret-dark green silk-
gold braid edge-white
ostrich plume-jeweled
ornaments-
French-
1st half
16th C.

béret-
black felt-
slashed brim-
white ostrich plume-
gold circle-
French-
1st half 16th C.

béret-
black velvet-
straight brim-
white ostrich
plume-gold
medal with
red enameled
center-
French-
1st half 16th C.

black felt-
gold braid
and tiny
ornaments-
white ostrich-
French-
1st half
16th C.

felt
hat-
rolled
brim-
pearls-white
ostrich-
French-
1540

black velvet
béret-white ostrich-
jeweled brooch-tiny
gold ornaments-
English-
1530's

béret-
black velvet or
silk-gold cord
and embroidery-
white ostrich-
French-
mid 16th C.

béret of
black velvet-
white ostrich-
pearls and gold
chains-gold and
topaz brooches-
English-
1537

bonnet for
common wear-
felt or moire-
Florentine-
2nd half
16th C.

bonnet of silk
with crushed band
and rosette-
Italian-
2nd half
16th C.

RTW

Renaissance Europe

"Spanish toque" of colored silk-jeweled band-single pearl earring-French-2nd half 16th C.

"Spanish toque"-silk or velvet-jeweled band and brooch-Italian-2nd half 16th C.

"Spanish toque" of black silk or velvet-jeweled band-Spanish-2nd half 16th C.

toque of black velvet-orange and white ostrich-German-1580

black velvet toque attached to velvet coif-jeweled brooch-English statesman-2nd half 16th C.

"Spanish toque" of silk or velvet-crushed band with bowknot-Flemish-2nd half 16th C.

iron helmet of the king's archers-ostrich and aigrettes-French-1559

"Spanish toque" of silk or velvet-with gold cord-attached to velvet coif-German-2nd half 16th C.

"Spanish toque"-black velvet or silk-pearl necklace-ostrich and aigrettes-Italian-1583

R-T-W

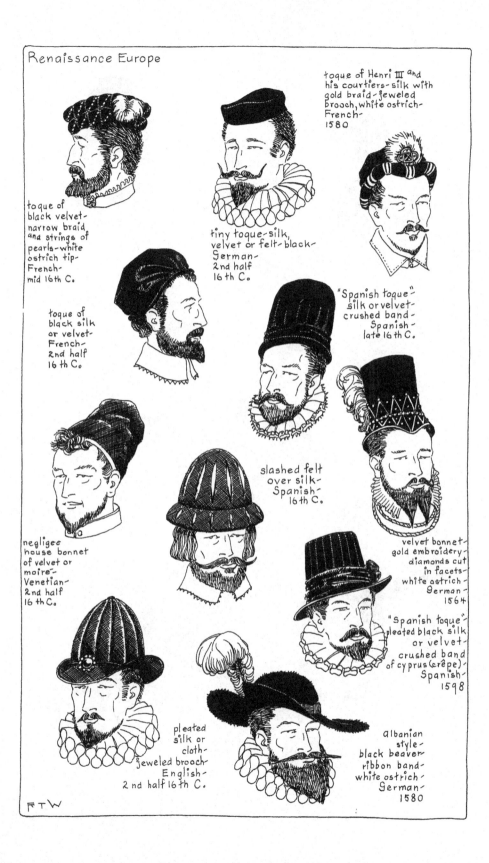

Renaissance Europe

toque of Henri III and his courtiers- silk with gold braid- jeweled brooch, white ostrich- French- 1580

toque of black velvet- narrow braid and strings of pearls- white ostrich tip- French- mid 16th C.

tiny toque- silk, velvet or felt- black- German- 2nd half 16th C.

toque of black silk or velvet- French- 2nd half 16th C.

"Spanish toque" silk or velvet- crushed band- Spanish- late 16th C.

slashed felt over silk- Spanish- 16th C.

velvet bonnet- gold embroidery- diamonds cut in facets- white ostrich- German- 1564

negligee house bonnet of velvet or moire- Venetian- 2nd half 16th C.

"Spanish toque" pleated black silk or velvet- crushed band of cyprus (crêpe)- Spanish- 1598

pleated silk or cloth- jeweled brooch- English- 2nd half 16th C.

Albanian style- black beaver- ribbon band- white ostrich- German- 1580

FTW

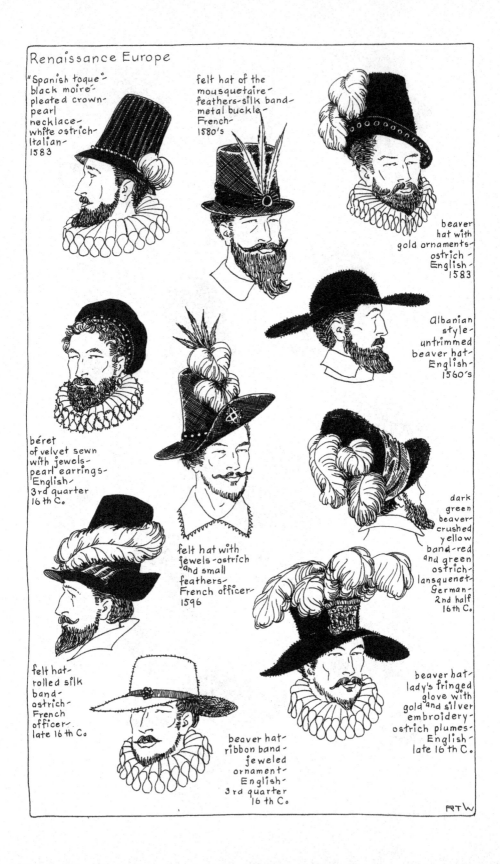

Renaissance Europe

"Spanish toque"-
black moiré-
pleated crown-
pearl
necklace-
white ostrich-
Italian-
1583

felt hat of the
mousquetaire-
feathers-silk band-
metal buckle-
French-
1580's

beaver
hat with
gold ornaments-
ostrich-
English-
1583

Albanian
style-
untrimmed
beaver hat-
English-
1560's

béret
of velvet sewn
with jewels-
pearl earrings-
English-
3rd quarter
16th C.

felt hat with
jewels-ostrich
and small
feathers-
French officer-
1596

dark
green
beaver-
crushed
yellow
band-red
and green
ostrich-
lansquenet-
German-
2nd half
16th C.

felt hat-
rolled silk
band-
ostrich-
French
officer-
late 16th C.

beaver hat-
ribbon band-
jeweled
ornament-
English-
3rd quarter
16th C.

beaver hat-
lady's fringed
glove with
gold and silver
embroidery-
ostrich plumes-
English-
late 16th C.

RTW

Renaissance Europe

calotte of gold embroidery-large jeweled brooch-pearl pendant-silk cord with jewels (ferronière)-hair ribbon bound-Italian-late 15th C.

flowing hair with braids-pearls over forehead-band of plaited ribbon around neck-Italian-circa 1500

center part-each half ribbon-bound-wound over ears-combed ends covered with gauze-crushed gauze across back-jewels-Italian-late 15th C.

coiffure of braids-large jewel with pearl pendant-pearl earrings-Spanish-late 15th C.

blond hair or yellow silk bunched up and held by gold fillets-Italian-circa 1500

braids looped up over velvet calotte edged with pearls-crimped front hair-German-1st half 16th C.

German adaption of the Italian fashion-ribbon and ostrich plume-1st half 16th C.

chaplet of gold wire and enameled flowers-spray of buddleia-German-1526

caul of tiny gold beads over white silk-ribbon bound hair-hanging ends-large jewel and pearls-Flemish-1470

coiffure with ferronière-jewels and pearls-back strand bound with ribbon-French-1500

coif of gold tissue over flowing hair-silk fillet-young Italian lady-early 16th C.

RTW

Renaissance Europe

coif of gold embroidery on black- pearls and large jewel- tiny strings- Italian- 15th C.

ribbon-wound strands of hair- two chased gold bandeaux- gold ring over forehead- French- 1550's

coiffure with narrow ribbon- ribbon-wound chignon-crimped front hair- Italian- late 15th C.

coiffure with gold galloon bandeau- twisted strands- ribbon wound chignon- Italian - early 16th C.

center part- two rows of braids- two strings of pearls- pearl earrings tied with string- French- 1560's

twisted strands drawn into high chignon- covered with calotte-silk with gold embroidery- Italian- late 15th C.

center part- rolled front sections-gold bandeau with rubies and pearls- large chignon wound with pearls-French- 1560'S

bridal headdress- caul of gold cord over silk- interspersed with gold beads- three pearls on forehead- Italian- 1523

calotte over chignon-velvet with pearls and jewels- pearl earrings- Italian- 2nd half 16th C.

attifet coiffure- front hair dressed over wire frames- satin calotte with pearls- German- 1560's

coiffure dressed in rolls-floor- length gauze headdress with pearls and jewels- Italian- 1581

RTW

Renaissance Europe

center part - tight curls
at temples - gauze scarf
over chignon - pearls and
jeweled hairpins - Venetian -
2nd half
16th C.

attifet coiffure -
two rows curls over wire
frame - back in chignon -
pearl earrings - Venetian -
1581

center
part - tight
curls at
temples - pearl hair
pins on left side -
pearl earrings -
Venetian -
2nd half
16th C.

hair dressed
over wire frame -
pearl and gold
ornament -
Spanish -
2nd half
16th C.

queen's
coiffure
with pearls
and jewels -
small tight curls
around face - pearl
earrings - English -
2nd half 16th C.

red wig - pearl and
jewel hairpins -
coronet of gold
wire, jewels and
pearls - pearl
earrings - English -
late 16th C.

attifet coiffure
over wire frame -
tight curls
round face -
jeweled pin -
pearl earrings -
French -
1590's

braids rolled
over ears - gauze
chou at back -
pearl earrings -
Italian -
2nd half
16th C.

coiffure over
wire frame -
pearls and
jewels -
pearl earrings -
French -
late 16th C.

attifet coiffure -
hair dressed
over wire frame -
bandeau of
gold enamel
and jewels -
French -
1585

FTW

Renaissance Europe

corno of silk-gold
framework-pearls-
silk flowers-long
scarf white silk voile-
Italian-2nd half
16th C.

tiny pillbox
over
chignon-
silk or velvet
with pearls and
gold embroidery-
Venetian-
circa 1500

"trembling cap" of
gold or silver cord-net
edged with pearls-
pearl earrings-
Italian-
late 16th C.

corno of pearls-
gold and pearl
diadem-silk
voile streamers-
Italian-late
16th C.

corno
of gauze
over chignon-
pearls-
two long streamers-
German-
early 16th C.

Venetian
princess
or dogaresse-
ducal costume-
corno crimson satin
or velvet-crimson
voile shoulder cape-
pearls and jewels-
16th C.

cap of
fine voile-
two long
streamers-
young Italian
noblewoman-
late
16th C.

cap
of gold
or silver cord-
over silk-
pearls-French-
2nd half
16th C.

corno of pearls-
aigrette in
jeweled socket
with petals-
pearl earrings-
Spanish-
late 16th C.

cap of gold
or silver cord over silk-
pearls-gold and jeweled
ornament-gold bands-
Italian-2nd half
16th C.

RTW

Renaissance Europe

hair rolled over pad-strings of pearls-ruche of pearl sewn gauze-French-1560's

hair dressed over wire frame-diadem of pearls and jewels-German-late 16th C.

wig-natural front crimped-chignon on top framed by pearl rings-aigrette in pearl socket-pearls and jewels-French-circa 1600

silk flowers edged with with tiny pearl blossoms-ostrich tips and aigrettes-Spanish-late 16th C.

attifet headdress or the widow's bonnet as worn by two queens-sheer voile with wired edge-Catherine de'Medici 1555, in black with scalloped piece over forehead-Marie Stuart 1560, in white with barbe-pearl-edged piece over forehead-French

queen's headdress-white velvet brim edged gold cord-gold crown-jewels and pearls-gauze streamers-pearl earrings-French-2nd half 16th C.

"Dutch coif"-lawn with wired edge-tiny pleats-embroidered silk coif with lace edge-single pearl center front-Dutch-1587

sheer lawn cap-wired edge-pearls and jewels-English-late 16th C.

RTW

Renaissance Europe

escoffion-stuffed gauze-
gold or silver cord-
jewels and pearls-
German-
early 16th C.

escoffion-
gauze and
silk wound
round stuffed
silk roll-
jeweled crown
and medal-
pearls-
streamers-
Spanish
queen-
late
16th C.

escoffion-
stuffed
roll-
natural
colored straw-
brown chenille
embroidery-gold medal-
Italian-
early 16th C.

Dutch coif-
sheer lawn
with stuffed
crest in
back-
gold ribbon
bands-
German-
early
16th C.

escoffion-
white silk
stuffed roll-
cord and pearl
mesh-pearl
sewn band-
jeweled brooch-
German-early
16th C.

variation
of the
Dutch coif-
padded back-
tapestry and
silk-wired
peak of sheer
lawn-jeweled
medal-French-
late 15th and
early 16th C.

the
"Dutch coif"
two caps
of embroidered
lawn-
under cap
with scarf-end-
English-
early
16th C.

Dutch coif with chincloth
or "muffler" of fine white
lawn embroidered in yellow-
German-early
16th C.

Dutch coif
with
padded crest-
white lawn-
ribbon cords-
French-
early
16th C.

padded back
of a popular
style of the
Dutch coif-
white lawn-
ribbon cords-
early
16th C.

escoffion-
stuffed roll
with ribbon
cords-pearl
frontlet-
English-
early
16th C.

RTW

Renaissance Europe

Dutch coif—two caps of embroidered silk—white lawn fold next face—string of jewels—velvet piece faced with colored silk—Flemish—2nd half 16th C.

bavolette—shoulder length folds of white lawn pinned over lawn coif—French bourgeoise—2nd half 16th C.

Dutch coif—cap of seed pearls—heavy jeweled band—large round ornament of jewels and pearls with crystal fringe—galloon over forehead—sheer white lawn wired—Flemish princess—1539

cap of fine white lawn with gold hoops—German—2nd half 16th C.

cap and streamers of gauze with gold thread—large pearl in front—pearl earrings—Italian—late 16th C.

crimped hair dressed over frame—pearls on wire—pearl earrings—French—1598

cornet—cap with two flaring wings—fine white lawn and lace—pearl earrings—French—late 16th C.

Dutch coif—red velvet or silk—gold cloth—gold embroidery and pearls—sheer white lawn front—German—2nd half 16th C.

cornet or Dutch coif—simple starched cap of white linen—Dutch bourgeoise—2nd half 16th C.

RTW

Renaissance Europe

RTW

hood of silk, velvet or cloth-gold cord caul over silk-lawn frills-jeweled ornament-frontlet of twisted strand of hair- English- 1470-1490

hood of cloth-edged gold or colored embroidery-cords with gold points at sides, to tie hood back- English- late 15th C.

hood of cloth-edged gold or silk embroidery- white linen coif-cords with aglets to tie the hood back-English-late 15th C.

widow's hood of dull black faced with white- worn over white coif- white linen gorget- French-early 16th C.

hood of brocade-silk border-coif of white lawn- English- 1st half 16th C.

severe type of gable hood, worn by older women-gable, wimple and gorget of white linen- long white veil in back- English-circa 1500

widow's hood in dull black lined with white- French- 1st half 16th C.

hood of red velvet-gold cord mesh and tassel- pearls and jewels-gold tissue coif-braided gold ribbon-French- 1524

gable hood-black velvet falls-one pinned on top- looped gold brocade lappets-white lawn coif-gold ribbon over forehead-gold frame with pearls and emeralds-English-1536

gable hood-black velvet falls-box like crown- front same as lower left- English- 1530's

Renaissance Europe

hood-fall of black
silk or velvet-silk
fold embroidered
with gold and pearls-
French-
2nd half
16th C.

hood-black
velvet fall and
front-white
lawn cap with
pearl-sewn strings-
gold frame with
pearls-English-1540's

hood-black velvet
fall over white linen
coif with stiffened
front-fine gold
crown-
Flemish-
early 16th C.

hood-pearls
with cale of fine
linen or lawn-
French-
2nd half
16th C.

hood-black
velvet fall-
white linen cap
with strings-
pluted gold ribbon next to
hair-gold framework-
English-1540's

bongrace of
embroidered silk-
wired edge-
French-
late 16th C.

bongrace of pleated
gauze with wired edge-
French-late 16th C.

bongrace of
black velvet-
pearl earrings-
French-
late 16th C.

RTW

Renaissance Europe

beret of silk with pearls and feathers-
attached to caul of pearl-sewn silk-
French-
2nd half
16th C.

velvet
béret-
white feather-
coif of
brocade,
gold framework
and pearls-
English-
2nd quarter
16th C.

velvet béret with
pearls-attached
to gold cord net
caul with pearls-
side cauls of
knitted silk-
German-
1540

large "flat cap" of
velvet, felt or silk-
coif of brocade, silk,
gold cord and pearls-
gold pendant with
pearls and jewels-
English-
1520's

velvet
bonnet-gold and pearl
embroidery-attached to
caul of gold cord and
pearls-ostrich tips-
French-
late 16th C.

velvet béret-
attached to pearl
sewn gauze caul-
feather with pearls
and gold stem
embroidery on
underside of brim-
German-
mid 16th C.

velvet bonnet
with pearls and beads-
caul of gold tissue
with gold embroidery
and pearls-
German-
late 16th C.

felt or velvet
hat attached
to gold cord
caul with pearls
over silk-young
English woman-
2nd half
16th C.

felt hat
attached to
caul band of
gold tissue
with pearls and
embroidery-
German-
1560

tiny béret of
black velvet
with gold net
and pearls-
gold net caul
over silk-pearls-
sheer lawn
front piece-
German-
1586

black
velvet
hat with
pearls and
jewels-
attached to gold
net caul with
pearls over silk-
German-
2nd half 16th C.

RTW

Renaissance Europe

"Spanish toque"- black velvet with pearls, strip of ermine, jeweled brooch, white ostrich and aigrettes- attached to elaborate pearl caul- pendant jewels and large pearl- Spanish- late 16th C.

Spanish toque- black velvet with pearls- velvet coif- gold crescents with pearls- long streamer in back- French-1572

Spanish toque- black velvet- pearl band- rose brooch- jeweled earrings- Italian- 1583

Spanish toque-velvet with pearls and ostrich -gold net caul over silk -white lawn front- German- 2nd half 16th C.

Spanish toque over long veil- black velvet with pearls, white ostrich, and tiny feathers- jeweled brooch with pendant pearl- French- circa 1580

Spanish toque of starched gauze with pearls -single pendant pearl-chou of gauze at side- French- late 16th C.

bongrace of white satin with pearls- aigrettes- Italian- 1583

Spanish toque- velvet or felt- ostrich and aigrettes- silk band- jeweled brooches or buttons-gold net caul with silk and pearls-English- late 16th C.

loo mask (French loup) black velvet lined with white silk- widow's coif- tissue or lawn with pearls- French- 3rd quarter 16th C.

mask for sun or cold-green or black silk -held by button between teeth- headkerchief of silk or gauze with bongrace- French- 2nd half 16th C.

Renaissance Europe

hood of
gold tissue
draped
with
gauze-
wired edge-
French-
mid 16th C.

beret-peacock
green felt with
slashings-threaded
ribbon-rose and
white ostrich-gold
net caul-knotted
rose silk chinstrap-
German-early
16th C.

large brim of fine
straw with crushed
silk crown-
golden net caul-
pearl earrings-
Italian-late
16th C.

black velvet-
wide brim with
fold attached
to calotte-
flat beret crown-
crimped hair-
German-early
16th C.

beaver or felt
with a fold in
brim-ostrich
tips-flat beret
crown-pearl
mesh caul-
German-
early
16th C.

beaver
hat with
silk band-
ostrich and
feathers-gold
cord caul-
English-late
16th C.

cap with bongrace-
gray silk-
English-
1590

black
silk hat-
pleated crown-
pale blue ostrich-
silver band-
English-
1590

hat of black silk or
velvet-pleated crown-
gold cords-yellow
ostrich-caul of
gold tissue-
English-
1590

RTW

Renaissance Europe

headkerchief
with
bongrace
of silk or gauze
with wired
edge-
French-
late
16th C.

black velvet
Spanish toque
worn over long
white veil-
Italian-
late
16th C.

velvet or felt hat-
pearl band-ostrich
gold cord caul-worn
over full length huke-
of sheer fabric-wired
edges over shoulders-
French-
late 16th C.

velvet or felt
hat worn over
voluminous
silk shawl
with scalloped
edge-
Italian-
late
16th C.

attifet coiffure
and bongrace-
black velvet with
pearls-pleated
black taffeta
lappets with
pearl pendants-
Italian-
1583

bongrace
headkerchief
of white voile
or silk-
starched or
with wired
edge- Italian-
2nd half
16th C.

RTW

Renaissance Europe

huke
with bongrace-
cloth mantle
mounted on
wire or wooden
frame-brocade
facing-white
lawn coif-
Flemish-
2nd half
16th C.

huke
with
bongrace-
wired hooded
mantle-black cloth-
three-quarter length-
Dutch and
German-
2nd half
16th C.

huke
with bongrace-
hooded mantle
of black cloth
with cloth
ornament-
seven-eighths
length-
English-
1590

full length
black cloth
mantle worn
over white
linen coif
and bongrace-
Dutch-
2nd half
16th C.

bongrace
of gold tissue with pearls-
full length voluminous
shawl of black silk-
Spanish-late
16th C.

RTW

felt or velvet bonnet with turned-up band - cluster of pearls - Spanish prince - early 16th C.

flat velvet béret with wide brim - English prince - end of 15th C.

French hood of velvet and pearls worn over white linen coif - English princess - late 15th C.

coiffure in two braids - black velvet béret - gold ribbon band - German - 2nd half 16th C.

flat velvet béret - brim sewn with tiny gold ornaments - attached to coif of silk with galloon - undercoif white lawn tied with strings - white ostrich - English prince - circa 1539

black velvet béret - pearls and ornaments sewn to underside of brim - gold filigree cylinders with pearl ends - white ostrich - English prince - 1543

white felt bonnet with gold embroidery and white ostrich - French prince - mid 16th C.

Dutch coif - quilted red silk caul - white lawn front with gold embroidery - pearl edging - German - 2nd half 16th C.

black velvet béret - brim tied with narrow ribbon and gold ornaments - large gold and enameled medal - white marabou - white linen coif - French prince - early 16th C.

velvet bonnet with up-turned flaps - white linen headkerchief - Spanish princess - early 16th C.

RTW

THE SEVENTEENTH CENTURY

CHAPTER TEN

THE SEVENTEENTH CENTURY saw the decline of Spanish influence in the mode and the Paris of Louis XIII (1601–1643) taking over as arbiter of court dress. Though the Venetians had their own definite style, Italians in general followed the Spanish fashion till about 1630, the rest of Europe adopting that of the French. The Chevalier or Cavalier costume of the first half of the century with its height about 1630 to 1640, had elegance in design and color. Although the Cavalier was supposedly a horseman, the young dandies of Europe strutted about handsomely and conspicuously booted but horseless. The great Flemish painter, Sir Anthony Van Dyck (1599–1641), has left so many admirable portraits of aristocrats of the time that the age is also known as the "Van Dyck period."

Fashionable dress in the American Colonies usually followed that of the English generally within the year, with English ships sailing regularly between the continents. The English adoption of the mode was more conservative than the French and the Colonists never indulged in the style extravagances of the Europeans. The Virginia planters were, however, given more to display than the people of the New England Colonies. Among the Puritans and Quakers, the costume was of the fashion in general but all furbelows were dispensed with and hats, though of the same style and quality, were not, as a rule, cocked or beplumed. We read of sumptuary laws being enforced, as, for instance, the two young women in Newbury who wore "silken hoods and scarfs" being taxed for the offense but released when it was proved that their husbands were worth two hundred pounds each.

Pertaining to the masculine head, the short locks of the first decade lengthened to the shoulders by the 'twenties. Men with luxurious hair wore it "à la comète" (comet): parted in back and brought over the shoulders, a long curl or "mustache" on one side. The mustache was also a long curl on the feminine head. The lovelock, as the English termed it, was named the cadenette by the French and here is its story: Monsieur de Luynes was made high constable and at the same time his younger brother, Sire de Cadenet, was made a marshal. Rumor had it that the honor was bestowed upon the latter because he was the proud possessor of luxurious blond hair and had the most beautiful single curl tied with a ribbon. The lovelock was thereafter called a *cadenette* and the ribbon bowknots, favors.

The wearing of the lovelock exposed the left ear and prompted the Count of Harcourt (1601–1666), a celebrated French soldier and cadet or "second born son" of the House of Lorraine, to wear a pearl earring. For this, he became known as "Cadet la Perle" and several portraits reveal him wearing the single earring. The lovelock and the pearl earring were introduced into England by Charles I (1600–1649). Earstrings disappeared with the advent of the gold wire hook attached to the earring.

A fringe of hair appeared over the forehead in the 1630's. If one's locks were sparse, pieces or "corners" of false hair were added. Some daring young dandies in the 'forties powdered their hair with fine flour but the idea did not take because of the unsightly effects upon the handsome fabrics of jacket and cloak. Curling irons were in constant use by both sexes in this age of curled locks.

An interesting American note is the following: among the rules laid down for the boys of Harvard College founded in 1636 was one, "nor shall it be permitted to wear Long Haire, Locks, Foretops, Curlings, Crispings, Partings or Powdering of ye Haire."

A pointed mustache, a tuft of hair on the lower lip and a "Van Dyck" beard accompanied the long hair. Beard and mustache were kept trim by a pomade of perfumed wax and by the aid of a tiny beard brush and comb. There was also a small gadget of Spanish origin, a metal contrivance to keep the mustache in shape when sleeping, and another device was a small "beard box" made of pasteboard. The great vogue of the trim beard and mustache caused the creation of the corporation of barber-hairdressers to whom, in 1637, Louis XIII gave letters patent.

The beard disappeared suddenly at the French Court one day in 1628 when Louis XIII amused himself by playing barber and trimmed the beards of his courtiers, leaving a tiny lip-beard "à la royale." Frenchmen were often clean-shaven in the 'forties, the fashion becoming general by the mid-century and lasting to the nineteenth century. The mustache became so diminutive in size that its disappearance near the end of the century was barely noticed. Many Englishmen wore the pointed beard and long mustache until the 'eighties.

The fanatic Puritan of England cut his hair short and round, barely covering his ears, to show his scorn of ringlets and ribbons whence the name "Round-head." The Puritan of the American Colonies also wore his hair closely cropped. In fact, a manifesto was issued in the Plymouth Colony against flowing locks on the masculine head. Other New England colonists however, adopted the long locks until the fashionable wig appeared in the 1660's. In Virginia and the Southern Colonies, the Cavalier style was wholly accepted even to the lovelocks.

Wigs came into favor in 1624 when the young King Louis XIII developed a slight baldness. Curiously enough, the wig was introduced to the French Court by an abbot. In 1620, the Abbé La Rivière wore a wig of long false hair at the court, and four years later Louis set the fashion by adopting the wig.

Wigs and false hair had been in fashion periodically over the centuries but the last revival and rage occurred about 1660. The original French word *perruque* became peruke in English, then perwyke, perewyke, periwig, ending finally in the short term wig by the middle of the century.

A set of ringlets or a single plait or curl was called a wig but it was not until the second half of the seventeenth century that the long full-bottomed wig appeared. It was a mass of tumbling ringlets of varied length and worn over a regularly shaved or polled head. What originated as a substitute for thin hair became in the late 'seventies a frankly artificial and decorative headpiece in which horsehair was employed, which retained its curl better than natural hair.

Excessive perspiration created by the heavy wig necessitated wearing a small cap or *calotte* of linen or serge next to the head. A negligee or "night cap" of silk replaced the wig at home, as the shaved head without its wig became very sensitive to draughts.

In France it became necessary to import hair for wigmaking, since such quantities were required that the demand was more than could be supplied by French peasant women. From Germany came a large amount of blond hair which meant much gold in exchange, a fact which disturbed the minister of finance under Louis XIV, Colbert, who ordered wigmaking to cease. The wig-makers' guild took the matter to the king and in the outcome, the importation of hair was curtailed but French wigs were permitted to be exported.

By the last quarter of the century, wigmaking greatly improved and French wigs especially were in demand all over Europe. In the earliest wigs, the hair was sewn to a calotte of silk but the strands were now drawn through canvas and held by individual knots. Dishonest wigmakers used the hair of goats and other animals and imported hair from foreign countries. Such hair and the wigs made of it were burned outside of Paris for fear of disease.

The abundant natural hair of Louis XIV (1638-1715) was copied by his courtiers but of necessity, they were forced to wig-wearing to simulate the long luxurious locks. From Versailles, the fashion spread over Europe. Though worn by most of his court, Louis XIV did not make use of the wig till 1673 when thirty-five years old. He then acquired a great number, even wearing a short bob when dressing. A corridor near his private apartment was fitted along both sides with stands to hold them.

The king's personal barber, Binette, who shaved him and trimmed his cropped head, was the only individual ever to see him "sans perruque." Upon retiring at night, the wig was passed out between the drawn bed curtains to his page, the performance repeated in reverse in the morning.

The wearing of wigs did not become general in England till the Restoration under Charles II (1660-1685). Charles I (1600-1649) wore a wig while in Paris but discarded it upon his return home. There, he and his Cavaliers wore the flowing locks which distinguished them from the "Roundheads."

Charles II, who had spent his exile at the court of Louis XIV, returned to England wearing a heavily curled full-bottomed wig. His graying hair having been black, he adopted a black wig, a style followed by his courtiers and also taken up in the American Colonies where wigs were quite generally worn by 1670.

The short bob wig of curls and the campaign wig dressed into two curls which hung down in back or over each shoulder were worn by traveler, sportsman and soldier. The wig of the Quaker was less pretentious and very often he wore his own hair in wig fashion; in fact, many European and American men did the same. Soldiers plaited their natural hair and are sometimes pictured with it tucked up in back under the cap. Occasionally when flowing hair was required for dress, horsehair hung in back, knotted to the back edge of the cap. About 1684, the hair began to be tied back for convenience and the silk bag appeared in the army before 1700.

The extreme size moderated about 1690 and powder in a grayish white and light brown or tan was used, pure white not until 1703. Wheat flour was generally employed but a contemporary writer speaks of a finely sifted starch as a base mixed with plaster of Paris. Scent was added to all powders: ambergris, musk, jasmine, orris root and bergamot. The hair was patted with a pomade, also scented, to retain the powder. Powder was costly and sometimes as much as two pounds was dusted on a wig.

The curls were tightened upon small rollers of pipe clay. There is controversy as to whether the hair was wound round hot pipes or wound round cold pipes and the whole then heated. The former method would seem to be the better for the health of the hair.

Almost at the same time in the 'nineties, we find the heavily powdered, elaborately curled wig as much worn in the American Colonies as by English and French courtiers.

Large pocket combs of ivory, silver or tortoise shell, chased and ornamented with gold, in handsome cases, were carried in the large pockets along with snuffboxes that were veritable works of art. Gentlemen conversed and combed their hair or wigs in public, in the box at the theater or on the mall. Men used perfume not only because it was smart but they considered it a necessity to disguise the odor of tobacco pipe-smoking, so heavily indulged in at that time.

In 1644, a work entitled *Les lois de la galantrie française* appeared, giving advice upon the toilet. It advised visiting the baths occasionally to have a clean body and everyday, "to take the trouble" to wash the hands and face, as often with almond bread and to shave the cheeks. The author suggests securing the services of a hairdresser, not the surgeon-barber whom one called when wounded or ill.

The "beever" hat worn by both men and women was the fashionable head-piece of the seventeenth century. Until 1600, hats of castor, the European species of beaver, came from the Low Countries. French and Spanish traders were the first to carry the desirable American beaver to Europe. The American Colonies exported great hogsheads of beaver pelts to England and Holland to be made into hats. The export fur list of the newly established colony of New Amsterdam gives an idea of the quantities shipped. From 1624 to 1632, from four to over seven thousand beaver pelts were shipped besides otter and other skins. The great vogue of the beaver hat naturally caused a serious deple-tion in the number of beaver in this country.

Charles I in 1604, incorporated by letters patent the felt-makers of London, granting them many privileges, thereby encouraging home industry and cur-tailing the importation of French and Spanish hats.

Beaver was most costly, in fact any good hat was costly in those days, valuable enough to be left among bequests in a will. And it was not an unusual occurrence for a man to be waylaid and robbed of his hat. Such hats required care and were kept in hatboxes when not worn. Hats were also made of velvet, wool, taffeta and silk or sarcenet.

The tall-crowned hat of the sixteenth century was still to be seen upon the heads of smart gentlemen in the first decade of this period. From the 'twenties to the 'forties, the swaggering Cavalier hat was conspicuous with broad brim either rolling or cocked and ornamented with long ostrich feathers, "weeping plumes." The broad-brimmed piece which drooped with much wearing came to be known as a "slouched hat." The crown was often encircled with a jeweled necklace or a silk band sewn with gems. A large gold ornament held the plumes.

In those days of free swordplay, the feathers were placed to the back or left side of the hat, permitting freedom of the sword arm. Too, the hat ornament was often a love token, and the position on the left side signified the heart or love. The decoration has ever since remained on the left side.

Puritans and Pilgrims favored the high crown with wide brim uncocked and a simple ribbon held in place by a small silver buckle. Many Puritans, however, adopted the Cavalier fashion with jeweled band and ostrich. Not all Puritans dressed in the "plain style" and though they wore "saad colours," those colors were lovely in grayed tones of red, orange, greenish blue and violet. The Pilgrims, simple and practical folk, wore good and durable clothes supplied them by the company of London merchants to whom they had mortgaged themselves. The Quakers, a plain people but whose garments were always of the finest quality and usually gray or brown, wore the broad-brimmed hat of felt or beaver, rolling or cocked. The Quaker never bared his head, refusing to raise his hat in salutation, that gesture being considered an affectation.

The shape of the crown varied constantly but by the 'seventies, the floppy brim was being cocked fore and aft, by the 'nineties cocked three ways, creating the tricorne, a hat to be worn for well over a hundred years. The brim was sometimes held to the crown by loops and buttons, by hooks and eyes and sometimes by a cord threaded through holes in the brim. The flaps could be let down at pleasure, one, two or three sides being lowered to protect the powdered head in bad weather.

Names were given the manner of cocking the hat by certain personages and from the military manner in which the Duke of Monmouth (1649–1685) son of Charles II, cocked his hat, came the "Monmouth cock."

Military headgear of the seventeenth century followed the mode of the large beaver hat, plumed and laced. In the first half of the period, though men often fought in their plumed hats, the morion and lobster-tailed helmets were worn to the mid-century. An "iron hat" shaped like the beaver, was equipped with a socket at the base of the crown to hold plumage. The iron "scull" or skullcap, carried in the saddle-bows when not in use, was for wear under the soft hat. When companies of grenadiers were added to the infantry in the latter part of 1600, the wide-brimmed hat was found inconvenient in throwing hand grenades and in the British Army, a fur-banded cap with hanging bag was substituted.

The Roman Church retained the biretta and the tonsure which the Re-
formed Church of England abandoned. English clerics wore the scholar's cap,
the squarish biretta or the cap with earflaps. French and English clergy in the
second half of the century adopted the wig and broad hat.

Men wore their hats indoors and out till about 1685 but there seems to be
no definite record of when etiquette forbade the wearing of the hat at table or
in church. Young men removed their hats in the presence of their elders,
except "at dinner" and hats were removed before royalty. The hat was more
often carried than worn with the heavy wig and also so as not to disarrange
the curls, thus the custom of removing the hat indoors would appear to have
been simply a desire for comfort. Though worn at the table of Louis XIV, that
custom had disappeared by the reign of Louis XV.

The montero cap, popular in Europe and the Colonies for negligee, hunting
and riding, is still worn today by farmers and hunters. It was usually of woolen
cloth with cloth or fur flaps, though a montero cap is mentioned of black
velvet. A simple round crown had a flap around the sides and back which
afforded protection when turned down.

The Monmouth cap, originally made in the town of Monmouth, England,
which is still known as Capper's Town, was a knitted woolen close-fitting
cap with turned-up band and overhanging crown, a stocking cap we call it
today. Sailors wore the cap and it was used in the Colonies by workmen.

Lace became very important as ornamentation, trimming all fine attire,
even hats being "laced." Documents of the period tell us that the nightcaps
of Charles I were lace-trimmed. James II, King of England from 1685 to 1688,
fled to France where he died in 1701, wearing a nightcap of lace which had
been sent him by Louis XIV. Etiquette of the Court of France demanded that
the head of a royal person be covered with a bonnet or cap when dying.

The various edicts of, first, Richelieu (1585–1642) and then Mazarin (1602–
1661) prohibiting the use of metal embroideries, galloons and passementeries,
created an extravagant use of "galants" or ribbon loops. Riband or ribbon was
originally the band or border of a garment. In the sixteenth century, a narrow
band of silk with two selvages was made in Milan but its tremendous vogue
as trimming is of the seventeenth century. Next, in 1656, Mazarin attempted
to stop the wearing of galants but with no success.

A Spanish note comes from a descriptive letter written in 1679 by a visitor to Spain, in which the writer describes the fashionable masculine hat as unadorned, save for a band of black crêpe or cyprus and very smart.

Feminine locks, usually crimped, continued to be dressed high over a wire frame in the first quarter of the century. Jewels and pearls attached to enameled pins or bodkins, were sprinkled over the coiffure. If necessary false hair was added and brown or blond wigs were worn, "heads" they were called. Dye was resorted to, saffron a favorite color and the hair set with a paste made of starch mixed with pomade, perfumed with iris for blonds and violet for brunettes.

With the above hairdo, English ladies were fond of wearing a halo-like headdress made of gauzy fabric with an elaborately embroidered or lace edge set on the back of the head.

A Londoner visiting Italy in 1617, wrote that young Italian women tied their hair with gold or silver lace.

The 1630's found the formal coiffure replaced by a lowered hairdo with cheek curls and a fringe over the forehead. The French called the bobbing curls over the cheeks "English ringlets." When the side sections were bobbed and crimped, that was the *coiffure à la moutonne* or sheep-like fashion. Long single curls resembling the masculine lovelock were heartbreakers; the loose curls at the temples, favorites. Kiss-curls were the tiny ringlets at the back of the neck and confidents were the curls next to the ears.

The Spanish Anne of Austria, who married Louis XIII, is said to have introduced the low headdress with cheek curls to the French Court and the French Henrietta Maria, who married Charles I, is supposed to have carried the fashion to England.

Gradually the ringlets lengthened to the shoulders. Strings of pearls were wound in the hair, flowers were worn or a drooping plume placed at the side of the head. Black ribbon bowknots were very smart. A letter written in 1640 described veils of colored taffetas worn by Venetian ladies, the veils weighted at the corners with lace tassels.

A center part appeared by the 'sixties and the falling curls were held away from the cheeks by means of wire frames or "set-out" combs. Very often, the curls were false, tied to the head with ribbons. Pepys, in his diary in 1662 speaking of his wife's coiffure, terms such pieces, "a pair of perruques."

This hairdo is associated with several well-known women of the seventeenth century and often given their name: Ninon de Lenclos (1620–1705) a noted French beauty; the Marquise de Sévigné (1626–1696) a woman of letters and great charm and the Marquise de Montespan (1641–1707) a favorite of Louis XIV, supplanting la Vallière (1644–1710). A note of 1661 says that Madame de la Vallière wore flowers and pearls in her blond curls which hung to her shoulders and two large emeralds in her ears. The coiffure was also worn by Nell Gwyn, the actress mistress of Charles I of England.

The "hurluberlu" or "hurlupée" appeared in 1671, a style originated by a woman hairdresser named Martin. In this madcap creation, the sides were cut in uneven lengths and crimped with two long curls, one over each shoulder. "A la Maintenon" was another name for it after Madame de Maintenon, who was wearing her hair in that fashion when first noticed by Louis XIV.

In the "tete de chou" or cabbage head, another style of the 'seventies, large bunches of curls were dressed on either side of the forehead. Curls tied into a bunch in back instead of a chignon, was also a chou, in English "boss" or "bundle."

Then came the inevitable reversal when the silhouette of the head narrowed and the curls were heaped on top and all because—but here is the story: It was in 1675 that the Duchesse de Fontanges (1661–1681), a beautiful young woman who succeeded Madame de Montespan as favorite of the king, when following the hunt, lost her hat in the wind and her hair tumbled down. She tied up her blond curls with a garter of ribbon and lace, the bow in front, whereupon Louis XIV was so complimentary that the ribbon of convenience became the rage.

The high curled coiffure with upstanding ribbon loops was the coiffure "à la Fontanges" and the bonnet which appeared about 1685 was the "bonnet à la Fontanges," later simply called the fontange, commode or tower cap. Every curl and every piece of fabric in the headdress had its special name; in fact so many were the various items that it was found necessary to publish a dictionary of the terms. The "tower," rows of curls one atop the other supported by a silk-covered wire frame called a palisade or commode, was often false.

The tiny cap was built up with pleated bands, first of lace-edged sheer linen or muslin, then of priceless gold and silver laces to which pearls and flowers were added, such a headdress sometimes costing from 1,000 to 2,000 pounds. The final disappearance of the fontange was a real hardship to the lace merchants.

The goffered frilled headpiece rose to absurd heights, which the king then complained of as ugly. Women were compelled to lower their heads when passing through doors and the roofs of the sedan chairs in which ladies were carried had to be raised. Louis ordered the headdress lowered and his wishes were complied with but in a few months, his displeasure forgotten, the fontange reappeared, reduced to two tiers.

It rose again until 1714 when the English ambassadress, Lady Sandwich with a simple low hairdo, was presented at the French Court and at once, the fashion changed. Louis, his pride piqued, could not refrain from remarking that what a king's authority was powerless to accomplish, an English lady had unwittingly effected.

The fashion was of shorter duration in England than in France and much modified. It was also adopted by those American colonists who followed the mode.

By the end of the period, the feminine coiffure dressed high, copied the twin peaks or curls of the masculine wig. Women from the middle of the century adopted the man's costume for horseback riding in coat, waistcoat, neckwear, beaver or felt hat and the powdered wig.

The coiffure of the Spanish lady followed the European mode but with a distinct Spanish flair. The high crimped hair over a wire frame of the early years of the century was higher and narrower than the rounded effect of the Northerners. The exaggerated Spanish version of the broad low coiffure of the 1630's is known to us by the wonderful portraits of Velásquez (1599–1660).

The hair, flat on top, was parted at the side, drawn across the forehead and held in place by a large ribbon rosette with jewels. The bushy, crimped and usually dyed blond hair to which false pieces were added if necessary, spread over a wire frame and flowed to the shoulders, its contour spreading like the broad skirts worn below it. Added to the headdress were bodkins tipped with diamonds, pearls or other colored stones and at the side of the head, a long drooping plume of ostrich or breast feathers, the whole resembling an ancient Egyptian wig.

Until this period, the lady's hairdresser had always been her maid. It did not occur to barbers to undertake the arrangement of the feminine coiffure until a certain insolent individual named Champagne appeared toward the middle of the century. He displayed a genius for creating new styles and it was said that he held his customers in his power by his threats to "walk out" on them. If they refused to kiss him, he would leave them with their hair but partly dressed. The smart fellow exacted gifts, not money as payment, thereby gaining twice as much in value.

He was hairdresser to Princess Marie de Gonzague, who was utterly dependent upon him and his conceit made him a great annoyance at the Court of Nevers. He arranged her head and crown upon the day of her wedding to the ambassador of the King of Poland in 1645. He accompanied her to Warsaw, traveled about the northern kingdoms, returning to Paris in the suite of Queen Christine of Sweden (1626–1689). His return to Paris was an event of great importance to the ladies of the court.

There is a story about a hairdresser, one of the early English dandies, Robert Fielding, Beau Fielding or Handsome Fielding, who was notorious for his love affairs at the Court of Charles II. He bribed the hairdresser of a supposedly wealthy lady to assist him in making her his wife. Though successful, the marriage evidently was not to his liking because in the same month and very same year, November, 1705, he married the Duchess of Cleveland, the former mistress of the king. The law took him over as a bigamist and he died in 1712.

In Paris, in the second half of the century, there were many women hairdressers, all wives of wigmakers.

The coif disappeared for formal wear but was retained for negligee. Lace caps and the attifet or bongrace, the pointed black cap with white lining, of Mary Stuart fame, remained the headtire of widows and elderly women of all nations. The widow's peak it was called, which name is still applied to the flattering pointed growth of the hair on the forehead.

The Dutch coif or cornet remained a favorite with the women of the Low Countries and was as important in the New Netherlands as in Holland. The corneted cap of fine linen batiste with exquisite lace sometimes had lace lappets or pinners pinned up at the sides of the face over the ears.

Children of all countries wore the embroidered bonnet in Dutch style. The English boy wore his until four or five years old and the little girl until eight or ten. The stitched or quilted linen bonnet, the béguine or biggin, was worn alike by baby and his feminine elders among the plain people. The coif or cap is worn today by the country people of France, Germany, Holland, Hungary and by many religious orders.

The French hood continued to be worn by women of all ranks and ages, especially in winter when it was often fur-lined. The hood, generally of black or brown cloth, by the end of the century was being made in colors and of velvet, lutestring, sarcenet, camelot and a gauze of thin silk called tiffany. The combination hood and cape known as the Dutch hood was popular in scarlet or orange-red cloth and called the "London Ryding Hood." And that brings us to the origin of *Little Red Riding Hood* or *Chaperon Rouge* published in 1697 by the French writer Charles Perrault (1628–1703) in his *Tales of Mother Goose*. The scarlet hoods or "cardinals" and cloaks were worn also by the masculine world, even the Quakers wore them.

In the 'forties appeared the kerchief-like hood, given the old name of coif though in no way resembling it. This headcovering of lace, taffeta or sheer dark fabric, usually black, was a square of material folded diagonally and tied under the chin, a fashion lasting well into the next century. Madame de Maintenon, the ascetic wife of Louis XIV, was always seen in one, either black or brown. It is noted that she discarded the headscarf after the performance of "Esther" in 1689, adopting the new high headdress.

The coif or sheer headkerchief edged with lace and pinned to the hair, often hung over the face supposedly protecting the complexion from disfiguring sunburn and freckles. Young women preferred one of black crêpe to the mask, as being more flattering to the skin, while older women continued to wear the mask. The later kerchiefs were of velvet.

That curious mantle of the sixteenth century, the huke, continued to be worn by the gentlewomen of Spain, Germany and the Low Countries. The hoops were gone but it was still made of black cloth and full length. The part covering the head was gathered to a small round disc of velvet from the center of which projected a pompon of black silk mounted on a little stick. In the same category was the wired cage-like hood with the name of the shell, conch. It was a garment worn by the French widow and attached to her cloak at the shoulders.

Spanish women did not wear cap or coif but when traveling, donned a small hat. They observed the Moorish fashion of going veiled in public and only married women were permitted to make use of cosmetics.

The feminine hat, when worn either for travel or hunting, was a replica of the masculine headpiece in felt, beaver or velvet, often placed over the white lingerie coif. A favored shape was that known to us as the postilion hat. When revived in the 1880's, it was called the Van Dyck, the Rembrandt or the Rubens, after those great painters of the seventeenth century.

The period of the steeple hat and the scarlet cloak in the second half of the century is that of the terrible witchcraft beliefs and persecutions in England and the American Colonies. The costume has remained the witch's garb ever since.

Down through the ages, each country has had its own summer shade hat woven of vegetable fiber. As today, the most valuable straw was grown in Tuscany, furnishing the famous Tuscan plaits and Leghorn hats. In England, the art of weaving strands of straw dates from 1552 when Mary of Scotland took plaiters back with her from France. Wheat straw was grown and the Duke of Buckingham (1592–1628) encouraged straw plaiting and straw hat making in his own country, not without good profit to himself.

Lords and ladies further encouraged the industry by wearing domestic straw hats. Straw-plaiting became an important craft in England and the foundation of sewn straw hats. It was done in the home by many thousands of women and children and remained a feminine occupation to the nineteenth century. In the American Colonies, a note written by a Pennsylvania Quaker in 1685, urges that girls be taught the art of making straw hats and baskets.

In wintry weather all women, even children, in Europe and the Colonies wore the hood, the chinband and the mask as a protection for the complexion. Though the wide use of the mask declined in the 'sixties, it did not disappear but was seen throughout the century and a strict code of rules governed its usage. The mask was usually black, of velvet, satin or taffeta though there were masks of green and white silk. White masks were worn by Venetian ladies in 1695, so writes an English visitor at that date with the further comment that the masks resembled those worn earlier by English ladies with their cloaks. The loo mask which covered but half the face, was secured by strings over the ears or a wire over the top of the head while the full-face mask was held by a glass button or small silver bar on the inner side and placed between the teeth. Plain glass was sometimes inserted in the eye openings.

"Patching the face" with gummed black silk patches became very popular in the second half of the century and ladies carried exquisite little patch boxes with a tiny mirror in the lid. Patches or *mouches* as the French named them because they looked like flies, were cut in various designs such as flowers, crescents, stars, even figures and animals. Patches worn in Venice in the mid-sixteenth century, made necessary no doubt to cover skin blemishes caused by impure cosmetics, were first worn by ladies of the court and there we have the origin of the term, "court plaster."

Cosmetics were still made of crude and injurious ingredients. The bourgeoise, the actress and the lady of quality, all made use of rouge but the coloring of the lady of quality differed in its being a very delicate tint. When the complexion was pale, vermillion was applied to the cheeks and if too rosy, was toned down with "Spanish white" which was wool saturated with white lead or chalk. Spanish papers, tiny books of red or white paint covered papers, were also used.

Ladies themselves made a powder of pulverized egg shells mixed with toilet water and slept at night with pieces of bacon applied to their faces to produce rosy cheeks. Often, a lemon was carried in the hand and occasionally sucked to produce red lips. Youthful cheeks were to be had by means of "plumpers," which were small balls of soft wax placed in the cheeks.

Pear-shaped pearls were the outstanding ornaments of the century in earrings and necklaces. The single string around the neck, choker length we call it, became classic. An ingenious Frenchman named Jacquin of Paris, about 1680, invented an excellent imitation of the opalescent bit. He filled hollow blown glass with an essence composed of the silvery particles left in the water in which white bait had been washed. "Temple stones" for which there arose a tremendous vogue, were produced by an artisan of the Rue du Temple in Paris, who discovered a process for coloring crystal and produced inexpensively, imitation rubies, emeralds and topazes.

Until 1626, when John Tilsby undertook to manufacture the articles in Gloucestershire, the common pins used in England, were principally of French make. Good pins in those days were made of brass while inferior ones against which legislation was passed, were fashioned of blanched iron and sold as brass.

1600 to 1700

beaver hat with jeweled band and ostrich plumes - English - early 17th C.

felt or beaver - band of galloon - gold ornament - small feather - English - 1606

beaver or felt - wing in gold socket - pendant pearl - English - 1602

cocked beaver with jeweled band and brooch - English - early 17th C.

cocked beaver hat - brooch with gold disks and pendant pearl - English - early 17th C.

Beaver or felt - rolled crêpe band - gold ornament - Dutch - circa 1610

negligee cap of embroidered silk - turned-up band edged narrow gold lace - English - early 17th C.

beaver or felt with wide crêpe band - English - circa 1600

felt or beaver - rolled crêpe band - ribbon rosette - French - circa 1610

RTW

1600 to 1700

Cavalier-coiffure á la comète-lovelocks-English-1620's

Cavalier-beaver or felt-jeweled brooch-ostrich plumes-French-1620

Cavalier-beaver hat cocked front and back-ostrich-jeweled brooch-pendant pearls-French-1620's

Cavalier-beaver or felt with rolled crêpe band-Dutch-early 17th C.

Cavalier-beaver with ostrich-silk band-coiffure á la comète-French-1628

Cavalier-cocked beaver-ribbon band-coiffure with lovelock-French-1629

Cavalier-cocked felt or beaver-Dutch-1624

French-1622

RTW

1600 to 1700

Cavalier-
large floppy
beaver hat
with ostrich-
circa
1630

Cavalier-
felt or beaver with
ostrich-silk ribbon and
rope band-
coiffure
á la
comète-
French
1630

Cavalier-
hair short on
right side-
long on left-
English-
1630's

short
coiffure-
Spanish-
1630's

the
cardinal's
red calotte
or zucchetto-
1630's

simple
coiffure with
center part-
German-
1630's

Cavalier-
beaver with
ostrich-
lovelock and
favor-
French-
1635

beaver or
felt-ostrich-
curled hair-
single pearl
earring-
English-
1630's

large felt hat-
ribbon band-
Dutch-
mid 17th C.

R T W

1600 to 1700

Cavalier-beaver hat-silk rope band-English-circa 1638

Cavalier with ribbon favor-French-1635

Cavalier-lovelock and favors in two colors-single pearl earring-French-mid 17th C.

Puritan-black felt or beaver-silver buckle-silk band-1630's

cardinal's red biretta-Spanish-1643

Quaker felt or beaver brim rolling or cocked commonly gray or brown-2nd half 17th C.

Pilgrim-felt with ribbon band-silver buckle-1620's

felt hat-fine gold chain-ostrich-ribbon loops-German-1650's

"laced hat" of felt-ribbon loops-aigrette-lovelock with favor-English-1650's

coiffure with lovelock-Swedish-1643

RTW

1600 to 1700

felt hat with
ostrich-
natural hair-
French-
1660

Puritan-
black felt
hat-natural
hair with
lovelock-
1650's

natural hair-
English-
1660's

black felt-
satin band
and loops-
natural hair-
Dutch-
1660's

natural hair-
Swedish-
1660's

black felt with
silk band and
jeweled buckle-
black full-bottomed
wig-
English-1660's

felt hat with
ostrich and
ribbon loops-
natural hair-
French-
1650's

the montero for
negligée and
traveling-fur or
cloth flaps, varying
in shape-
2nd half 17th C.

RTW

1600 to 1700

full·bottomed
black wig·
English·
circa
1670

felt or velvet·
ostrich fringe·
ribbon loops·
campaign wig·
French·
1670's

felt hat·
ostrich
fringe·
galloon edge
and loops·campaign
wig with "favors"·
French army officer·
1670's

beaver
or felt
cocked hat· brown
full·bottomed wig·
French·
1679·

brown double·peaked
full·bottomed wig·
French·
1690's

felt cocked hat·ostrich·
brown full·bottomed wig·
French·
1680's

powdered full·bottomed
wig· English·
1690's

beaver or felt
with ostrich·
wig or natural
hair with favors·
French cavalry
officer·
1670's

R T W

1600 to 1700

cocked hat-
beaver, felt
or velvet-
ribbon
loops-
natural hair-
French-
1680

cocked
hat of
beaver
or felt-
ribbon
loops-brown wig-
French-1670's

cocked velvet hat-
brim satin-faced-
gold lace and
ostrich-black wig-
French naval
officer-
1690's

cocked
hat-
felt or velvet-
ostrich and
ribbon-short
bob wig-
French army
officer-
1689

beaver or felt-
gold or silver
braid-ostrich-
ribbon loops-
campaign wig-
French army
officer-
1678

cocked hat
or tricorne-
felt with gold or
silver braid and
buttons-ostrich-
gray powdered
wig- French
1693

cocked hat or
tricorne -ostrich fringe-gold
or silver braid and band-brown
wig-French-1695

cocked hat or
tricorne-felt with
gold or silver braid-
ostrich-French musketeer-
1700

RTW

1600 to 1700

hair dressed over
wire frame-jeweled
brooch and pearls-
black velvet
headdress with
gold lace-
English-
1610

widow's coif-
black crêpe-
rope band-
French-
1613

felt hat faced
with velvet-galloon
band-jeweled
brooches-worn
over lace coif-
Dutch-
1610

beaver hat
worn by the
Princess
Powhatan
Pocahontas-
galloon band-
English ringlets-
earrings-
American-
1616

turban roll of
gauze or metal
tissue-tight
curls-pearl
earrings-
English-
1621

hair dressed over
wire frame-rubies
and pearls-black
velvet bows with
pearl drops-German-
1620's

beaver hat
with ostrich-
crimped hair-
pearl earrings-
German-
1612

hair
dressed
over wire
frame-
jeweled
pins-
French-
1620

Dutch coif or
cornet
of sheer
transparent
lawn-wired
edge and lace-
Dutch-
1620's

RTW

1600 to 1700

beaver hat-
ostrich-
ribbon band-
Dutch-
circa
1610

widow's cap-
half mourning-
white lined
with black-
French-
1620's

Dutch coif
or cornet of
sheer lawn
with thread
lace edge-
fine tucks-
Dutch-
1630's

headkerchief
pinned to
hair for
street wear-
silk gauze-
French-
1629

hair dressed over
wire frame-
pearls and
jewels-pearl
earrings-
aigrettes-
French-
1625

beaver hat with
aigrettes-velvet
and pearls-hair
dressed with pearls-
pearl earrings-
Dutch-
1630's

hair dressed
over wire frame-
gold diadem-
square jeweled
pins-ostrich-
pearl earrings-
German-
1629

crimped hair-
gold ornament
with pearl
drops-gold
leaves-
German-
circa
1630

RTW

1600 to 1700

center part-
pearl and velvet
coif over chignon-
paradise plummage-
Italian-
1620's

Dutch coif or
cornet
of lingerie
fabric with
wired edge-
French
bourgeosie-
1630's

hair dressed
over wire frame-
heartbreakers-
ribbon bowknot-
pearl
earrings-
French-
1630's

loo mask-black
velvet-hair
dressed over wire
frame-ostrich tip-
pearl earrings-
French-1630's

Spanish queen on
horseback-crimped
hair-ostrich tip-
gold or silver ribbon-
pearl earrings-
1630's

Dutch coif or cornet-
sheer black lawn-
wired edge-
white embroidery-
pearl earrings-
Dutch-1635

cornet or
Dutch coif-
transparent white lawn-
wired edge-pointed
undercap with
embroidered
bands-
German-
1630's

bongrace
of black
taffeta or
velvet-hair
dressed over
wire frame-
French
bourgeoisie-
1630's

RTW

1600 to 1700

widow's mourning headdress attached to cloak-transparent black fabric topped by silk bongrace-silk covered wires-French-1630's

front hair fringed-side hair crimped-chignon in back-blue and white ostrich-French-1630's

natural colored straw hat worn over lingerie coif-embroidered Chinese blue band-Dutch-1630's

black beaver hat Cavalier fashion-white ostrich-English ringlets with a heartbreaker-English-1630's

à la moutonne-hair fringed over forehead-crimped sides-chignon in back-crocheted loosely hanging hood-pearl earrings-French-1630's

huke-long mantle of black cloth-bongrace with pompon-English ringlets-Flemish-1630's

à la moutonne-fringe over forehead-side hair crimped-chignon in back-pearls and jeweled flowers-jeweled earrings-note pearls on string left side-Dutch-1632

English ringlets-chignon wound with strings of pearls-English-1630's

RTW

1600 to 1700

fringe over forehead-
sides cut and
waved-high
chignon-ostrich
plume-pearl
earrings-
Dutch-
1640's

fringe over
forehead-high
chignon-felt
hat-ostrich
and ribbon
rosette-
German-
1640's

chignon wound with
string of pearls-
ribbon
fillet-
kiss-curls
on neck-
earrings-
Dutch-
1650's

huke-long
mantle of black
cloth-bongrace
with pompon-
German-
1640's

English ringlets-
pearls and ribbon
round chignon-
pearl earring
and heart
breakers on
left side-
English-
1640's

felt hat with
ribbon band-
German-
1644

general back view-
chignon with pearls-
ribbon loops-
English ringlets-
1640

widow's headdress-
black crêpe-full length mantle attached to
shirred coif-wired and pleated bongrace-
English ringlets and chignon-German-1640's

pearl coif
over
chignon-ostrich
plume-English ringlets-
English-1644

RTW

1600 to 1700

black silk
widow's coif-
heartbreakers
or favorites
tied with
ribbon-chignon
in back-
Flemish-
1648

straw hat with
ostrich-worn
over white
lawn hood-
lace edge-
crimped
hair-chignon
in back-
Flemish-
1647

black mask held by
wire over top of
head-black cloth
hood over silk
headkerchief-chin
band-English-
1640's

coiffure
with
ribbon-
kiss-curls on neck-
Dutch-
1650's

corno
of silk and pearls-
heartbreakers-
kiss-curls on neck-
Dutch-
1647

beaver hat worn
over white lawn
coif-scalloped
edge-
English Puritan-
1650's

coronet of hair
with strings of
pearls-chignon
in back-
pearl earrings-
Swedish-
1640's

hood of
white muslin
with fine
lace-
English-
1648

RTW

1600 to 1700

wired
ringlets
tied with gold
or silver ribbon with jeweled ends-
metal ribbon rosette with jewels-
plume of spotted breast feathers-
Spanish-1650's

widow's coif-
black and
pearl-edged-
wired
heartbreakers-
chignon in
back-
French-
1660's

heartbreakers
with velvet
bowknots-
silk hood
tied under
chin-French-
1660's

hood of fine
white muslin-
scalloped edge-
English ringlets-
Swedish-
1660's

wired
heart-
breakers-
braided
chignon-
Dutch-
1660's

wired
heartbreakers-
pearl and jeweled
ornaments-pearls
round chignon-pearl
earrings-Dutch-
1668

coiffure dressed over
wire frame-gold or silver
ribbon-large rosettes on top
and sides-fringe attached
to bowknots-of
small thin gold
leaves-
Spanish-
1650's

widow's coif-black
with pearls-heartbreakers
and chignon-French-1663

RTW

1600 to 1700

comb with
leaf motif in gold
and pearls-
chignon wound
with pearls-
Dutch-
1670

hood of colored
silk worn over
hood of fine
white muslin-
lace frill-
English-
1670's

lace calotte
with bowknots
à la Fontanges-
back curls tied
into a "chou"-
pearl earrings-
French-
1670's

coiffure
"hurluberlu"
over wire frame-
larger on left side-
pearls and garnets-
Flemish-
1670's

favorites at temples-
high chignon-
ribbon loops
and band with
jewel-earrings-
French-1679

coiffure with ribbon loops
à la Fontanges-"confident"
curl next to ear-
pearl earrings-
French-
1680's

coiffure
"tête de chou"
with loops
of galloon-
pearl earrings-
French-
1680's

black taffeta hood
lined white satin-
black ribbon
loops-black
mask and patch-
French-
1689

RTW

1600 to 1700

the fontange-
curls dressed
over wire frame
called commode-
pearl hairpins-
jeweled brooch-
temple curls
called favorites-
French-
1690's

riding
habit-black
felt tricorne-metal
ribbon edge-ostrich-
black wig-
1690's

fontange of
pleated white
lawn and
lace-black
taffeta
ribbon-
patches-
French-
1680's

fontange
with lappets-
lawn and
lace-ribbon
loops-gold
and pearl
diadem-
earrings-
patches-
ringlets-
English-
1690's

a
"transparent"
sheer white gauze-
green and rose
ribbon-fluted
lappets-pearl
hairpins-patches-
French-1688

fontange
of lawn and
lace covered
with scarf
for street-
French-
1680's

negligée headdress-
sheer white lawn-
ribbon bowknot-
French-1690's

fontange of lawn
and lace-tiny
lace edge-net
square with frill-
taffeta ribbon
loops-
French-
1680's

RTW

1600 to 1700

boy in beaver hat-
ostrich plume-
lovelock-
French-
1615

baby girl
in lace
Dutch coif-
German-
1628

boy in black
beaver Cavalier
hat-
Dutch-
1625

boy in silk bonnet
with lace-
feather-jeweled
ornament-
German-
1628

young girl in
lace hood-
hair drawn
back into
chignon-
English-
1630's

"Baby Stuart
cap"-three
rows of shirred
lace-narrow
edging-
English-1634

boy with
lovelock-
English-
1636

young girl with
ringlets-hair
drawn back
and tied-
pearl earrings-
English-
1645

boy
with
velvet béret-
Spanish-1630's

little girl in
fontange-fine
lace-lace
loops at
side-
French-
1695

young
girl-hair
dressed over wire frame-orange-red plume
and rosettes-pearl fringe-Spanish-1650's

baby boy in
silk hood over
lawn cap-
American-1670

FTW

THE EIGHTEENTH CENTURY

CHAPTER ELEVEN

THE EIGHTEENTH CENTURY is conceded to be the most brilliant period in the history of French costume with the French Court setting the mode in clothes and social manners for Europe and the American Colonies. The American colonist paid special attention to the new fashions which were generally taken up within a year following their appearance.

The newest clothes came from France and England in the merchant ships which plied their routes regularly across the Atlantic. London tailors and wig-makers sent their new creations along with beautiful fabrics from China and the Indies, other luxuries and household articles. Many colonists kept their measurements in London for especially made attire. Fashion dolls or "fashion babies" were sent regularly to London from Paris. The small mannequins dressed in the very latest fashions were sometimes sent direct to the Colonies but not so frequently, usually making the trip by way of London.

The American preference in the early part of the century was for English fashions, then from 1760 to 1780, both French and English were followed. After that, with the exception of the period of the French Revolution, the

French mode became the thing in the feminine world, Paris holding the scepter till the fateful year of 1940. During the French Revolution, London took over as arbiter of man's dress, a position she holds to date.

Except for court affairs, English women gave less thought to dressing than did American women. Letters of foreigners of the times, especially after the American Revolution, comment upon the neatness of the attire of our women but criticize the fact that the wives of bankers and merchants of the New Republic were always dressed in the latest and costly French style.

Of the English dandies, there was Ambrose Phillips (1671-1749) a famous beau nicknamed "Namby Pamby." He wore the full-bottomed wig, was an author and a wit of rank at Button's Coffee House in London where smart men held forth.

He was followed by Richard Nash (1674-1761) known as Beau Nash or "King of Bath" which he presided over as master of ceremonies. He wore a tall white beaver hat, was a leader of fashion and a professional gambler.

The tiny lipbeard and mustache, which had become mere patches late in the preceding century, disappeared in the early years of this century.

The full-bottomed wig with its high peaks remained in fashion through the first two decades but from 1730 was worn only by professional and elderly men. "Corners" of horsehair were inserted in concealed parts of the wig to add to its contour.

Young men grew tired of the heavy wig, parting it in the center and in summer, tying the back into knots, then letting the hair hang in the winter. This practice created the "knotted wig."

In the "tye" or "tie wig," the hair was simply drawn back and tied with a black silk ribbon.

The bagwig worn first by soldiers before 1700, had the hair encased in a bag of gummed black taffeta drawn tight by a string and covered by a rosette or bowknot of the same material. It is said that this style originated among the servants who thus covered their hair while at work but another source tells us that it originated in the stables where the horses' tails were covered when in the stalls. By the 'thirties, gentlemen had also adopted what was at first considered too negligee and disrespectful for the social world. The bag which increased in size to the 'forties, served as a protection to the coat from the grease and powder of the wig.

The ribbon ends of the tie wig and the bagwig were brought around to the front of the neck and tied in a bow. This was the solitaire and the beginning of the man's black silk tie: A jeweled barette or diamond pin sometimes fastened the solitaire.

The pigtail wig, also early eighteenth century, had a tightly braided tail, sometimes two, spirally wound with black ribbon. The queue, pigtail or whip of the soldier and sailor was often false, made of black leather or chamois with a tuft of hair or "paintbrush" at the end and cleaned and polished along with his boots. Late in the century when the pigtail was discarded in civil life, it was retained by the military. Eighteen hundred and eight saw the end of the pigtail in the United States Army.

The dressing of his wig was most important in the soldier's life and often when there were too few barbers, a whole regiment of soldiers would tie each other's wigs. Veterans continued to powder long after the fashion had passed. The curled and powdered hair in the American Army required stores of flour and tallow, a pound of flour was each man's ration for a week.

The Ramillies wig, also a favorite in the army, got its name from the Battle of Ramillies in Belgium in 1706, fought between the English and the French. It was an English victory under the Duke of Marlborough (1650–1722) and men's and women's styles were named for the battle and the duke. In this wig, the pigtail was tied top and bottom with black ribbon. Sometimes, the braid was looped under and tied with ribbon.

The bushy short bob wig, a favorite of the clergy, was worn on ordinary occasions and for negligee by men and boys.

The cadogan, catogan or club wig of the 'seventies, named after the Earl of Cadogan of earlier date, was first worn by the English Macaronies. The cadogan was looped up and tied by a string or the black solitaire, sometimes held in place by a small comb or like the ladies', confined in a silk net. The Macaronies or "exquisites" were a group of idle young men who made a tour of Italy in the 'fifties and upon their return to London in 1760 inaugurated the Macaroni Club in opposition to the Beefsteak Club. They adopted everything extreme in the fashionable world and it followed that everything extreme was named after them. The term with the same meaning was also in use here in America.

"Pigeon's wings," the soft rolls at the sides of the face, in the first quarter of the century were replaced by set rolls or puffs, *cadenettes* in French, the same name as that given the lovelock of the previous century. The front hair or toupet was dressed in pompadour fashion, often natural and combed into the wig, then powdered to conceal the joining. About 1770, coinciding with the rising headdress of the opposite sex, appeared the Greek or horseshoe toupet. It was waved and dressed in a single roll, often over a wire frame, over the front of the head from ear to ear.

Very fashionable and very costly in the first quarter of the century was the Adonis wig of fine snow-white hair with gray next in popularity. Less fashionable than the gray or white wig was the "brown wig" dusted with brown powder.

Pure white powder appeared in 1703, covering not only the wig but, as a contemporary writer says, "also the coat." Louis XIV, alive to 1715, disapproved of powder and did not use it until his last years and then, sparingly.

An interesting story connected with hair powder is the discovery in Saxony of the long-searched-for material for making white porcelain in the royal factory at Meissen in 1715. A wealthy iron manufacturer on horseback observed that his horse had difficulty in extracting his hoofs from the soft white earth over which they were traveling. With the great demand for hair powder in mind, the rider wondered if such an adhesive powder might not prove a substitute for the wheat flour then being employed. As such, it was used in great quantities.

Böttcher, the superintendent of the porcelain factory, dusting it upon his wig, remarked upon the unusual weight of the powder. Upon investigation, he found it to be an earth powder and experimented with it in his ceramics with the happy result of at last finding the long-looked-for ingredient to produce white porcelain.

Gray and blond powders were also used, gray the more popular. In France many gave up the use of powder because of the scarcity of bread among the poor but the fashionable world went its way in its flour-powdered wig. Rousseau said, "The poor are without bread because we must have powder for our hair." The fashion of powdering was at its greatest height from 1760 to 1776 and there were also such colors as grayish pink, blue and violet scented with violette, chypre and others. Pulverized starch was also used and another item is that hair powders were made by the makers of perfumed gloves.

With the French Revolution (1789-1795) the use of powder, a fashion of one hundred years, went out but many partisans of the old regime and also many patriots refused to give up the custom. In England, the Tory continued to dust his cadogan or club wig to distinguish himself from the sympathizer with the French Revolutionist. Pitt's tax in 1795 however, had a telling effect and the high price and the poor wheat harvest brought the end of powdering in 1790. It cost the individual one guinea a year to powder, such a person being nicknamed a "guinea pig."

One might wonder at a century of such a practice of powdering the hair over a base of grease but it had its advantages, important enough to counteract the disadvantages. First, it flattered the face and second and most desired, it eliminated that sign of age, gray hair.

As wigs were more commonly worn, they became distinguishing signs of class and profession which very reason was the death-knell of the style for fashionable folk. That the wig was beginning to go in the 'sixties, is apparent in the petition of the Master Peruke Makers of London to George III, complaining that gentlemen were returning to the fashion of natural hair. Many men powdered only upon occasions of ceremony and by the 'seventies, many ceased shaving the head.

Natural hair began to appear in the mid-century, dressed in a black silk bag with a bowknot of ribbon, many young men discarding the bag as soon as they grew a sufficient length of hair. The ribbon-tied queue was also worn during the growing process especially by army officers and if the tail or whip required extra length, false hair was added. French and German regulations designated the two waist buttons in back as the point at which to terminate the whip.

The black ribbon remains part of today's khaki uniform of the Royal Welsh Fusiliers. The "flash," a bunch of black ribbons with pinked ends, is worn attached to the back of the collar of the tunic. So fond of the flash is the regiment that one retired officer wears it on the collar of his civilian dinner coat today.

The wig was retained by doctors and clergymen into the early nineteenth century and survives to date in the British Empire in the costume of judges and barristers, certain professions and in the uniform of the coachmen of the sovereigns.

All classes of men in the American Colonies wore the wig although in the South with its warm climate, great distances between plantations and many poor people, the wig was often discarded in favor of a cap. Those of better circumstances wore a cap of fine holland linen while the common folk wore one of wool. Negro slaves wore half-worn and secondhand wigs, also less expensive ones of white horsehair or goats' hair made up in the simpler styles such as the bob wig. Small boys too, wore wigs. The wig was not spurned by the Quaker, who wore one of less pretentious dimensions, but often he was content with his own hair dressed in wig fashion.

Fastidious persons had their wigs especially dressed for Saturday night and Sunday wear and the barbers' boys were to be seen late Saturday afternoons carrying wigs to and fro from house to shop. The wig was sent in an especially built box to the barber to be dressed and powdered on a block. Curling papers, irons, a paste of pomatum and flour and hot clay pipes around which the curls were rolled, ended with the dusting of powder. Many large homes had built-in wig closets where the gentleman sat, a great cloth around his neck, his face protected by a glass or paper cone while his valet powdered his freshly dressed wig.

Natural hair was curled by means of paper curlers or "papillotes." Not only European but many an American gentleman kept a French valet to perform such tasks.

Interesting in today's wigless times is the fact that the stage dressed its characters in the fashionable costume of the day regardless of country or period. David Garrick (1717-1779) played Othello in a Ramillies wig as did Spargner Barry (1719-1777) with a small cocked hat. James Quin (1693-1776) performed Othello with blackened face and powdered wig and the Hamlet given by John Kemble (1757-1823) also wore a powdered wig.

A distinctive coiffure of the 'eighties was the "hedgehog" in which the top and sides were cut in a studied dishevelled crop. There were many different fashions of wearing the hair, the most popular having the sides bobbed and a tie in back or the parted hair simply flowing to the shoulders.

The cocked hat or tricorne was the masculine hat of the eighteenth century. Generally carried under the arm, "le chapeau bras" became a mark of gentility, a sign of professional and social rank as contrasted with the lower classes who wore their hat uncocked. The clergy wore the large uncocked, unadorned hat while the headpiece of the gentleman and the army officer was ornamented with gold or silver galloon, ribbon cockades, lace and ostrich fringe or plumes. Gold and silver galloon disappeared from civilian clothes in the first quarter of the century when its cost became prohibitive. Although a new galloon was invented with the metal worked on one side only, the fad for such ornamentation had passed, its use surviving on uniforms and livery.

The heavy wig was the cause of carrying the hat under the arm when indoors and resulted in the disappearance of the age-old custom of men wearing the hat in the house, in church and at table.

The most popular hat of the century, both civilian and military, was the Swiss military hat, a large comfortable piece that set well down on the head. It really was a bicorne with high front and back flap, the highest point being the spout-like crease in center front. To the French, it was the Androsmane; to the English and Americans, it was the Kevenhuller of simplified spelling, named after the famous Austrian field-marshal Khevenhüller. An English note of 1753 calls the hat *démodé* but it was worn through the 'eighties.

Then there was the "Ramillies cock" with flaps higher than the crown. The back flap sharply turned up was higher than the front flap which was scalloped out in center front, creating a tricorne.

Hats became smaller by the middle of the century and black, the color for ceremonial and general wear. The tricorne was made in straw for summer wear.

The Nivernois was a diminutive tricorne, a favorite of the English Macaronies and worn by them with the cadogan wig in the 'seventies. The name derives from the Duke of Nivernais, Louis-Jules Mancini Mazarini (1716–1798), a royalist who refused to flee during the French Revolution, was imprisoned and although he became Citizen Mancini, remained the gentleman of former days.

The bicorne which supplanted the tricorne in the 1790's, was another evolution of the cocked hat. It folded flat and was also a "chapeau bras." It became the ceremonial dress hat and is worn today by high ranking officers of the American, British and French navies.

In the 'seventies and 'eighties there developed in Paris a tremendous vogue for things American and English. The American trend was the result of our own Revolution and the influence of our popular ambassador to Paris, Benjamin Franklin, who lived there from 1776 to 1785. Men wore for country use the Holland or Pennsylvania hat, a round hat with low crown and rolling brim made of felt in gray, brown or green.

Anglomania brought forth the jockey hat, which came from England where it was first worn by grooms then adopted by their masters. It had a low crown, the brim bent down in front to shade the eyes.

Late in the 'eighties appeared the tall round hat of felt napped with beaver with narrow rolling brim, the "stovepipe" of the next century. A hat of polished beaver was invented in Florence, Italy, in 1760 but was not to be perfected till the 1830's.

Hatmaking was one of the first of American industries with the men of New York, New Jersey and Pennsylvania wearing domestic hats while importing most of their other wearing apparel. By 1740, exportation of American hats to Spain and Portugal reached such figures that the London feltmakers protested to Parliament against the "outrage," as detrimental to home industry. Forthwith many restrictions were placed upon the Colonial hatmakers.

In France in 1792 appeared the red woolen Phrygian cap, "le bonnet rouge," sign of the Revolutionist. The elegantly dressed patriot was known as a *muscadin,* a name acquired by overdressing and the excessive use of musk perfume.

In portraits done in the 'nineties we occasionally find men wearing earrings, usually tiny hoops. Such baubles are to be noted also in some American portraits.

The age-old blue woolen beret or Scotch bonnet worn by shepherd, soldier and gentleman in Scotland was woven in one piece without seam or binding. It was also called the "blue bonnet" and had either a red or blue tuft on top. A ribbon cockade, a sprig of native evergreen and a feather or feathers, signified the wearer's rank in his particular clan. Three feathers were permitted the chief or head of the clan, two for the gentleman and one for the clansman.

The Prince Charlie bonnet of today is rather full-crowned and has a wide band. It got its name from the young pretender Prince Charles Edward (1720–1788) or "Bonnie Prince Charlie" who in 1745 and '46 made an unsuccessful attempt to regain his father's throne.

Till the eighteenth century great laxity was permitted in European military dress with the exception of the Prussians, individuals even wearing mourning. From that period, the rules of costume and even tactics were set by Prussia, of which a surprised visitor in 1729 says, "Uniformity reigns in all details in the army, even to the shoe buckles." And further, "The Prussians have a custom which has never been practiced by any troops; to refurnish anew each year."

The distinction by uniform between army and navy was not officially established among European nations till the first half of the eighteenth century when a marine uniform appears to have originated in England. The sailor's hat was a small flat version of the tricorne, described in an English note of 1762 as a "hat with its sides tacked to the crown, the whole pressed flat and looking like an apple-pasty." In the 'seventies, first appeared the shape known as the sailor, a hard round hat with narrow brim and made of varnished or japanned leather.

Late in the century, the great British Admiral Horatio Nelson (1758–1805) made the round hat of straw summer regulation for the crew. The "boater" the English called it. To counteract the softening effects of the damp atmosphere, the sailor took to varnishing the straw hat. Sennit straw, today's name for the shellacked straw sailor, is also of nautical origin, coming from seven-knit, a technique of rope-plaiting which the plaited straw resembled. At Eton, the hat was adopted in honor of Nelson, and every year on Boat Day held June 4, the boys wear the boater or "skimmer" with flowers stuck in the ribbon band.

The colors of companies in the army followed those established in heraldry by lords and leaders for the liveries of their retainers and domestics. In England, scarlet and blue, in accordance with armorial hues of the royal family since the reign of Edward III (1327–1377) had been the cloth ordered for the king's troops; thus it followed that in this period of Queen Anne (1702–1714) the colors were red and blue. During a period of mourning, military hats were denuded of lace and banded with crêpe.

A regulation order of 1702 to the Royal Scots reads: "As nothing disfigures hats or dirties the lace more than taking off the hat, the men are for the future only to raise the back of their hands to them with a brisk motion when they pass an officer." However, the salute of the open hand with facing palm was a direct and frank assurance that the passing individual was friendly, a custom of Medieval Times when civilians were armed and the streets very narrow. The gesture was also practiced by the knight who wore a visored helmet and flicked back the visor to greet a friend or to be recognized.

The ribbon rosette of the mode became the insignia of the military world, worn from the beginning of the century and usually black. Cockades were of leather and silk and Washington in orders of 1776 assigned green to subaltern officers, white or buff to captains and pink to field officers. In 1780, the officer's cockade was changed to black with white relief signifying the expected union of the American and French armies.

With the American Revolution in mind, the French Revolutionists decided to have a cockade of their own and adopted the colors red and blue of the City of Paris. After the fall of the Bastille, Lafayette ordered the white of royalty added as a sign of accord with the king. The red was placed between the blue and white but in 1791, the white was placed between the blue and red.

Varied indeed and constantly changing were the many designs and colors of military bonnets and helmets of the eighteenth century. The iron skullcap or "scull" was still worn under the fabric hat in battle. The very large cocked hat of the Prussian grenadier of 1730 was found to be a great inconvenience when throwing hand grenades with the long rifle butt slung in back. The hat with the protruding corners was easily knocked off the head by the musket. Frederick William I of Prussia (1713–1740), father of Frederick the Great, substituted the shako of Hungarian origin, the sugarloaf-shaped bonnet of copper with high point and metal plate, the design so familiar to us in our pet andirons of the "Hessians" of the American Revolution.

To give the hat a more martial air, the king had a covering of bearskin added. The headpiece was popular in the French Army where it was introduced by the German mercenaries and worn by the horse grenadiers. The British grenadier also wore the miter-shaped cap but of cloth or velvet with the arms and supporters on the frontal embroidered in colors, gold and silver and very handsome it was.

The hussars, originally a Hungarian cavalry, wore a cap with a wide band of fur and a pointed cloth bag which hung to one side. Originally, the point of the bag was fastened to the right shoulder to ward off sword thrusts. In that period of the wig, a distinctive and ferocious mien was effected by shaving the head save for a tuft of hair on top and wearing a mustache with long drooping ends. By the 'sixties, they had changed to side locks, braided and ribbon-tied. The hussar later adopted a cloth cap with the hanging bag.

The uhlans of Poland or Lithuania, originally of Asiatic origin, wore a casque of imitation gold encircled by a turban-like band of leather, later of fur. A tail of horsehair flowed from the crest.

American uniforms in general followed those of European design. A note concerning headgear in 1781 is the following taken from the orders upon uniforms of the Committee of Officers of the Massachusetts Line: "A fashionable military cock'd hat, with a silver loop, and a small button with the number of the Regiment."

The feminine coiffure of the first half of the century was dressed close to the head, the front drawn up off the forehead, a small topknot usually covered by tiny lingerie cap completing the "small head" contour. Delicate and small ornaments of blonde lace, artificial flowers, striped ribbons, aigrettes and strings of beads were artfully perched on top of the simple hairdo. We know this style by the various portraits of the lovely Marquise de Pompadour (1721–1764), a favorite of Louis XV and who ruled the social, fashionable and intellectual world from about 1745 to 1764.

Set curls arranged over the front of the head appeared about mid-century. There were French curls, English curls and Italian curls. The front hair was cut short and shaped into flat ringlets by means of a paste of pomatum and flour over a small black taffeta cushion, "the patted coiffure" the French called it. The hair was drawn up to the crown of the head in back and for court attire, curls hung over the shoulders.

In 1750 ladies adopted the century-old masculine fashion of the perruque or wig. From 1730 until this time the powdered "mannish wig" or a false chignon with cocked hat, had been worn only on horseback. The feminine wig was a cap-like affair covered with short curly hair or wool over which the natural hair and all the extra puffs and ornaments were dressed. There was also the elaborately dressed separate wig, a great convenience to ladies without hairdressers, especially in America. In this period of the built-up head, it was impossible to do one's own hair and the separate piece could be sent to the barber to be dressed.

A lady with her head dressed for a ball, often done the day before, would be compelled to sleep sitting up. New York and Philadelphia boasted a few hairdressers who did a thriving business. The fashionable woman paid as much as two hundred pounds a year to have her head dressed.

After a lady's hair was dressed, she, like her lord, covered her face with a paper or glass cornucopia while the powder was dusted or blown through a tube over the hairdo. This operation made powder mantles or dressing jackets of embroidered muslin a necessity. Powdering puffs, powdering bags and powdering machines were invented.

An advertisement from the *London Magazine* of 1768 notes: "False locks to supply deficiency of native hair, pomatum in profusion, greasy wool to bolster up the adopted locks, and gray powder to conceal dust." A Boston paper of 1768 advises: "Black and White and Yellow Pomatum is from Six Coppers to Two Shillings a Roll," and from a New York paper we have: "Orange Butter for Ladies' Rolls," "Hair Powder Plain and Scented, Blue, Brown, Maréchal and White" and another shop mentions a special gray powder for mourning.

Hair powder was a feminine fashion for more than half a century; it flattered the complexion, added brilliancy to the eyes and was always used for full dress. Gray and light brown or blond powder appear to have been the favored colors and white was often lightly dusted on to give a frosted effect.

Certainly dusty, and more than that, must have been heads dressed for a period from two to nine weeks though retouched daily and anointed with strong essences. The many contemporary notices of poisonous compounds for application to eliminate vermin tell the story. A writer advised the necessity of "opening up the head" once a week and a pretty gadget which afforded relief was a "scratcher," a dainty stick with a hook, to be had in ivory, gold or silver and sometimes encrusted with diamonds.

The higher coiffure of the 1770's was really artistic and elegant but it became extravagant and fantastic in height and ornament in the 'eighties. The hair was built up over cap wigs, horsehair cushions, wire frames, cotton wool foundations to which were added false puffs, cadogans, tulle, fresh and artificial flowers and fruits, jewels, ribbons, lace and feathers. Every puff or curl, each piece of decoration had a name. For grand occasions there were models of ships, coaches and windmills executed in blown glass. The death in 1774 of Louis XV, who had speculated unwisely in wheat, was a relief to the people and to show their great hope in the new regime, women wore spikes of wheat in their hair and on their hats.

Small flat bottles shaped to fit the head were concealed in the coiffure, holding water with fresh flowers. The manufacture of artificial flowers was not perfected till the early years of the nineteenth century though they had long been made by the nuns in Italian convents for altar decorations. This latter fact inspired the commercial production in France.

There was the fashion of puffs of gauze, strips or folds of the newly invented tulle. Tulle, a very fine net of silk or cotton, is supposed by some to have originated in Tulle, France but it was first made in Nottingham, England in 1768 on a stocking machine. It was a loosely woven tricot stitch which unraveled easily. The first French tulle made in 1778 by one Caillon, was as unsuccessful as the English attempt. Despite its poor quality, tulle became very popular and was even made in the French barracks, soldiers selling the stuff in the streets.

Yards and yards of tulle were required for the headdress and huge mobcap and during the blockade caused by the American Revolution, our ladies suffered for want of gauze and pins.

Feathers became the rage both in the hair and on hat or bonnet. The standing plumes of the English Court dress coiffure of today, date from the French fashion of Marie-Antoinette (1755–1793). One day, so the story goes, upon the completion of her toilette, she playfully added some peacock and ostrich feathers to her coiffure. Louis XVI, entering her boudoir, admired the get-up and the fashion was on its way.

Upon another occasion and during the visit of her brother Emperor Joseph II of Austria, the French queen turned to him for compliments upon her elaborate feathered headdress. But instead of offering the expected admiration, he made the remark that "though some people would consider it pretty, it was too fragile to support a crown."

Lord Stoment, ambassador of George III at the French Court in 1774, presented to the Duchess of Devonshire an ostrich plume three feet in length and that is the story of the introduction of the feather vogue into England.

Of the large built-up "heads" of the 'eighties, the most popular and most conservative was the "ingénue coiffure" named for Molière's stage character, Agnes in "L'Ecole des Femmes." It was dressed high in front with side puffs, the back in loose curls or a cadogan. Sometimes the cadogan was looped up in a silk net or held in place by a small comb. The hedgehog cut which men also wore, appeared in 1778 and became popular in the 'eighties. In this style, the front hair was cut short and frizzed to the ends, the back hanging in loose curls or a cadogan.

The "baby coiffure" which lasted but a short time, was the result of the queen's illness necessitating cutting her hair. She had lovely blond hair which inspired the fashionable color called "Queen's hair."

Among French women when horseback riding in the 'eighties, the wig gave way to hanging hair, either tied at the neck or in a long braid, English women preferring unbound flowing ringlets.

The 1780's are the years of the earliest publication of periodical illustrated fashion journals and the papers devoted their space not to the costume but to the mode in hairdressing. The most conservative coiffure required from one to two hours of the hairdresser's time. It was smart, therefore, for the fashionable lady to be surrounded by her admirers, intimates, tradespeople and servants during the ceremony, her toilette upon rising from her bed consuming hours.

According to a note of 1769 there were twelve hundred hairdressers in Paris. They called themselves artist-hairdressers and many took pupils, charging a high fee for instruction. For more than a century there were men and women hairdressers but the preference was now for men, it being considered that the man displayed more originality in his work.

A famous personage of the profession was Dagé, hairdresser to Madame de Pompadour. After Dagé came Le Gros, a former cook, who revolutionized the coiffure in his creation of the towering silhouette. He founded an academy in Paris where he taught his art to men and women, presented medals instead of diplomas and wrote a book upon hairdressing which was translated into several languages.

A master in the arrangement of tulle puffs was the hairdresser Léonard Autier, known simply as Léonard. He was coiffeur to Marie-Antoinette, who granted him many favors. Her regular man was an unoriginal fellow named Làrseueur whom she would not discharge but permitted him to do her hair regularly, with Léonard as regularly undoing the work and building anew.

Court etiquette prescribed that an attendant in close contact with royalty was not permitted to carry on his profession with the public. In this case, the queen, fearing that Léonard's skill might lessen if he confined his talent to only one head, insisted that he cater to his regular clientele. He made the trip daily from Paris to Versailles driving his own coach and six-in-hand. It was he who with the Duc de Choiseul carried the queen's personal jewels to Brussels. From there, the treasures were sent on to Vienna, a hoped-for haven which the unfortunate queen never reached. After the fateful flight to Varennes, he became an émigré, fleeing to Russia, where he continued his work.

A gruesome task fell to the lot of a certain hairdresser who was forced by the revolutionists to dress the decapitated head of the Princess de Lamballe so that "her friend Antoinette would recognize her." The poor fellow almost died of horror. The face was rouged and the hair frizzed and powdered and then hoisted upon a pike before the window of the royal prisoners.

A reform or move toward equality in dress took place in the 1780's with both the court and the public adopting simpler clothes. Powder, less frequently seen, and the high coiffure were reserved for court affairs. Contributing influences were the writings of Jean-Jacques Rousseau, English country life with a less formal way of living, the loss of great fortunes and the country clothes of the queen and her ladies worn "playing farming" at the Petit Trianon. False hair, wigs and powder disappeared in France during the Reign of Terror (May 1, 1793 to July 24, 1794). They reappeared, however, directly after. In England the queen and the ladies of the court ceased powdering in 1793.

In headgear, the first years of the eighteenth century found the tall fontange fashioned of such costly laces as Brussels and Mechlin. It then disappeared, replaced by the small dainty bits of white lawn or batiste with or without lace-edged lappets and tiny silk flowers familiar to us in the charming pictures of Watteau (1684–1721), the French painter and engraver.

After the middle of the century, the cap grew in size, in the 'seventies becoming a large bonnet, "chapeau-bonnette," the French name. This is the first time that the term "bonnet" was applied to feminine headtire.

The "Ranelagh mob," mobcap or just plain "mob" which it later became, with its deep hanging frill, originated in England, suggested by the cap worn by the market women. "Ranelagh" is from Ranelagh Gardens, a smart place of amusement gotten up by Lord Ranelagh upon his estate.

Another cap was the "dormeuse" or sleeping bonnet, a cap with frills which hugged the cheeks and tied under the chin. Bonnet-hats and demi-hats were of English origin, huge soft crowns with drooping ruffled brims and made of sheer muslin, lawn, taffeta, satin, velvet, lace and ribbon-trimmed with the ribbon ends pinked. Other trimmings were feathers, artificial flowers and fruits and buckles. Such bonnets were so large that the small lingerie cap was often worn underneath.

Bonnets were to be seen upon all occasions other than full dress. The citizeness and the Charlotte Corday, named for the youthful French heroine of the Reign of Terror, were variations of the mob ornamented with the tri-color cockade. The late 'nineties saw the decline of the vogue of the cap except in the boudoir but it was to remain a favorite of the elderly woman for nearly a century more. At the French Court of the eighteenth century, a lady wore under her cap, upon reaching the age of forty, a black lace coif tied under her chin. The cap survives to the present day in many European costumes and lasted into the twentieth century as the housewife's dust cap.

Lace caps were very costly affairs, one of Brussels net costing thirty pounds and another of Flanders or French point, eighty pounds while a "lace head" ordered by George Washington for his wife cost over five hundred dollars.

Country or "milkmaid fashions" originated in England, where the wide-brimmed hat of the village damsel worn over a lingerie cap and tied under the chin, became a feature of the English mode of "fashionable undress." Straw, not new to country women, acquired smartness in the social world, not the plaited straw or rush used by country folk but horsehair and fine yellow straw manufactured in Leghorn, Italy. Such shapes were of beaver too. Varied were the names: the shepherdess or gypsy hat, also "Churchills" after the beautiful sisters of the Duke of Marlborough. The very wide-brimmed flat-crowned straw of the mid-century was the "skimmer hat." The straw hat was popular in the American Colonies.

Straw became more fashionable than ever in the last quarter of the century, enormous quantities being exported from Italy. Fine leghorns, black horsehair and chip were especially in demand and worn winter and summer. Leghorn hats have always been woven of Tuscan straw, the most valuable straw grown. Four to five days are required for the making of a good quality hat but one of the highest quality may take six to nine months for its execution. Straw-plaiting was a feminine industry done in the home, in England especially by young women of limited incomes, a form of work copied by American women.

The large hat was secured to the hair by long hatpins or ribbon tied under the chin or held on by a diagonally folded kerchief which passed over the crown and tied under the chin. This latter was a long-lasting popular fashion, a silk piece of white, scarlet or green, regardless of the color scheme of the hat. Bright green was the color most generally used, the large brim of the leghorn hat often faced with green.

The two great English portrait painters of the day, Thomas Gainsborough (1727–1788) and Sir Joshua Reynolds (1723–1793), wielded a definite influence over the feminine head. The black Gainsborough or Marlborough hat of velvet or taffeta with large crown and wide brim and graceful sweep of line and plumes was the most elegant feminine hat of all time. To the French, it was the Marlborough, after the popular "Chanson de Marlborouk" which the French queen was heard singing to herself one day, causing a revival of the famous name and song.

Sometimes very small hats, doll hats we call them, were part of the tall headdress and pinned firmly on top, a style which coincided with that of the masculine Macaronies in England where ladies of the same ilk were also dubbed Macaronies. There were also Macaronie ladies in Cadiz, according to a note written by a feminine English visitor there in 1773 and they wore yellow powder in their hair.

There were turbans and toques of muslin, gauze or tulle made over a wire frame and trimmed with ribbons, feathers and jeweled ornaments. Turbans were also fashioned of silk scarfs with fringed ends, of crêpe, silk and ribbon, a style which carried over into the next century.

For horseback riding as already noted in the first half of the century, the black silk tricorne and powdered wig was the feminine headtire. In the 'eighties the wide-brimmed hat was worn and the postilion shape, while in the 'nineties there was the jockey-like cap, a brimless close-fitting hat. But the tricorne was definitely the riding hat of the century, remaining the formal equestrienne headpiece in France to date. Silk, felt, velvet and beaver were the fabrics used with plumes, ribbons and buckles as trimming. Many ladies preferred the riding hood, to be spoken of in a later paragraph.

The fashionable ladies of Venice wore the tricorne and with their inherent love for black and lace, placed the hat over a black lace mantilla draped like a Medieval wimple. It was usually a black silk hat with white silk edge or lining, sometimes ornamented with a plume and the black lace mantilla hanging to the waist. The concealed hair hung simply, in ringlets, unpowdered and the lady's face unrouged, in fact, a pallor was effected by white powder. In public she carried the mask.

The black lace head scarf, loosely tied under the chin, was also sponsored by European ladies of the eighteenth century. The mantilla, which later came to be particularly associated with Spanish women, appeared in Spain later in the period and was French-made, the black lace of Chantilly which a lace authority writing in our time states "is without rival even today." The Chantilly lacemakers associated by their work with the aristocrats, were wiped out in 1793 and some unfortunate individuals suffered the fate of their royal patrons on the scaffold.

The French hood held its own throughout the century, worn by women of all nations and stations. It was made of silk, velvet or sarcenet attached to a long cape or separate with short shoulder cape and then called "capuchin." Quilted, fur-lined or fur-edged for winter wear, the hood of the early period was usually scarlet, cherry red or cardinal and called a red riding hood or cardinal.

The huge English mobcaps or "mobs" and the exaggerated coiffures necessitated enormous hoods for traveling and very popular was the calash, calèche or "bashful bonnet" supposedly designed and introduced in 1765 by the Duchess of Devonshire. The calash was first made of green silk, later of various fabrics and colors. The material was shirred over whalebone or reed hoops which could be raised or lowered like a carriage top by a string attached to the front and held in the hand. The Quakeress called her black silk calash the "wagon bonnet."

The thérèse was of gauze or tulle or of black taffeta with deep gauze frill, also made over reed or whalebone hoops.

The black silk hood lined with white silk and finished with a short shoulder cape was part of the bridal costume of the Pennsylvania girl of the eighteenth century. It is mentioned by several contemporary writers who say that the rest of the costume was light colored, of rich fabric and of the mode of the moment.

Brides wore white and occasionally a veil but these two features of our bridal costume of today do not appear to have been the custom in those times. The general use of the bridal veil dates from the end of the century which witnessed the invention in England of a machine for the manufacture of net and lace wide enough to be used for veils and shawls. The first American bride to wear a veil, so they say, was the adopted daughter of Washington, Nellie Custis. Her wedding was held on the President's last birthday in 1799 and her veil, a wedding gift, was a beautiful scarf which she wore pinned to her coiffure.

The use of the mask, not so general as in the previous century, lasted past the second half of this period. The black velvet mask was carried in winter, a green mask protected the lady against sunburn when horseback riding and young girls wore one of linen which was tied on under the hood. Masks were worn in the American Colonies, as a bill of sale of Washington's testifies in an order for masks from abroad for his wife and "Miss Custis."

"Face-patching" continued in fashion to the French Revolution when patches, paint and powder, which savored of aristocracy, disappeared in the debacle. Patches were of all sizes and shapes and worn by all ages in the feminine world. They were carried in small costly patch boxes of ivory, tortoise shell, silver, gold, enamel, brass or china with a tiny mirror in the box cover. There were also beautiful vanity boxes and rouge pots.

"Face-painting" in France was definitely the mark of the upper class, required at court and at all fashionable assemblies. White and vermilion paints were used, the cheeks entirely rouged. A letter written in 1733 by some English ladies visiting Paris states that they were compelled to rouge, their natural coloring being conspicuously pale by contrast. Face-painting was not carried to such excess in other countries. More often, the English disapproved of paint and since the Americans followed the British way of living, the use of cosmetics here was on a more moderate scale.

Nevertheless, the many advertisements of wonder-working beautifiers in toilet waters, perfumes, wash balls, cold cream, lip salve, sticking plaster, court plaster, scent eggs, patches, pomatum, hair dyes, powder boxes and puffs which arrived in every cargo, is evidence that the ladies of New York were as eager to enhance their looks as the French and English beauties.

Face powdering was the result of hair powdering with the discovery of the flattering mat texture given the skin by this means. Pulverized rice was employed for the face. Wash balls composed of a mixture of rice powder, orris and white lead were held to be most beneficial. There was a choice in rouge, French red, Chinese red, Spanish red, carmine and Bavarian red liquor, the latter also taken internally. Spanish paper and Spanish wool were, as previously stated, items impregnated with rouge to rub on the skin. Myriad were the lotions and toilet waters but plain water for washing was carefully avoided. Venetian ladies sponged their faces with water but immediately coated them with paint and Venetian gentlemen of fashion also painted, powdered and patched.

At the beginning of the century, an Italian perfumer living in Cologne,

Germany concocted a toilet water which became famous and is in use today, Eau de Cologne. It was prepared from vegetable extracts, oils and rectified spirit but he kept the formula a trade secret.

The use of toilet water and perfume was not confined to the feminine world, there are such items noted in the personal accounts of our own George Washington. However, after the French Revolution, perfume for men declined in favor. Frenchmen used Eau de Cologne and Englishmen, lavender water but American men frowned upon scents of any kind, a prejudice which was to last till after the First World War.

The choker-length string of small pearls was worn in the first half of the century, then the flattering black velvet ribbon took its place, from which often hung an exquisitely jewel-framed miniature, locket or tiny "perspective glass."

Ladies and gentlemen made use of the perspective or single glass carried on the black silk ribbon or cord around the neck or mounted on either a short or long handle of tortoise shell or silver. A pretty way of employing the spectacle glass by nearsighted fashionable ladies was to have the glass set in a fan, particularly in a jeweled painted fan. There was also the double-lens lorgnette. Opera glasses appeared early in the century and "temple spectacles" about 1720, followed by "bridge spectacles," built for the nose without side supporters.

Jeweled hair ornaments, turban pins and long earrings of delicate design were the fashion. Diamonds became the rage, the stones having acquired greater brilliancy in the improved cutting by Dutch lapidaries. The demand for the sparkling gem led to the invention of "strass," lead glass set in silver.

This was the century of the craze for paste jewelry or by its European name, strass, invented by a German jeweler, Joseph Strasser. Paste was not considered an imitation but more as a substitute for valuable ornaments and was worn by the aristocracy. The periods of Louis XV and Louis XVI are designated by connoisseurs as the "golden age of paste," the French strass having a quality, its setting a finish and its design an unsurpassed grace and delicacy.

When the Revolution broke in France, the people responded to the call to liquidate the national debt by giving up their art treasures, gold, silver and jewelry. Following which, instead, were worn earrings, hair ornaments and turban pins and rings in crystal, paste set in marcasite and enamel in the three colors of the cockade. The fashion of inexpensive jewelry was adopted by "le beau monde" of other countries, with pearls and garnets worn on formal occasions.

Marie-Antoinette and her famous modiste, Rose Bertin, who ran an establishment in London, were the authors of many new fashions. The Anglomania fad in Paris was due in no small degree to Mlle. Bertin who, when the crash came, fled with her workwomen to London where she continued to design for English ladies and French émigrées. Fearing the confiscation of her property as a non-patriot, she hastily returned to Paris in 1792 and reopened her shop. She then sold bonnets to the citizenesses for three pounds each instead of her former prices to the aristocracy, which ran as high as two hundred pounds.

It is said that styles in hats between 1784 and 1786 changed seventeen times. In this period of extravagant ornamentation on costume, the milliner occupied an important position. The milliner, who made bonnets, capes and mantillas, also trimmed the dresses which the tailor and the seamstress supplied. Till the French upheaval, the Paris-made hat was the thing and all fashionable women, even in the American Colonies, wore a Paris creation.

The first style publication in the manner of our modern fashion magazines containing colored plates was the *Cabinet des Modes* founded in Paris in 1785. It enjoyed a tremendous success in its short life before the Revolution. A partisan of the Revolution, the paper endeavored in its contents to suit all tastes but alas, it found that a world of frivolity was necessary for its survival. Till the late 1790's, when several French fashion journals appeared, our fashion notes must be had from England and German sources.

The fashion term "silhouette" originated in 1759 when Etienne de Silhouette (1709–1767), controller general of France, displeased the people by imposing new taxes. The public retaliated with thousands of scornful jokes and cartoons and "silhouette" became the popular term for any object, pictorially reduced to its simplest form. Thus an outline portrait of the head in profile became a silhouette. Quite a vogue ensued for such a style of portraiture, the outline filled in with solid black.

1700 to 1795

full-bottomed
wig-two peaks-
white hair or
white powder-
French and English-
1st two decades

gray
full-bottomed
wig
with bobs-
Dutch-
1724

powdered
wig-black
felt tricorne-
French bourgeois-1710

powdered wig of
ringlets worn by
a Dutch colonist-
1st quarter
18th C.

powdered bob wig-
English and French-
early
18th C.

black felt
tricorne-silver
braid-white
cockade and ostrich-
brown wig-half
over shoulder-French
officer-1st quarter
18th C.

powdered tie wig-
any wig tied in
back-pigeon's
wings at sides

knotted
blond wig
with front peaks-
French-1718

curled natural
hair of a
Dutch patroon-
American-
early
18th C.

RTW

1700 to 1795

cocked "laced hat"-
black felt-silver or
gold lace-buttons
and loops-powdered
pigtail wig-black
ribbon-pigeon's wings-
French-
1731

cocked "laced
hat"-black
felt with
gold lace-
loops and
buttons-powdered
bag wig-pigeon's
wings-black silk
bag and ribbon-
French-
1728

gray wig with
tonsure-French
abbot

cocked hat-
black felt-
black cockade-
powdered
Ramillies wig-
ribbon bows
and solitaire-
English cavalry
officer-1740's

uncocked black
felt hat-brown
bob wig-
French abbot-

gray
powdered tie wig
with toupet-
black ribbon
solitaire-
English-
1730's

negligeé cap
of light red
velvet-shaved
head-American-
1767

uncocked black
felt hat-brown
bob wig-
German archbishop

curl papers-
natural hair-
black ribbon solitaire-
French-1745

powdered wig-
Greek or
horseshoe toupet-
cadogan-puffs-
English
1774

RTW

1700 to 1795

riding hat-
black felt tricorne-
braid edge-ostrich fringe-
loops and buttons-
powdered bagwig-
black silk bag
and solitaire-
French-
1733

hunting hat-
cocked black felt-
white braid edge-
buttons and loops-
natural hair in tie-
English-1750's

nivernois-black felt
tricorne-braid edge-powdered
wig with cadogan-English-1770's

hunting hat-
varnished leather
with visor-
powdered
bob
wig-
French-
1753

double
pigtail wig-
black ribbon-
Greek
toupet and
puffs-
French-
1771

English jockey
hat-felt or
leather-
ribbon
band and
buckle-
powdered wig
with cadogan-
French 1779

black felt
tricorne-
knotted
cord-
powdered
bagwig-Greek or
horseshoe toupet
and puffs-
black silk bag
and ribbon-
French-
1770's

exaggerated
nivernois-
black felt-cords and
button-powdered wig with
Greek toupet and puffs-
English Macaroni-1770's

cocked
black felt-
unpowdered
natural
hair in
in tie-
American-
1750's

cocked
black felt-
natural hair
or bob wig-
Quaker
1774

RTW

1700 to 1795

white bob wig of elderly, clerical and professional men— American— last quarter 18th C.

brown wig with Greek toupet and puffs— French—1780's

negligée cap over shaved head—bright colored satin— English— late 18th C.

natural toupet brushed over wig— cadogan fastened at crown— American— late 18th C.

Holland or Pennsylvania hat— light brown felt or straw—brown band—brown wig with cadogan— French—1780's

Quaker hat as worn in Paris— beaver with ribbon and buckle— natural hair or wig with cadogan— 1780's

hedgehog style— natural hair or wig— French— 1785

felt hat—natural hair or wig in cadogan— French—1780's

powdered wig with plaited cadogan held by comb— English—1790's

felt riding hat— ribbon band and cockade—natural hair or wig— French—1786

negligée cap of white satin with green and rose design—gold braid— French— 2nd half 18th C.

RTW

1700 to 1795

felt hat with ribbon-wig or natural hair-"single glass" English-1786

the fur cap of the American frontiersman-fox, squirrel, coonskin or bear

black felt riding hat-ribbon and buckles-powdered cadogan wig-English-1789

white or gray wig of professional men-English-1790

full-bottomed white wig-English and American judges-late 18th C.

mortarboard-doctor of civil law-American-late 18th C.

felt cocked hat-braid edged-buttons and cord-powdered bagwig-English-1786

black felt with ribbon band and buckle-natural hair in tie-English-circa 1790

black felt cocked hat-mauve ribbon-bobbed natural hair-French-1790

gray wig with pigtail-black ribbon-American-end of 18th C.

RTW

1789-1795
French

Phrygian bonnet or "le bonnet rouge" of the Revolutionist - of wool with tricolor cockade - natural hair in pigtail - earrings

black felt tricorne - braid and button - tricolor cockade - bobbed natural hair

army general - black felt tricorne with metal braid - natural hair in pigtail

felt hat with fringed scarf and feather - bobbed natural hair

"le bonnet rouge" of the Revolutionist - red woolen cap

general's bicorne - gold braid - tassels - ostrich and aigrettes - tricolor cockade

felt hat with ribbon and ostrich worn over silk scarf tied round head - a royalist

felt hat with white royalist cockade - worn over silk scarf tied round head

sailor hat - varnished leather - hair bobbed at sides with short queue in back

sailor hat - varnished leather - hair in cadogan

RTW

1789-1795
French

royalist
wearing
white
powdered
wig

"patriote élégant" with
curled natural hair

patriot wearing
white powdered
wig with
cadogan

felt hat with
ribbon and
buckle-
natural
hair

the coiffure of
napoléon Bonaparte-
natural hair

"patriote élégant" wearing
felt hat with
tricolor
cockade-
powdered
wig

"patriote élégant"
felt hat with
tricolor
cockade-
powdered
wig

patriot-beaver hat-
small tricolor
cockade-natural
hair in tie-earrings

bobbed hair
parted in
center

natural hair
bobbed at sides-
back hair
in tie

patriot
wearing
powdered
wig

RTW

1700 to 1795

"Kevenhuller cock" tricorne
of black felt·blue cockade·
light brown bob wig·Austrian
soldier·1st
decade

"Kevenhuller cock"·
Swiss military or
"Androsmane" in French·
black felt tricorne·
white ostrich·buttons
and loops·pigtail
wig·pigeon's wings·
black ribbon·
French officer·
early 18th C.

"Ramillies cock"
tricorne in
black felt·
high flat back·
braid edge·
powdered bagwig·
black silk bag
and ribbons·
pigeon's wings·
French·
1729

tricorne in
black felt·
gold braid·white
powdered
pigtail wig·
black leather
queue·German
officer·
1st half
18th C.

red cloth
and fringe·
metal
frontal·
brown bob
wig·Austrian
soldier·
1st decade

bonnet of
cloth and
copper·
white stripes
and band·
metal insignia·
powdered hair in
braided queue·
Prussian grenadier·
1760

blue cloth bonnet·
white stripe·
bearskin frontal·
metal insignia·
powdered pigtail
wig·Austrian
grenadier·1730

red
cloth bonnet·fur band·
shaved head with tuft on top·
French hussar·1721

blue cloth bonnet·
gold braid·black pompon·
foliage·powdered hair
in queue·black ribbon·
Austrian hussar·
3rd quarter 18th C.

RTW

1700 to 1795

shako-
bearskin
bonnet-metal
frontlet-white
feather pompon-
cord and tassel-
hair in
queue-
French-
1780's

casque of imitation gold-
leather roundlet and
bands-horsehair-
shaved head-
French uhlan-
1746

calpac,
busby or
bearskin bonnet-
green ribbon-white
cords and
aigrette-
hair in
queue-
Prussian
hussar-
1760

bonnet of cloth-
aigrettes-cockade-
cords-hair in queue-
French hussar-
1766

metal casque-
leather visor-
horsehair-tied
band-hair
in queue-black
ribbon-
American
cavalry major-
late 1770's

cap of
varnished
leather-
bearskin
and aigrettes-
hair in queue-
English general-
1780's

embroidered
cloth and velvet-
pompon-
hair in
queue-
English
guard-
1745

the
Prince Charlie-
Scotch bonnet-
blue woolen cap
with red tuft-
feathers-spray
of laurel-ribbon
cockade-officer of
Highland Regiment
1740's

bearskin and
blue cloth-
metal shield
and tassel-
brown bob wig-
German grenadier-
1738

RTW

1700 to 1795

Androsmane, Kevenhuller-
or Swiss hat – French
musketeer of the 18th C.-
black felt with
white braid, ostrich
and ribbon
cockade-
powdered
bagwig-
1745

the
Kevenhuller-
black felt with white
ostrich- ribbon cockade-
cord and button-Prussian-
3rd quarter 18th C.

black felt tricorne-
white braid-
black ribbon
cockade-
English life
guard-
1746

black felt
tricorne-
brown bob
wig or natural
hair-English
sailor-1730's

Kevenhuller-
black
felt-black
cockade-white
feather pompon-
natural hair-
Prussian cuirassier-
1760

black felt
Kevenhuller
with black
cockade-powdered
hair-black ribbon-
American Marine officer-
1775

black
japanned
leather-
hair
in queue-
American
naval captain-
1777

black
japanned
leather-
white edge-
black cockade-
powdered hair in
queue-American
Marine-1775

black japanned
leather-white
edge-black cockade-
natural hair-
English sailor-
1780

black felt tricorne-
galloon edge-
black cockade-
cord and button-
powdered hair in tie-
English general-1780's

RTW

1700 to 1795

bearskin bonnet-metal
shield-red leather pompon-
powdered hair in queue-
American-
1775-1785

powdered hair in queue-
cap black varnished
leather-silver
braid-buck's tail-
Philadelphia Cavalry-1775

cocked hat-
black felt-
white edge-ribbon
cockade-black feather
pompon-powdered hair in club-
American officer-1780's

natural hair in queue-
large unlooped or
uncocked hat
recommended
by Washington
for troops early in
American Revolution

Kevenhuller
style-
cocked black felt
hat-black and white cockade-
powdered bobbed natural hair-
American colonel-1780

Nivernois-black felt
cocked hat-braid
edge-black cockade-
American general-
1770's

cocked black
felt showing trend
toward bicorne-
ribbon cockade-
American general-
1780's

cap of
varnished leather-
"Liberty" on
metal shield-
ostrich feathers-
powdered hair-
American rifleman-
1790

Kevenhuller style-
black felt cocked
hat-black and white
cockade with buttons-
powdered hair in queue-
American general-1780

RTW

1700 to 1795

fontange and cap
of white lace-black
lace scarf-pearl
clusters in hair-
French-
early 18th C.

fontange-sheer
black cap
with red
galloon edged
pearls-black
velvet loops-
single pearl
earring-
Swiss-
early
18th C.

French hood
of sheer
black silk-German-
early
18th C.

black silk
tricorne-gold
lace-black
net and lace
mantilla-black
velvet mask-
Venetian-
1st half 18th C.

brown taffeta
hood-white
ribbon lappets-
lorgnette-
French-
1718

capuchin-
turned-back
edge-short
cape-black,
brown or
light colored
silk-light
lining-
French-
1st half
18th C.

riding costume-
black silk tricorne
over black
mantilla-
blue ribbons-
white frilled
cap-
Swiss-
early
18th C.

RTW

1700 to 1795

Quaker cap of sheer white lawn American early 18th C.

white batiste cap-lace edge-artificial roses-French-1731

tiny cap-lace edged white lawn rose ribbon-artificial roses-French-1718

tiny lace edged white lawn cap-colored ribbon-French-1731

milkmaid, shepherdess or gypsy hat of leghorn blue ribbons-ruffled white muslin cap-English and American-2nd quarter 18th C.

lace edged white lawn cap-New York-1750's

riding hat-tricorne of leghorn ribbon cockade-ostrich tip-French-1740's

leghorn hat-wide brim cocked in front-ruffled white lawn cap-English-1750's

riding hat-black silk tricorne-black ribbon bowknot-French-1735

RTW

1700 to 1795

light colored beaver over pearl·sewn cap·ribbon and ostrich plumes· English· 1750's

"skimmer hat"·leghorn with green silk facing·silk or velvet ribbons· frilled white lawn cap· English· 1750's

powdered hair· with puffs· jeweled piece· tiny aigrette· earrings· French· 1750's

powdered coiffure with set curls over small cushion· Madame de Pompadour· 1764

black velvet mantilla over fine lace cap· French· 1739

cap of sheer white muslin· black taffeta ribbons· powdered hair· German· 1770's

straw or beaver in Watteau style·colored ribbon· English· 1760's

calash· collapsible like carriage top· silk shirred on hoops· English· French· American· 1770's

triangular head kerchief·taffeta with lace·pearls in hair· American· 1770's

RTW

1700 to 1795

powdered
hair in
puffs and
cadogan-
ribbon
bowknot-
English-
1770's

Watteau hat-
ostrich, small
feathers and
ribbon-
powdered hair
in puffs and
cadogan-
French-
1776

Watteau hat-
straw or felt-
ostrich and
ribbon-
powdered
hair in
puffs and
cadogan-
French-
1770's

riding hat-
beaver with
ostrich and
ribbon-
powdered
hair in cadogan-
French-
1770's

cap, fall and scarf
of sheer silk-pleated
fans with velvet edge-
silk rosebuds-
Austrian-1770's

turban of
Oriental scarf-
beaded fringe-
English-
1770's

dormeuse bonnet
with lappets-
shirred lawn
and lace-
taffeta
ribbon-
French-
1770's

dormeuse
bonnet-sheer
lawn and fine
shirred lace-
satin ribbon-
English-
1770's

RTW

1700 to 1795

queen's coiffure-powdered hair-small jeweled crown-ostrich plumes-French-1770's

woman's wig over which natural hair was dressed-French

queen's coiffure-powdered hair-ostrich, pearls and ribbon-large square jewel-French-1777

powdered hair-black velvet ribbon-pearl earrings-English-1780's

coiffure à l'ingénue-powdered hair-French-1780's

powdered hair in hedgehog style-English-1780's

hedgehog coiffure-powdered hair-back lappets of hair set with paste-French-1780's

white straw faced with brown-white taffeta ribbon-English-1780's

powdered hair with huge cadogan-straw hat with taffeta ribbon-English-1780's

RTW

1700 to 1795

unpowdered
coiffure-
artificial roses
and foliage-
taffeta
ribbon-
French-
1780's

white straw faced
with gauze-
pale blue
ribbon-brown
hair lightly
powdered-
English-
1780's

powdered
hair-
artificial
red roses-
green foliage-
violet ribbon-
French-
1788

hair lightly
powdered-
taffeta
ribbon-
French-
1780's

toque of ribbon,
tulle, ostrich,
and artificial
flowers-
powdered
hair-
French-
1786

coiffure
with cadogan-
white muslin
hood with
red ribbon-
French-
1780's

RTW

1700 to 1795

turban style in
velvet, silk,
metal striped
ribbon and
pearls-
powdered
hair-
French-
1780's

thérèse of silver
spotted pale blue
gauze-
French-
1780's

hat of pleated
gauze-tinsel
ribbon-sheer
white muslin
cap-
powdered
hair-
English-
1789

riding hat-pale
colors-cylinder
shape draped with
folded gauze
scarf-metal
striped border-
powdered hair-
cadogan-
French-
1780's

riding hat of
straw or felt-
ribbon and
ostrich-
powdered
hair-
cadogan-
English-
1784

"bonnet hat"
sheer white
lawn and
fine lace-
faced with
pale color-
English-
1780's

RTW

1700 to 1795

blue taffeta hat-white
ostrich tipped with
rose-pearls-powdered
hair-cadogan-
French-
1780's

silk riding hat
with ostrich-
button and loop-
powdered hair-
French-1785

headdress of tulle,
spotted net-pearls-blue
taffeta fillet-white satin
loops poised on lappets-
rose and white ostrich-
powdered hair-cadogan-
English-1780's

taffeta hat-
satin bowknot-
ostrich-feather-
powdered hair-
French-
1780's

black velvet hat-
satin ribbon-ostrich-
worn over white lawn
mobcap with taffeta
ribbon-
English-
1780's

leghorn hat with
light brown facing
and ostrich-blue and
white striped satin ribbon-
sheer white frilled
lawn cap-
French-
1787

RTW

1700 to 1795

the Gainsborough or
Marlborough hat-
black taffeta-
mauve plumes and
taffeta ribbon-
powdered hair-
English-1780's

powdered
hair-
bonnet hat-
white taffeta-
fur band-
red velvet
crown-white
ostrich and
aigrette-
sheer white
scarf with
lace-
French-
1780's

riding hat
of
black straw-
black satin
band-beige
ribbon ties-
English-
1780's

riding hat of beaver
draped with net
veil-ribbon bands-
large buckle-
cock and ostrich
feathers-hanging
hair in knot-
French-
1786

white straw with
white tulle loops
on brim and back
of hair-blue
velvet hoops and
bowknots-
powdered hair-
English-
1780's

RTW

1700 to 1795

hair in cadogan-
mobcap of sheer
white lawn-colored
taffeta ribbon-
American-
1780's and '90's

mobcap of
sheer white lawn
over wire frame-ribbon-
powdered hair-German-
last quarter 18th C°

bonnet
of sheer
white muslin over
wire frame-pale
pink satin ribbon-
powdered hair
in cadogan-
English-
1780's

leghorn
hat with
silk facing
and ribbon-
tied on with
silk scarf-
English-
1790's

mobcap of
black taffeta,
black gauze
and white
lawn-black
bowknots in
front-
English-
1789

draped silk
turban-
powdered
hair-pearl
earrings-
English-
1780's

leghorn hat
with tulle
and ribbon-
yellow powder
on hair-
Spanish-
1780's

RTW

1700 to 1795

béret of slate blue velvet and satin white ostrich plume powdered hair pearl pendants French 1780's

black lace and tulle mantilla red satin ribbon rosette in hair Spanish 1790's

toque in the first colors of the Revolution, red and blue - red and blue taffeta French 1789

red and white taffeta - ostrich dyed red and white - gold leaves on green band hair in cadogan English 1791

crown of ribbon and ostrich tips - long plumes, white and color powdered hair with cadogan - silk and pearl flowers jeweled earrings American 1794

RTW

1700 to 1795

mobcap of
sheer white muslin-
taffeta ribbon-ruched
muslin and ribbon ties-
powdered hair-
American-
1790's

Charlotte Corday's cap of
sheer spotted white muslin-
fluted frill-taffeta ribbon-
French-1793

Revolution
Phrygian cap-
white muslin-
tricolor ribbon-
French-1795

turban of
tulle with
ostrich plume-
French-
1790's

black
taffeta crown
and flutings-
red taffeta
ribbon-red
taffeta petals
with aigrettes-
French-
1790's

turban of tinsel
striped ribbon and tulle-
American-1790's

crownless
turban of
taffeta-
English-
1790's

turban of tulle with
aigrettes, pearls and jewels-
American-1790's

PTW

1700 to 1795

riding hat of beaver-buckle and ribbon band-powdered hair in cadogan-English-1790's

straw hat-striped and plain taffeta ribbons-artificial flowers-hair in cadogan-French-1792

black velvet faced with beige silk and white taffeta ruching-crown corded black spotted rose colored silk-rose ribbon-black ostrich-English-1795

riding hat of black taffeta-black satin loops-red silk band and rosette-English-1790

black straw-royal blue ribbons-rose and white ostrich-stalks of wheat-sheer white muslin cap-hair in cadogan-French-1790's

straw hat with satin ribbon-hair in cadogan-French-1790's

riding hat-black taffeta-narrow black ribbon-silver buckles-French-1790's

RTW

1700 to 1795

infant boy-
be'ret of
velvet-ostrich
feather with
jeweled brooch-
German-
1st quarter
18th C.

infant boy-
black tricorne-
white edge-
white ostrich-
worn over
white cap-
new York-
early 18th C.

small girl in
embroidered
lingerie cap-
American-
early 18th C.

young
girl-tiny
lingerie
cap-
taffeta
ribbon-
French-
1731

infant
boy in frilled lace
cap with ribbon
and ostrich tips-
French- 2nd decade
18th C.

small girl-
coiffure
dressed
with
ostrich
tips
and pearls-
American-
1730's

small boy in
powdered
wig with
black
ribbon-
French-
1730's

infant
boy-
frilled cap of spotted
net with tassel-pink
silk fold round head-
French-
1739

small girl-
hair dressed
into topknot-
ornament of
crystal beads
and silver foliage-
English-last quarter
18th C.

straw bonnet-
taffeta crown
and bowknot-
spray of cherries-
English-
1779

small boy in
cocked hat-black felt-
natural hair-black
silk bag and bowknot-
American-1760's

R.T.W.

1700 to 1795

little girl in felt hat-
velvet edge-ostrich-
ribbon bowknot-
English-1780's

boy-cropped head-
English and French-
1780's

tiny girl
in black
taffeta calash
over lingerie
cap-
English-last
quarter 18th C.

infant-spotted white
lawn cap-fluted frill-
taffeta ribbon-English-
1780's

taffeta
hat with
ostrich tips
and ribbon-
English-
1780's

small girl in
toque of white
lawn- pale blue
ribbon- high
unpowdered
coiffure-
French-
1780's

boy in black
beaver hat-
satin ribbon-
Spanish-
1790's

tiny girl-gauze
bonnet made over
wire frame-small
silk flowers-
aigrette-
English-
1770's

little girl in
dormeuse bonnet-
sheer white lawn-
taffeta ribbon-
English-
1780's and '90's

small boy in
"sailor hat" of
white straw-
red ribbon-
French-
1780's

RTW

DIRECTOIRE, 1795-1799

CHAPTER TWELVE

THE FRENCH REVOLUTION changed the manners and clothes of Europe and America but in France, the desire to eliminate the old, evolved fashions as extreme and as absurd in simplicity, as the exaggerated extravagances of the effaced aristocracy.

The muscadin of the Revolutionary period was followed by the "incroyable" or "unbelievable" of the Directoire. He was the dandy or fop of the times who made a cult of the extreme in dress. He was fond of peering at people and things through his perspective glass, a single lens mounted on a tortoise shell, gold or silver handle. He penciled his eyebrows and used quantities of amber perfume.

The incroyable wore his hair cut in dog's ears, the back raggedly short or done in a cadogan or the club style of the seafaring man. Another seafaring fashion he liked was the wearing of hoop earrings.

This latter notion was not confined to the French dandy but is seen, less conspicuous in size, in several portraits of American gentlemen. These particular pictures are the work of Saint Memin, a French refugee artist who worked in New York and Philadelphia from 1797 to 1814. He was an aristocrat who had fled to Switzerland, traveling from there to Canada in 1793.

Returning *émigrés* showed their disapproval of the eccentric coiffure by the adoption of the shaggy Brutus style, the short haircut of the Roman Consul Brutus of the sixth century B.C. The hair was cut unevenly and the front brushed forward over the forehead. Napoleon while in Egypt changed to the short cut. Englishmen adopted it also; in fact, in the last years of the century, the shaggy short hair of Paris and London was taken up by fashionable men of Europe and the American Colonies. The well-groomed man of 1799 was the prototype of the well-groomed man of the nineteenth century. However, some conservatives, particularly older men, continued to wear their hair in a short queue and powdered.

Other returning émigrés adopted the blond wig and black collar, a sign of mourning, in opposition to the red collar and dog's ears of the *incroyable*.

The tricorne disappeared after the Revolution, leaving in its place the bicorne and the tall crowned hat, the "stovepipe" of the nineteenth century. The folding bicorne of the 1790's was a variation of the cocked hat and also called the "chapeau bras," of which the incroyable wore an exaggerated version. The bicorne is worn today in France for ceremonial affairs and by ranking officers of American, British and French navies.

A law regulated the official costume of the members of the French Directoire, the "Five Hundred" as they were called, a costume intended by its classic design and magnificence to inspire respect for the lawmakers. The hat for general use resembled the Spanish toque of the sixteenth century while the large plumed hat cocked in front was worn upon gala occasions.

Wigs and false hair, which disappeared from the feminine head during the Reign of Terror, were again worn directly after and if one could not afford a whole wig, one at least wore a large false chignon or a cadogan confined in a silk net. Some wigs which were worn over a cropped head were fashioned of short curls arranged in a studied profusion. Blond, red and black were the smart colors with blond the favorite. Madame Tallien, later Princess Chimay, a leader of fashion of the period, usually wore black, the color of her own hair but it is also recorded that she had thirty wigs in various colors.

There was a classic trend in hairdressing, the inspiration furnished by the portrait busts of ancient Greek and Roman goddesses and empresses. The hair was waved, plaited or curled, drawn back into a Psyche knot and made glossy with "antique oil." A fillet of ribbon or jewels ofttimes encircled the head.

In the disheveled style, the "coiffure à la Titus," after the Roman Titus of the first century A.D., the raggedly trimmed short hair was brushed from the crown of the head over the forehead and cheeks. It was not unlike the wind-blown bob of the 1920's.

The masculine "dog's ears" were copied with strands of straight long uneven hair hanging over the face. Lugubrious, indeed, was the coiffure "à la victime" which had its origin in the hastily cut hair of the French unfortunates about to be guillotined. And a "whimsical touch" was the narrow red ribbon around the neck.

The "merveilleuse" or "marvelous one" was the feminine counterpart of the incroyable. Her classic costume was extreme, bordering on nudity and her hats were exaggerated versions of the mode. A favorite style was the jockey bonnet, a style not confined to the French lady as is attested by a contemporary colonial fashion note which states that a "jockey" was worn by a fashionable American miss.

Important was the helmet bonnet and especially so the capote or poke bonnet, a style which was to last more than a century. Bonnets were usually tied under the chin with ribbons and were of straw, silk, felt, beaver and velvet. White, considered classic, was much worn, also black, cherry color, violet and deep green.

The dress of the Quakers or Friends always reflected the prevailing mode in a thoroughly simplified form but in fine fabric. Interesting to observe, is the fact that the Quaker bonnet always gray or brown, is of the Directoire period and a modification of the Paris fashion. There is fine distinction in the details of the Quaker bonnet, pleat and flare designating the sect. The crown of the English Quaker bonnet was gathered, not laid in pleats and had a cape. New Jersey Quakers were warned thus, "Nor to wear superfluous Gathers or Pleats in their Capps or Pinners, Nor to wear their heads drest high behind, Neither to Cut or Lay their hair on ye Forehead or Temples." The stiffly pleated bonnet when first worn was frowned upon by some Quakers as a frivolous get-up.

The late eighteenth and the early nineteenth centuries witnessed a decided vogue for that most wearable and artistic headdress, the Oriental turban, especially for evening wear. The fashion of the turban, supposedly inspired by Napoleon's Egyptian campaign, is said really to have originated in London where the draped headpiece was seen on the heads of visiting Indian nabobs.

The classic mode brought in the pale complexion for which rice powder was employed. In 1798, the pearly tones of the picture "Amour et Psyché" exhibited by the French painter François Gérard, was the inspiration for white pearl powder for the face.

Cameos and medallions were of all colors and sizes, worn at the throat, in earrings, in the hair and in the folds of the turban.

Directoire 1795-1799

tall beaver hat-
cockade, ribbon
and buckle-hair
in short queue-
French

seaman-tall
felt hat-cockade
left side-hair
in tie-
French

"incroyable"
bicorne or
chapeau bras-
ribbon and
cockade-
hair cut in
"dog's ears"-
French

"incroyable"
hair cut
in "dog's
ears"-hoop
earrings-
French
1796

member of the
Directoire-
pleated blue
béret-crushed
red silk band-
white feather
panache
1795

cocked hat-
ribbon
cockade-
"dog's ears"-
French
1795

beaver hat-
tricolor cord-
cadogan wig-
dog's ears and
braids-
French
1797

member of
the Directoire-
dress hat-black
beaver-tricolor
cockade-white V-
red, white and
blue ostrich
1795

curled hair-
hoop earrings-
French
émigré in
America

American
version of the
incroyable
haircut

RTW

Directoire 1795-1799

coiffure from
a portrait of
Josephine -
1798

side part -
high chignon
with ribbon -
curled on
one side

coiffure
à la Titus -
long earrings

coiffure
à la grecque -
ribbon
fillets -
silk kerchief -
1797

fringe and
braided
chignon

classic
coiffure -
velvet fillet
with jewel -
1799

classic headdress
of silk
and ribbon -
1797

rows of curls
and strings
of pearls

center part -
sides bobbed -
back in cudogan
with ends
dressed into
puffs

RTW

Directoire 1795-1799

black silk
edged and
embroidered
with
gold-gold
feather ornament-
curls and
cadogan

exaggerated
headdress of a
"merveilleuse"
stiffened
taffeta loops-
frilled white
lawn cap

gauze turban-
chinstrap-aigrette-
Titus hair-
earrings-
1797

velvet
turban-
Titus
hair

bonnet
of taffeta, tulle
and ribbon-wheat
stalks and
pine cones-
hair in
cadogan

silk
turban
in two colors-
wheat stalks-
knot at side-
hair in cadogan-
English-1796

classic
headdress-
white silk caul-
rose ribbon
fillet-
long green
veil

cap of straw-ribbon
bowknot-artificial
flowers-hair in
cadogan-1796

silk or velvet
turban-jeweled
socket and
band-
aigrette

FTW

Directoire 1795-1799

a "merveilleuse" silk hat—ribbon—ostrich—hair in puffs, cadogan and dog's ears

red silk bonnet—white lawn frills—black velvet and red ribbon—hair in cadogan—1797

cottage bonnet—natural straw faced with green—green silk kerchief

bonnet of white silk with rose colored ribbons—black lace frill—1799

hat of silk, felt or straw—striped ribbon—ribbon ruche—ostrich and aigrette—hair in cadogan—1795

beaver hat—ribbon band—silver buckle—side hair bobbed and crimped—back in cadogan—1795

ancient tutulus shape—velvet, silk or straw—satin petals, rosette and ties—1796

straw hat with velvet ribbons—1799

RTW

Directoire 1795-1799

straw helmet-
ostrich crest-
rosette with
button-chin
strap of two
pieces ruched
ribbon-
English-
1799

coal scuttle,
capote or
poke bonnet-
yellow bonnet
with ribbons-
worn over
lingerie cap-
English-
1797

a "merveilleuse"
jockey cap
of velvet,
silk or straw-
ribbon bowknot
with tassels-
Titus
hair cut-
1796

the Quaker
or Friends'
version
of the
Directoire
bonnet
in gray
or brown-
cabriolet
or "wagon
top" style

sheer lawn bonnet-
striped gauze
lappets-
frill edged-
roses, foliage
and ribbon-
hair in
cadogan

silk bonnet-
silk frill of
contrasting color-
ribbon ties-
torch lily blossoms-
veil draped
over front-
English-
1796

silk bonnet-
striped yellow
and white-
brown ribbon
trimming

poke bonnet of
straw-shirred
silk crown
and facing-
ribbons-hair
in cadogan

RTW

FRENCH CONSULATE AND EMPIRE, 1800-1815

CHAPTER THIRTEEN

THE NEW FASHIONS WERE launched at the public winter balls and the summer gardens instead of the former way of being first worn at Versailles.

The short haircut of the Roman emperors was the prevailing coiffure among men, the ends brushed over forehead and cheeks. The long side pieces to the front of the ears paved the way for whiskers which the fashionable man had not worn for a century. About 1809, curled hair in loose ringlets came into fashion and by 1812, short side whiskers were again the mode. The mustache is also to be noted, worn by army officers, particularly the Germans. Shaving became important in this new era of bodily cleanliness, many men shaving themselves. The finest razors were made in Sheffield, England, and were much prized.

The wig or natural hair in a queue and sometimes powdered, was worn only by elderly men and some soldiers. The American soldier's queue in 1804, was shortened to seven inches and entirely cut off in 1808.

The simple ribbon-banded masculine headpiece of the nineteenth and twentieth centuries was firmly intrenched. Its silhouette varied and it was fashioned of felt napped with long or short angora or beaver, also fashioned of straw. The colors were gray, beige or black and the silk ribbon was tied into a bow or fastened by a small steel buckle. Quakers retained the broad-brimmed, low-crowned hat. Clergymen too, wore the shallow-crowned hat and the tricorne for formal wear.

The tall hat of silk or polished beaver which appeared about 1803 was not a success, the process of polishing not perfected till 1823. It will be recalled that polished beaver was an invention of Florence, Italy, as early as 1760.

The postilion or post rider of the swift traveling coach, or post chaise of the early nineteenth century, wore a top hat with tapering crown whence our name "postilion" for that shape. The hat was a revival of a sixteenth century style.

In the tall hunting hat was an inner band threaded with a string which was drawn up tightly to secure the hat to the head, the same idea as used in the Renaissance beret. The small bow in the leather sweatband of the modern hat is what remains of the drawstring.

The dandy and the army officer wore the large bicorne or *chapeau bras*. The bicorne with ostrich fringe, gold lace or both, accompanied the habit for full dress. The bicorne or military dress hat of the European and American armies is known to us as the Wellington hat after the Duke of Wellington (1769–1852). A tassel hung from each of the two corners. The famous cocked hat of Napoleon, also a bicorne, with its tricolor cockade was a small version of the Swiss military hat.

Quakers retained the low-crowned hat with wide brim and some clergymen still wore the tricorne of the eighteenth century. Liveried servants also wore the old-fashioned tricorne.

The Scotch bonnet known as the "Glengarry," akin to today's overseas cap, dates from the early nineteenth century. The blue woolen cap rising to a point in front, with center crease, was laced in back to fit the head. A novelty then, it is not even today considered correct or comfortable by the old conservatives.

The name Glengarry applied also to a feminine riding habit of the period belonged to the contemporary MacDonell of Glengarry, the last representative of the Highland chief of history. He and his body of retainers who invariably accompanied him were always attired in full Highland dress.

Military headdress, in general, was the same for European and American armies, varying only in color and insignia. The modern cap with soft full crown, leather band and visor, appeared for the first time in this period. New, was the stiff felt shako with flaring bell-shaped crown the "tarbucket," adopted by many regiments and still the bonnet of the West Point cadets. Leather was substituted in the United States Army in 1813 with cotton pompons instead of feathers. Our generals wore the cocked hat for dress and officers of lower rank, the bicorne. The bicorne has remained the dress hat for naval officers to the present day.

The tall black polished felt was prescribed by Congress in 1810 as a military hat for the American army. It had a standing feather pompon on the left side toward the back. It must have proven a fragile headpiece and appears to have lasted only a few years.

Of this period was one of England's greatest beaux, George Bryan Brummell (1778-1840), known as Beau Brummell. He held sway from 1800 to 1812 and revolutionized "le beau monde" with his cult of bodily cleanliness, immaculate white linen and simple, beautifully tailored clothes. He left a worthy costume work on male and female dress from the ancient Greek and Roman periods to 1822.

In the early years of the period, the short Titus cut in the feminine coiffure vied in popularity with the classic style. Those who changed from the short locks wore wigs, false braids and chignons, false fronts and bunches of curls attached to combs till nature supplied them with longer hair. Many heads were dressed "à la Psyché" with a chignon or "à la chinoise" with the hair drawn to a knot on top of the head. The "coiffure à la Ninon" reappeared with clusters of curls at the sides of the face, the hair up in back with a center part.

There was a vogue between 1805 and 1810 for one-sided effects in hairdressing, either side of the head dressed differently, flat on one and clusters of curls on the other. The hair was dressed and the curls set with "antique oil" and throughout the period, the ears completely exposed.

Combs of antique design, works of the jeweler's art, were set with pearls, diamonds and small cameos. There were also gold wreaths of laurel with jewels and diadems encrusted with gems. A hair ornament to be seen in many contemporary portraits, was a long gold hairpin, five or six inches in length in the form of an arrow. Another long hairpin had dangling gold balls. The ferronière of the Renaissance was revived, a fine chain around the head with a jewel in the middle of the forehead.

Pink or white artificial roses were favored evening hair ornaments. It is in this period that the making of flowers, long since an art in Italy, became perfected in France. Violets in the hair or as a corsage became the fashion, an imperial insigne during those dramatic Hundred Days of Napoleon's return from Elba in 1815.

The great Parisian coiffeur of the Empire was Michalon, considered an artist in dressing milady's hair. His visits to his clients were made in a cabriolet driven by himself, a Negro groom mounted behind and it is said that he charged a gold louis (twenty-four pounds silver) then thought a high sum for such services.

The poke bonnet of varied name, size and shape was worn quite generally by women and children of every age. Satin, velvet, silk plush, panne velvet, crêpe, rep, muslin, tulle, lace and straw went into its making, adorned with flowers, ribbons and plumes. Fashion's decree in color was white and delicate shades. Beaver becoming scarce, we hear of false beaver, a fabric of wool felted with a facing of long beaver fur.

As in the late eighteenth century, some hats were still tied on by a silk kerchief folded diagonally or by a triangular silk piece in green or scarlet, regardless of the color scheme of the hat. Ribbon ties held the wide brim of the Pamela bonnet pressed against the cheeks.

The mode was influenced by the martial events of the times and many hats took on a decided military air suggested by helmet and shako. In England, hats and bonnets were named for Wellington. The crowns of feminine headgear grew very high, coinciding with the growing popularity of the masculine top hat. By 1813, bonnets were so tall that ladies were compelled to hold them on their knees when in a carriage.

A collapsible bonnet called a "chapeau bras," rather like the calash of the eighteenth century, was brought out in London to cover hair and bonnet in bad weather. The shop which advertised the invention boasted that the piece could be folded and carried unseen when not in use.

The bonnet was often worn over the lingerie cap or "cornet" and sometimes the cap was simulated by lingerie pieces being sewn to the hat. The frilled laced lingerie cap was given the old name of cornet though minus the lappets of the original Dutch piece of that name. The embroidered, lace-trimmed sheer muslin cap was often worn for evening affairs and there were close caps of embroidered tulle for morning wear and dainty lace caps for sleeping.

Turbans were very popular, especially for evening, and were fashioned of brocaded, embroidered and spangled fabrics, moiré, satin, velvet, silvered gauze, fringed crêpe and knotted silk scarfs. Draped "desert turbans" were open in back with curls tumbling out.

The successful English machine for the manufacture of net and lace in large pieces made for the popularity of veils and shawls. From the fronts of bonnets hung long or short veils and the lovely and costly pieces were often draped over the head in place of a hat. The filmy length of net and lace was occasionally worn by the bride with a jeweled diadem though the all-white bridal gown had not yet become custom.

The national Spanish headdress, the lace mantilla worn over the high carved ivory or tortoise shell comb, dates from this period.

At the turn of the century, women adopted a pale or white complexion to accompany the classic white and delicate-hued costumes. And the discarded rouge, it is stated, was taken up by the opposite sex. Scented soaps and toilet waters became essential in this new era of bodily cleanliness and very few, simple and abbreviated clothes.

The practice of make-up was still too reminiscent of the aristocratic regime to which the French Revolution had dealt the deathblow. English and American ladies were always more conservative in their use of cosmetics than their Latin sisters. Gradually, however, beauty aids returned to favor, particularly among women of "advanced age" as a contemporary writer puts it. One reads that the Empress spent 3,000 francs a year for rouge.

Rice and pearl white powder were used, Eau de Cologne and a cake of soap. Many ladies made their preparations at home, a toilet water of glycerine and rosewater, lampblack for mascara and often, a wet red ribbon for a delicate rose tint on the cheeks. "To rouge and pearl" was the expression.

The ordinary pin of brass and wire-wound head of English make, was still a luxury costing as high as a dollar for a small package as late as 1812.

Consulate and Empire 1800-1815

Highland Soldier-red and white bonnet-black ostrich-white aigrette-silver button- 1807

hair parted round the head and brushed to the front- French- circa 1809

O hair brushed up off forehead- side whiskers- American- circa 1810

side part and long side pieces- English- 1810

fringe and pompadour- side whiskers- French- 1804

straight hair- side part- Spanish

cropped head of the 19th and 20th centuries. French- 1811

part over top of head- American- circa 1805

American Indian-British Army Captain- bonnet with ostrich plumes- son of Joseph Brant- 1812

RTW

Consulate and Empire 1800-1815

beaver hat in white, gray or beige- English- 1805

black felt- ribbon band- French- 1809

postilion shaped crown- polished black beaver or angora- French- 1810

black felt- ribbon bands and cockade- French circa 1810

marine summer dress hat-black straw-white ribbon- red and white feather pompon- English- 1815

sailor in dress uniform- hat of varnished leather-tricolor cockade- French- 1808

stove pipe- black beaver- ribbon band- French- 1814

black straw or felt-ribbon band- French- circa 1810

black straw or felt with ribbon band- steel buckle- German- 1802

cloth with embroidery and insignia-band and visor of varnished leather- Prussian Army Officer-1814

RTW

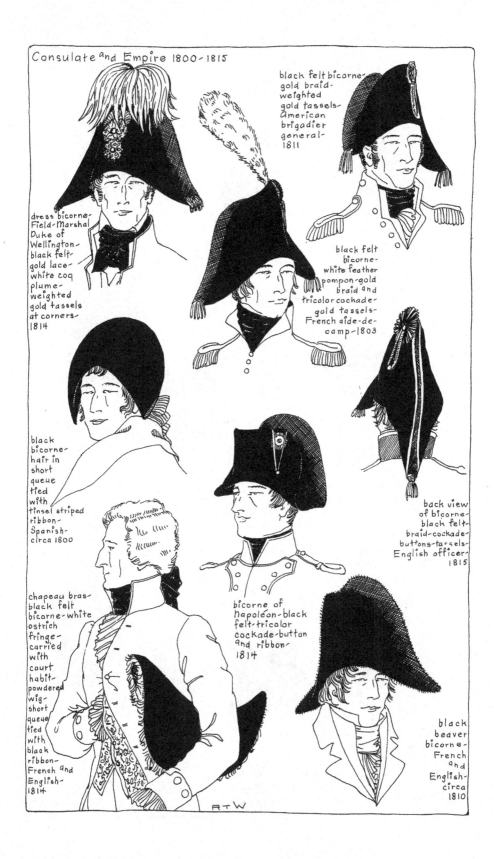

Consulate and Empire 1800-1815

black felt bicorne-
gold braid-
weighted
gold tassels-
American
brigadier
general-
1811

dress bicorne-
Field-Marshal
Duke of
Wellington-
black felt-
gold lace-
white coq
plume-
weighted
gold tassels
at corners-
1814

black felt
bicorne-
white feather
pompon-gold
braid and
tricolor cockade-
gold tassels-
French aide-de-
camp-1803

black
bicorne-
hair in
short
queue
tied
with
tinsel striped
ribbon-
Spanish-
circa 1800

back view
of bicorne-
black felt-
braid-cockade-
buttons-tassels-
English officer-
1815

chapeau bras-
black felt
bicorne-white
ostrich
fringe-
carried
with
court
habit-
powdered
wig-
short
queue
tied
with
black
ribbon-
French and
English-
1814

bicorne of
napoléon-black
felt-tricolor
cockade-button
and ribbon-
1814

black
beaver
bicorne-
French
and
English-
circa
1810

RTW

Consulate and Empire 1800-1815

black polished felt-feather pompon-U.S. Army-1810

the Glengarry-Scotch bonnet-cloth-ribbon-sprig of evergreen-cockade-feathers-early 1800

casque japanned leather metal crest and shield-braid-horse plume-English cavalry-1813

blue cloth cap with red bands-Prussian guard corps-1815

shako-waxed leather-metal shield and scale chinstrap-chenille pompon-white cords and tassels-Russian officer-1813

helmet of waxed leather-metal plate and scale chin strap-horse hair crest-Russian cavalry officer-1813

leather cap-Russian soldier-1813

black felt cap-brass plate-white cord and tassel-red and white woolen pompon-English cavalry officer-1811

shako of black felt-white braid-red woolen pompon-English officer-1813

RTW

Consulate and Empire 1800-1815

felt or cloth shako-chenille pompon-powdered hair in leather queue with ribbon bowknot-English artillery-1807-9

metal casque-scale and leather chinstrap-black or red chenille plume-English cavalry-1811

bearskin shako-white chenille pompon-scale and leather chinstrap-artillery officer-English-1811

shako-black cloth and leather-white cords-white cotton chenille pompon-gilt insignia-scale chinstrap-U.S. Infantry 1813

helmet-varnished leather-gilt braid and tassels-white ostrich-officer-French lancer-1806

shako-blue and black cloth-white braid, cord and tassels-red, white and blue chenille pompon-French general-1800

dress shako-black cloth-gilt insignia braid and tassels-black leather chinstrap-red coq feather pompon-French marine-1810

cloth shako-gilt cord and tassels-coq feather pompon-Prussian hussar officer-1814

black cloth shako-leather visor-colored cloth bag-gilt cord and tassels-silk rosettes-scale chinstrap-chenille pompon-major-general-English cavalry-1811

RTW

Consulate and Empire 1800-1815

capote or
poke bonnet-
satin with
straw visor-
lace net veil-
French-
1801

poke bonnet- black velvet
or beaver-pink ostrich-
blue rosette-white silk
kerchief-
French-
1802

"desert
turban" with
"mameluke point"
printed silk
in red shades-
French-
1803

jockey helmet
of beaver-
ribbon and
buttons-
earrings-
French-
circa 1804

jeweled arrow
hairpin-white
silk scarf-
gold embroidery-
hoop earrings-
French-1803

casquette à la minerve-
satin with
ostrich plume-
beads-
French-
1800

turban of pleated
gray gauze-gilt
spangles- gilt band
with jewels-
earrings-
French-
1803

riding cap of
beaver with
band of gilt
military braid-
ostrich plume-
american-
1800

RTW

Consulate and Empire 1800-1815

shingled coiffure
with false front
of curls-
French-
1800

white silk turban
with
Mameluke point-
long gold arrow
hairpin-
French-
1804

Titus
coiffure with
velvet ribbon
fillet-
French-
1802

Lavinia
hat of
white satin-
rose colored
facing
and ribbon-
French-
1804

Bonapartian
helmet-gilt
laurel wreath
on black velvet-
white silk
crown-white
ostrich-
French-circa
1802

tiny straw
evening turban-
artificial roses-
ribbon-
French-
1806

coiffure
with
diamond
hair
ornament-
Spanish-
1806

cottage bonnet-
straw-worn over
lingerie cap with
frill-artificial
flowers-ribbons-
French-1804

RTW

Consulate and Empire 1800-1815

Bonnet of corded
rose silk-
lace
veil-
French
1806

military bonnet or
Polish casquette-
pleated satin-ribbon-
feather pompon-
French-
1806

evening turban
of pearl sewn
striped white
satin-
earrings-
French 1806

cornet-
lingerie cap-
lace frills-
colored
ribbon-
French-
1809

military
riding
hat-beaver
with fur
pompon-
braid button-
German-
circa 1808

turban with
Mameluke
point-white
satin-pearl
fringe-
French-1806

"conversation
bonnet" with
brim turned
back-red
and yellow
striped silk-
French-
1805

coiffure in
one-sided effect-
American-
circa 1809

spangled
silk turban with ostrich plume-
French-1809

RTW

Consulate and Empire 1800-1815

striped satin turban-
aigrette and jeweled
brooch-
French-
1809

satin
bonnet-
ribbon ties- English
name "Regency cap"-
French-circa 1811

variation of the mob-
tulle and lace-
cording-satin facing-
English-
1811

the
Slengarry
riding
hat-
interlaced
ribbon over cork-
ostrich- small
feathers-ribbon
cockade-
English-
circa 1808

cornet
cap of eyelet
embroidery and
ribbons-
English-
1812

evening coiffure
embodying new
features of the
period-high
headdress à la
chinoise-ivory
comb-floating
veil 36 inches
long-pearl
beads and
earrings-
ferronière-
French-
1814

shirred white tulle
with double
ruching-tea
roses-green
foliage-
French-
1813

classic coiffure-
braids and
puffs-pearl
diadem-
artificial
roses-
French-
1811

R·T·W

Consulate and Empire 1800-1815

velvet bonnet
with
ostrich plumes-
ribbon bound
edge-
French-
1814

yellow straw-
rose colored
ribbon-
artificial
daffodils-
Pamela
bonnet-
French-1813

morning
bonnet of
shirred sheer white
muslin-eyelet embroidery-
French-
1815

cap of moiré and
velvet ribbon-
tulle frill lace edged
English-
1814

military hat-
peacock blue
velvet and
plume-velvet
rosette-
French-
1815

taffeta bonnet
with tulle
over crown-
ribbons-
French-
1814

Polish cap
of satin-
rope cord with
bead pendants-
eyelet embroidered
frill
English-
1814

RTW

THE ROMANTIC PERIOD, 1815-1840

CHAPTER FOURTEEN

IN THIS, THE ROMANTIC PERIOD, ringlets were the fashion, men with straight hair making use of the curling iron to acquire them. Like the feminine coiffure there was often a profusion of curls at the temples and over the forehead. It is said that Beau Brummell found it necessary to employ three coiffeurs to arrange his hair, one for the front curls, another for the side curls and a third for the back of the head, each section requiring a specialist.

The hair was cut moderately short and usually parted to one side. It was dressed with Macassar oil, and there we have the origin of the antimacassar, a protective doily placed at the back of the upholstered chair. Some men were clean-shaven, some wore a small mustache or short whiskers framing the face or both but always very trim.

The high beaver hat was the fashionable headpiece with crown of varying shape and narrow rolling brim. The full rolling brim of the late 'thirties has survived under name of the d'Orsay roll as worn by Count Gabriel d'Orsay (1801–1852). An amateur of the fine arts and a leader of society in Paris and

London, he was noted as "the greatest swell of the day." He settled in England in 1821.

The beaver was worn in fawn, gray, white for day and black for night. An improved version of the polished beaver appeared about 1823 but its popularity dates from the 1830's. The birth of the silk hat, so the story goes, was in Canton, China about 1775, made by a Chinese hatter for a Frenchman named Betta who carried his new headpiece back with him to Paris. The collapsible silk hat still called by the name of its French inventor, Gibus, appeared in Paris in 1823 and was patented in 1837. This practical hat was designed to be carried under the arm and was the outcome of the tall hat being worn to the opera and occupying too much space in the cloak room, whence its general name, the opera hat.

The London policeman, who dates from 1829, wore the tall straight-sided hat in black. His nickname, bobby or peeler, was a play upon the name of his creator, the Home Secretary, Sir Robert Peel.

The cap with visor, new in the beginning of the century and first worn by the military officer, was taken up by jockeys, small boys and coachmen, eventually becoming the sports headcovering for the well-dressed man. It was made of cloth to match the coat. Straw and felt were used for country hats. At home with his lounging suit or robe, the gentleman wore a "smoking cap" of velvet.

A tremendous vogue for everything Celtic swept the romantic 'thirties, influenced by the Ossian poets, Byron and Scott, all having an effect upon the costume of the day. The appearance of a collected edition of the poems of Robert Burns (1759–1796) in 1834 was responsible for the name of Tam-o'-Shanter. Men, women and children in the fashionable world wore variations of the Scotch bonnet called tam-o'-shanter after the famous character in Burns' poem of that name. The Scotch bonnet known today as the tam-o'-shanter or "tam," is of beret style in heavy brushed wool and is especially worn by men when curling, a game played with flattish stones on the ice.

Protestant clergy followed, as they do today, the layman's style of hairdressing and hat.

The military trend in uniform was toward a more practical and comfortable design, the cap being generally adopted. In 1825, in the United States Army, a cloth shako or "foraging cap" was permitted to company officers and enlisted men in place of the heavy leather shako or "tar buckets." The French regiment of Zouaves organized in 1831, made up of Arabs from North Africa and later of Arabs and Frenchmen, wore the tasseled red felt chéchia or the white turban scarf wound round the chéchia.

An American, J. R. Williams about 1820, invented the first mechanical process for the production of felt and though many improvements have since followed in the machine, the principle remains the same.

In America, the duty on imported leghorn straw and grass hats and the intense summer heat made the palm leaf hat popular, introduced about 1826. The leaf was imported from Cuba and the hats, varying in price from twenty-five cents to two dollars were made by young girls in their homes.

All the latest feminine fashions were of Parisian origin but, in this age, were launched by the queens of the stage instead of royal ladies. Coiffure and headgear were the distinct features of the costume.

The hair was dressed to the top of the head, "à la chinoise," leaving the ears exposed. Bunches of curls were worn at the temples and topknots were shaped into fantastic forms. Tightly braided sections were twisted into loops, urns, wings and whatnot to which ribbon, flowers and strings of beads were added. Wire, long pins and carved shell combs held the topknot secure. The upstanding lacquered loops of hair were "Apollo's knots." False curls and switches were in common use and dyeing freely resorted to.

Beloved was the ferronière, a fine chain round the head with a jewel over the forehead. Narrow velvet ribbon, strings of beads and tiny artificial flowers too, formed the ferronière.

About 1834 came a change with the temple curls dropping to the sides of the face, a return of heartbreakers or English ringlets. Braids were looped low over the cheeks, a style especially favored for horseback riding. "Chaste bands" of straight lacquered hair were dressed in the same fashion. As in the masculine coiffure, the new sleek effect was aided by the use of Macassar oil.

By 1840, the change in hairdressing was an accomplished fact with the chignon low at the back of the head, the top of the head flat but the center part retained. The lowered chignon was often held by a large ornamental comb of tortoise shell or ivory or by decorative hairpins from Italy.

The feminine head was nearly always enhanced by some form of headtire, indoors or out. For full dress, the young married woman wore in her hair artificial or fresh flowers, lace, plumes, gilt wheatstalks, aigrettes or handsome jeweled combs. At the beginning of the period, with the white flag of the French Restoration flying from the dome of the Tuileries, white, especially for evening, became more fashionable than ever, white ostrich, white cock feathers, white lilies, white lilacs and white roses appearing in the headdress.

Matrons wore turbans of costly brocaded fabrics, white cashmere, figured gauze, some sewn with pearls or spangles. The black turban for mourning wear was ornamented with dull jet. The large hat heaped with luxurious ostrich plumes was worn to dinner parties and to the opera.

The white and gold turban, "à la Rachel," so popular, was inspired by Halévy's play "La Juive" in which Rachel (1820-1858) the celebrated French tragedienne, appeared.

With the return of the Bourbons to the throne, there appeared a formal headdress for court wear, a white satin toque like the Spanish toque of the sixteenth century. It had white standing ostrich feathers and lace or silk lappets embroidered in gold or silver.

Unique to the period, about 1830, was the cornet or "fly-away headdress" for evening. It was a fantastic affair consisting of large flaring fans of, usually, sheer white embroidered organdy or Indian muslin. The fans were starched or wired, sometimes of silk or blonde lace augmented by flowers and ribbons, a jeweled brooch, buckle or hairpin of elaborate design.

Though the cornet or cap was of all sizes and shapes, adapted to every costume and every occasion, the decline of its vogue dates from the 1830's. There were nightcaps, "rising caps," morning caps and lacy theater caps which were worn under the large hat. Sometimes the cornet was simulated in lacy frills sewn to bonnet or hat.

Of the late 'thirties was the arcade, a flattering headpiece. It was a half-cap which sat far back on the head, of lace ruffles, ribbon and rosebuds and often tied under the chin with ribbon.

The masculine bandbox of the seventeenth century returned to use, not, however, for the gentleman's bands or collars but for the lady to carry her cap in to the party. When there, she changed her bonnet for the frivolous lacy bit.

In the 1820's, the very large hat and the very large poke bonnet vied with each other for first place, attaining an extreme size in 1830 and 1831. Finally the bonnet reigned supreme and noteworthy is the fact that, from this period, the term has been reserved for the feminine hood-shaped hat which ties under the chin.

There was the capote or cabriolet with wide "carriage-top" front, the Pamela with the wide front held against the cheeks by the ribbon ties and, about 1835, appeared the smaller version of the poke, the "bibi," ribbon-tied under the chin. In the bibi, tiny artificial flowers and lace frills often entirely framed the oval of the face, very charming indeed. The bavolet had a frill at the back of the neck, which gave it the name of "curtain bonnet."

Horseback riding was very popular between 1830 and 1835, women wearing the tall silk or beaver hat, occasionally beplumed but nearly always with floating green veil. The *casquette,* a riding cap, was of tam-o'-shanter shape with visor.

Veils were very much of the mode, in plain net with hemstitched edge, Limerick lace or net appliquéd with Honiton or Brussels and in crême or white. The veil was fitted with a drawstring, tied round the crown and left to hang in front or float in back. Hat brims were often edged with deep shirred ruffles of lace.

The bride in white dress and veil was occasionally seen but as often, she simply wore a wreath of white roses on her head. American girls followed this English bridal custom of roses in the hair and June, the month of roses as the time to marry. Orange blossoms, so definitely associated with the bride in our day, was a French fashion. To America, in 1838, from the south of France, came a goodwill shipment of the delicate blossoms from which time, our brides have worn orange blossoms on their wedding day.

Hats and bonnets were of beaver, felt, velvet, silk, plush, gros de Naples, leghorn and chip straw. They were ornamented with several different trimmings of which there were ribbons, flowers, feathers, marabou, paradise, aigrettes, padded borders, ruchings, twists and jeweled buckles. Brown velvet in a shade called "Lord Byron" and combined with white, was very smart. Green, in every shade from "early spring bud" to "bottle green," was worn. The melancholy mood of the period was evident in the preference shown for dark and grayed colors, Marengo black, Russian green, wine lees, pure Ethiopian, pigeon breast and lilac.

Ribbon was the rage, ribbon bowknots and floating ribbon streamers, the ends cut into points. Shot, damask and watered silk were designed in rich combinations of colors. Broad ribbon of colored gauze was striped with silver or gold and plaid and checked ribbons were inspired by the novels of Sir Walter Scott.

Fabrics, colors and trinkets were given names, some very surprising. In 1827, when the Pasha of Egypt presented a handsome giraffe to Charles X, Paris in a few days had named all kinds of costume accessories for man or woman, "à la giraffe." The coiffure with lacquered loops of hair, earlier called Apollo's knots, was renamed à la giraffe.

The 1820's witnessed the return of jewelry to the mode, with earrings, necklaces, bracelets, brooches and rings often all worn at the same time. The wearing of jewelry in the 'thirties was confined to earrings and hair ornaments. Especially of the period were cameos, pearls and garnets. Earrings were long and elaborate, though the pearl drop was often seen.

Black jet in jewelry became a vogue which was to last throughout the century. Black jet came from England where it was found in layers of shale and had been in use for centuries. The extensive employment of it in the nineteenth century for feminine baubles diminished the supply and jet of inferior quality was supplied from Spain. White jet came from Norway and black glass imitation jet from Germany.

The quizzing glass or single lens, mounted on tortoise shell or jeweled handle, was carried by the lady and the gentleman.

Romantic 1815-1840

English-circa 1820

American-circa 1819

English-1830's

English-1830's

French-1828

French-1840

German-1840

French-1840

German-1840's

Romantic 1815-1840

beaver
or felt-
ribbon band-
French-
1816

light colored
beaver-
ribbon band-
French-
1822

black silk-
brim
with
d'Orsay
roll-
English-
1830's

black silk
chimney
pot-ribbon
band-
French-
1825

straw
sailor hat-
ribbon band-
pompon-
French-1831

cap for
shipboard-
leather band
and visor-
cloth crown-
braid-
French-
1820

Quaker hat
of beaver-
1840

hunting cap-
japanned
leather-
French-
1833

cloth
cap for
country
wear-
German-
circa 1833

cap of velvet
worn with
smoking
jacket or
robe-
French-
1839

RTW

Romantic 1815-1840

Cossack cap of fur-cavalry officer-1830

red cloth béret-black fur band-black braid motif-green ostrich feather-silver button-Polish cavalry-1831

helmet-black waxed leather and gilt-red horse plume-scale and leather chinstrap-Russian drum major-1830

blue cap-leather visor-gold braid and insignia-lieutenant navy-French-1815-1840

cap of blue cloth and silver braid-black fur band-Circassian officer-1830

cocked hat-green felt-green coq plume-gilt insignia-black leather chinstrap-Austrian rifleman-1840

black cloth cap-red bands-Russian corporal-1830

shako of japanned leather-gilt insignia-scale and leather chinstrap-Russian-1831

1.I.P.

white muslin turban draped round red chechia (Berber skullcap)-tassel-French Zouave-1830's

sailor's hat of japanned leather-black ribbon-French-1840

R.T.W.

Romantic 1815-1840

coiffure of 1815

Russian toque-white satin-brown velvet ribbon-French-1816

royalist bonnet-white satin-white cock feather-fleur-de-lis-French-1816

formal toque for court-white satin-white ostrich-lappets with gold or silver eyelet embroidery-French-1815

shako-ermine with white satin bands-gold cords and tassels-English-1817

turban of draped silk-wheat stalks-pearl ferronière-French-1821

polished beaver with ostrich-over theater cap-lace frilled white muslin-English-1820

English coiffure 1820's

traveling hat-tam-o'-shanter-blue silk-red band and pompon-French-1820's

RTW

Romantic 1815-1840

Apollo's knots-
satin striped ribbon-
French-1825

evening
headdress-
taffeta ribbon
fringed edge-
French-
circa 1824

Pamela bonnet-black velvet-
black paradise plumes-black
satin ribbon- French-1821

yellow straw-
reseda green
ribbon-white
ostrich-
French-
1824

hat of
white satin-
artificial
mignonette-
French-
1826

evening
coiffure-
Apollo's
knots-
jeweled
ferronière-
flowers-foliage-
butterfly-
French-
1826

hat of
shirred bottle
green velvet-
crown of broad
wired loop-
black striped
green ribbon-
French-
1828

mourning
turban-
black crêpe
loops-
French-
1825

RTW

Romantic 1815-1840

black velvet-
satin facing-
black lace-
uncurled
ostrich-striped
gauze ribbon-
French-
1830

evening
coiffure-
Apollo's
knots-braids-
carnation-
lily of the
valley-
moss
rose-
French-
1830

evening
coiffure-
Apollo's
knots-
striped gauze
ribbon-wreath
of flowers-
tortoise shell
comb-
French-
1829

bridal
veil tied
with
wings-lace
net-Apollo's
knot-large
shell pins-
French-
1831

turban
à la Rachel-
white satin-gold spangles-
white aigrette-looped up
braids-French-1833

evening
coiffure-
Apollo's
knots-
curls-wheat
stalks-
French-
1832

"fly-away headdress"
evening-embroidered
white organdy-
peach colored gauze
ribbon-white roses-
green foliage-
French-
circa 1830

"fly-away headdress"
for evening-coral
taffeta-black velvet
stripes-coral uncurled
ostrich-French-1830

RTW

Romantic 1815-1840

the "bibi"-white satin faced with apple green velvet-green plumes and ribbon-white flowers and lace frill-French-1833

cornet-organdy or Indian muslin-wheatstalks and roses-French-1835

tam-o'-shanter riding cap-plum colored velvet-silk cord and tassel-French-1836

riding hat-fawn colored beaver and veil-looped up braids-French-1835

riding hat-black silk-green veil-English-1838

Quaker bonnet in bavolet style-white silk-1830

evening coiffure-curls, braids, pearls and bowknots-French-1834

bavolet-bonnet with curtain-yellow-straw-black satin-wheat and poppies-French-1836

RTW

Romantic 1815-1840

evening coiffure
Apollo's knots-
pearl
ferronière-
French-
1837

evening
coiffure-
pleated silk
fans attached to
combs-Apollo's
loops-
cherries-
French-
1831

brown velvet-
pink ostrich-
gold brooch-
English
ringlets-
French-
1836

sky blue taffeta
and ribbons-
white velvet loops
round crown-
deep lace frill
sewn to edge
of brim-
French-
1838

front view
of the
above
coiffure

evening
coiffure-
carved ivory
combs and
ostrich-
French-
1840-

the arcade-
evening, boudoir
and general
wear-
lace
and
flowers-
French-
1838

evening coiffure-
lacquered twists of
hair-fillet of
pink roses-
French-
1839

RTW

Romantic 1815-1840

straw bonnet
with ribbon-
French-
1817

young
girl's
coiffure-
French-
1817

boy's
cap-
cloth with
leather
visor-
American-
1818

boy's
tam-o'-shanter
cloth
with
pompon-
English-
1820's

small
girl-
English
ringlets-
American-
1828

silk bonnet
with veil-
French and English-
1821

boy in
black silk
hat-
American-
1830

"military"
cloth cap-
leather and
visor and
chinstrap-
French-
1830

bavolet bonnet
of muslin-shirred
over cording-
French-
1830

little girl-
dotted muslin-
embroidery-
French-
1830

small boy-
cloth tam-o'-shanter-
French-
1830

small boy
in large
straw hat-
French-
1823

Sources and dates are given
but the above styles are typical
for American, English, French
and German children of the period

RTW

VICTORIAN AND SECOND EMPIRE, 1840-1870

CHAPTER FIFTEEN

MEN'S FASHIONS IN THIS PERIOD settled down to a fairly standard design ruled over by London and readily followed by the metropolitan well-dressed man. Such is the case today, a full century later.

Luxurious hair was the thing, curly locks brushed forward or back, worn moderately long but trimmed up higher in back. The fashionable man dressed his hair with perfumed Macassar oil while the backwoodsman made use of tallow or bear's grease to slick up his hair. Many men wore the "cowlick," a lock of hair brushed into a curl over the forehead.

Side whiskers, longer in the 'forties, attained a luxurious growth in the next two decades. To the English they were mutton chops or "piccadilly weepers" and to the French, favoris or cutlets. "Dundrearys," we in America called them after Lord Dundreary, the famous English character in "Our American Cousin" by Tom Taylor in which the English-American comedian A. E. Sothern in 1858 made his debut. The term "sideburns" was an American colloquialism after the general and politician A. E. Burnside (1824–1881).

A clipped beard sometimes framed the chin and the mustache or "pair of moustachios" was popular with or without beard. The "imperial" was smart, a pointed tuft on the chin named in honor of Napoleon III, Emperor of France from 1851 to 1870.

The "topper" or "silker" of black silk plush or brushed beaver remained the hat for all formal occasions, especially in black. The hat of beaver was disappearing with the diminishing supply of beaver and Prince Albert's acceptance of the black silk hat made for its extreme popularity. The silhouette in crown and brim varied from year to year. The "John Bull" model was five and three-quarters inches high, then followed the "stovepipe" of seven inches, the "chimney pot" of seven and a half, topped by the "kite-high dandy" with its height of seven and three-eighths inches. The light-colored toppers in fawn, gray or white were usually of cloth.

Because of the uncomfortable though smart shape of the top hat, it is not surprising that the newly observed slouch felt of the Tyrolese peasant should meet with general adoption. The soft felt which originated in the Italian and Austrian Tyrol dates back to the Middle Ages when it had its beginning in the felted coif or hood of hare fur worn as a head covering and also as a padding under the helmet. The hat became popular with men of romantic and democratic opinions, the so-called bohemians of Europe, especially artists and musicians. It also signified a protest against the silk-hatted dandy; in fact, wearers of the "democratic hat" were persecuted in Germany for many years.

Many new shapes followed the improvements in the 1840's of the felt-making machine. The first really efficient machine was devised in the United States and introduced into England about 1858.

The popularity of the slouch hat in England and America dates from the visit of Louis Kossuth, the great Hungarian patriot, to both countries in 1852 and 1853 when he wore such a hat in black felt. The Hungarian hat it was called, with brim turned up all around and a ribbon band with short ends hanging in back. About the same time, a pork pie shape with floating ribbon ends in back was popular on the Continent.

In the United States, the Westerner and the Southerner, especially the planter and the frontiersman were very partial to the large broad-brimmed felt, the Mexican sombrero. The sombrero, Spanish for "shade," goes back to the fifteenth century and was fashioned of fur felt. Our Western version came to be known as the "cowboy hat."

The black stovepipe was worn by both the London bobby and the American constable of the mid-century and top hats with light-colored bands became the headgear of grooms and coachmen. Side whiskers eventually became the distinguishing mark of butlers and footmen who wore them well into the twentieth century.

A new and very important hat made its appearance in 1850 designed by William Bowler, the English hatter. It was a hard round felt with flat brim and low melon-shaped crown, and "melon" is what the French have always called it. It became the "bowler" after its originator but was also known as the "billycock," a contraction of William Coke, the first daring Englishman to sponsor the new headpiece by wearing it. The Earl of Derby helped popularize the hat by wearing his gray bowler with black band to the races at Epsom Downs and that is the origin of our American term "derby."

There was a tall round-crowned hard felt, a style worn by New York policemen. Another police hat seen in illustrations of the 'sixties was the visored cap. Broad-brimmed panama hats were worn in summer.

The establishment of the railroads brought about a great social change. The use of steam made traveling possible for many and in Europe, for the first time, aristocracy and the upper middle classes mingled in their trips to seaside and inland watering places. Men adopted more casual hats, wearing them with light summer suits of nankeen, foulard and alpaca. A favored summer headpiece was the straw sailor hat, forerunner of the stiff hard boater of the next decade.

The cap with visor, fashioned of the coat fabric, woolen plaid or check, was worn for hunting, fishing and the like. The cap with tam-o'-shanter crown was popular for men and boys for sportswear and was adopted by navies for the sailor.

The Scotch bonnet, the "Balmoral," the blue woolen beret cap, came to the fore in the 'fifties when Albert, Prince Consort of Queen Victoria erected the new Castle of Balmoral as a royal residence in Aberdeenshire, Scotland. The queen loved the Scottish garb and customs and dressed all the princes in the Highland costume.

In eyeglasses, the gentleman made use of the monocle and the pince-nez in square or round frames which hung on a fine chain, cord or ribbon of black silk worn round the neck. The Englishman, who uses the monocle to this day, became adept in the handling of the single unframed glass.

Climate and terrain now began to influence military costume. The stiff uncomfortable shako was replaced by the cap. French troops in Africa found the soft cap or kepi a more practical headpiece which we adopted in the Civil War, calling it the forage cap. Further protection was afforded in the havelock, a curtain of white washable material which covered cap and neck. That, too, we copied. Though worn by the ancient Persian soldiers, it bears the name of Sir Henry Havelock, the British general in the Sepoy mutiny of 1857.

The "slouch" or broad-brimmed felt was adopted in 1861 by the officers in the American war between the States, dark blue for the Northerners and gray for the Southerners.

New in this period was the pith helmet of Hindu name, topee or topi, made from the pith of the Indian spongewood tree and first worn by the English Army in India. Very light in weight, covered with white cotton and faced with green cloth, it really is insulated against the hot sun.

In feminine hairdressing, the Madonna style of center part and the head flat on top remained the fashion. English ringlets became demoded in the early 'forties but were worn a longer time in England than on the Continent. The smoothly oiled or lacquered side sections which covered the ears were drawn back into a huge netted cadogan or dressed to simulate the style.

The wedding of the beautiful Spanish Eugénie to Napoleon III in 1853 took place in Paris and the fashionable world copied her coiffure in which the hair was drawn up off the face and rolled back in Pompadour style. The Empress with her great beauty, her rare taste and distinction, was the first royal leader of fashion since Marie-Antoinette and her influence with that of her court, particularly in hairdressing, was rivaled by few celebrities of the stage.

Evenly placed waves at the sides of the head, resembling the later marcel wave, appeared in the 'fifties. The popular Manier bandeau was a tightly braided section of front hair held in position by a comb over which the hair was dressed in Pompadour fashion. In the 1860's, a horsehair cushion was substituted, the side fullness increased and the back dressed in heavy plaits, a loose chignon or a cadogan. Then to give greater bulk, especially in the "waterfall," the back hair was loosened and dressed over cushions necessitating the use of quantities of false hair and the net.

That ancient and artistic accessory of the headdress, the caul, now termed net, became extremely fashionable. In the 1850's it was of braided silk and velvet ribbon bordered with bias bands and fastened with gilt buttons and buckles. There were nets of chenille and in the 'sixties, nets of human hair made of the wearer's own hair which she furnished to her hairdresser.

By the late 'sixties, the hair was dressed high in back and the sleek coiffure disappeared with a disheveled effect replacing it in rolls, ringlets, bandeaux, braids and cadogans. Venetian blond and Titian red were the rage, many women dyeing their hair such variations of the desired color as yellow, tomato red and mahogany. What with bleaching, dyeing and the use of curling irons, the head of many a fashionable woman was an unkempt mass of lusterless hair.

Curling tongs were employed even on the hair of little girls in this latest craze for curls. Round combs and steel springs covered with silk or velvet ribbon were worn over the top of the head from ear to ear holding the young lady's locks in place.

The evening coiffure was ornamented with artificial flowers, silk and velvet ribbon, gilt and silver fillets and veils of blonde lace stitched with gold thread. The most favored decoration was that of artificial flowers, worn singly, in wreaths and in sprays, often sprinkled with glistening dewdrops.

The World's Fair held in Paris in 1855 gave great impetus to the French manufacture of flowers. Beautiful replicas were to be had of tulips, pansies, roses, lilacs, auriculas, primroses, wreaths of convolvuluses and bunches of long drooping leaves. However, it should be noted that women of means wore fresh flowers sometimes sewn to their voluminous tulle gowns and both men and women made use of small vials of water in lapel or hair to keep their posies fresh. The great vogue for fresh violets, especially Parma violets, had its beginning in this period and lasted nearly half a century.

The coiffure was named according to the ornament used, oak leaves with acorns for the "Druid," water flowers for the "Naiad," small feathers for the "Leda," wildflowers for the "Proserpine" and cornflowers and wheatstalks over the forehead for the "Ceres." There were also wreaths of ash privet with berries, aigrettes, gold diadems and combs composed of diamonds and many different stones with the settings often changed each year.

The "net à la Napolitaine" which encased the back hair was of strings of pearls finished with fringe and tassels. A short-lived evening fashion was the powdering of the headdress with gold or silver dust. A New York weekly paper of the 'sixties speaks of fashionable ladies gilding their hair with gilt or silver dust at fifteen dollars a dusting.

Eugénie, with her wedding veil of Alençon lace, wore a shell comb, a small wreath of orange blossoms and a coronet of sapphires. Her marriage to Napoleon created a vogue for the black lace mantilla in France. The national Spanish headdress evolved into three distinct mantillas: the blonde lace, white or black edged with a deep frill for fête days and one of black silk bordered with velvet for all ordinary occasions. In Spain, the law protects the feminine mantilla from seizure for debt.

The cloud or fascinator was the light fluffy three-cornered head scarf of lace, net or loosely knitted silk or yarn, worn in the evening especially in winter. This flattering age-old headcovering lasted to the end of the century and among its many names were opera hood and molly hood.

The bonnet remained definitely the headcovering for the greater part of the period but the cap and the hat were much worn too. The small "bibi" bonnet with bavolet or curtain and the "fanchon" or kerchief bonnet (so named because of its resemblance to a diagonally folded kerchief) were the prevailing styles. They were of velvet, satin, crêpe, lace and straw, trimmed with ribbons, feathers, flowers and fruits, encircled with gauze, tulle or blonde lace and tied with broad ribbons under the chin. Drawn bonnets were of silk, crêpe lisse, Mechlin net or tulle shirred on heavy cords and finished with lace frills. The drawn bonnet of the older woman was usually of black lace.

Beaver bonnets were a fashion for several years but the hat, though costly, was too heavy for evening wear and did not retain its color. The bonnet became very small in the 'sixties, the poke front fitting closely round the face.

Straw for summer hats staged a revival in 1850 and especially liked, were the wide drooping brims called "flats" and sometimes edged with a tulle or lace ruffle, a "protection against the sun." Such hats were held on, not by ribbon ties but by means of long pins made especially for the purpose. This hatpin appeared first in 1853, to be followed by jeweled ones.

Leghorn was the expensive and desired straw from Tuscany but there were also Swiss and Belgian straws, rice, chip and English "sewn straw," worn by those unable to afford the Italian product. In the 1860's, China with her very cheap labor copied the Western plaits and entered the straw industry. The Chinese variety, though inferior to the fine Italian and English straws, threatened the supremacy of England in the "sewn straw" craft.

Caps were dainty diminutive affairs with lappets, ribbons, flowers and sometimes a veil. The small flat bandbox was still in use for the tiny cap but a larger ornamented box held milady's dressiest bonnet when traveling.

THE MODE IN HATS AND HEADDRESS

The appearance of the small hat in the early 'sixties sounded the death knell of the flattering poke bonnet. There was a feminine version of the pork pie, a tiny round hat with upturned brim, flowers and ribbon. The Empress hat of 1859 was revived in 1931 as the Eugénie hat. As the coiffure rose in back, the small hat tipped forward to the eyes as in the "shepherdess or Watteau hat." Long streamers or "flirtation ribbons" either floated from the back of the hat or were threaded through the hair, "suivez-moi, jeune homme," the French term the ribbons (follow me, young man).

The fashion of the nose veil or "Empress demi-veil" worn with the tiny hat of network, tulle or point d'esprit and edged with a narrow frill of blonde lace lasted for years. The veil which covered the face appeared about 1863. A three-quarter length veil with orange blossoms in the hair was the thing with the all-white bridal costume. An enveloping black veil, bordered with crêpe hung over the small black crêpe bonnet of the widow.

All colors, especially delicate shades, were popular with dark tones late in the period. A yellowish brown called Theda was a favorite of the French Empress and after the death of the English Prince Consort in 1861, black was much worn. In the late 'sixties, reds prevailed under such names as magenta, Solferina, red currant, Shanghai and Pekin.

As to make-up, white face powder and rouge were sparingly used in this period, even in Paris. A new and harmless powder base was discovered in oxide of zinc but another generation was to pass before face powder came into general practice.

Jewelry was of several different colored golds and varied stones, all in one piece. Diamonds, rubies, sapphires, emeralds, pearls and topazes were fashionable, also coral, black jet and onyx. Fine gold was worked into tiny tassels, delicate fringe and pliable ribbon bracelets. It was a period of "sets," a pair of earrings, a brooch and a pair of bracelets all of matching design. Earrings were long and elaborate. Very small girls wore tiny earrings in their pierced ears, a custom from the 'forties on. The operation was either performed at home or at the jewelry shop where the baubles were purchased and was thought beneficial to the eyes.

Mourning jewelry was very important and fashionable, of gold with black enamel, dull jet, often with a coil of the hair of the "beloved departed" cleverly inserted in ring, brooch or locket. Lockets were often worn on an inch-wide black velvet ribbon round the neck.

Victorian-Second Empire-1840•1870

gray or tawn colored cloth top hat-English-1840's

melon shape-felt or straw-bow on left side-worn in London, Paris and New York-1862

black silk hat-French-1842

the pork pie of black felt with ribbon-German-1861

fawn colored felt-black ribbon band-English-1870

bowler, melon or derby-of hard felt-English-1862

mourning top hat-black silk with black faille-worn by Abraham Lincoln-1862

the "Hungarian" hat of felt or straw-French-1852

summer hat-light brown felt French-1857

gray silk top hat-German-1861

RTW

Victorian-Second Empire 1840-1870

side part and "cowlick" mustache- French- 1849

sports cap- red and green wool plaid- black leather visor- tiny feathers- French- 1844

center part, curls, whiskers and mustache- English- 1840's

country hat of felt- American- 1850

pompadour and sideburns- American- 1852

hunter's cap of patent leather- French- 1849

"slouch" hat of felt- American- 1856

English- 1850's

cap of suit cloth for traveling- English- 1861

sports hat of cloth- English- 1860's

montero cap for traveling- cloth with gray fur turn-ups- chinstrap- French- 1858

center part- curls and mustache- New York- 1868

RTW

Victorian-Second Empire 1840 • 1870

the képi-
red cloth-
gold braid-
black
leather
visor-
French
officer-
1840

Zouave cap-
chéchia of
red cloth-
blue
tassel-
French-
1854

képi-
red cloth-
gold braid-
black
leather-
French officer-
1845

képi-
blue
leather-red
cloth-white
braid-silver
buttons-
Italian-
1848

Bersaglieri-
black glazed
felt-black
coq plume-
ribbon-insignia-
chinstrap-
1850's

sailor
hat-
blue
japanned
leather-
blue ribbon-
French-
1860's

fringed blue
and yellow
cloth turban-
gold color
conical cap-
British
Indian army
officer

Balmoral-
blue
cloth-
feather,
ribbon and
evergreen
of clan-red
and white
diced band-
Scotch

képi-red-
blue cloth
band-black
leather visor
and chinstrap-
gilt insignia-
gray horsehair
plume-
German 1864

blue cloth béret-
red pompon-
white braid-
French-
marine-
1870

black cloth
cap-red and
black diced
band-insignia-
British Rifle

pith helmet-
white cotton-
green facing-
French and British colonial-
1860's

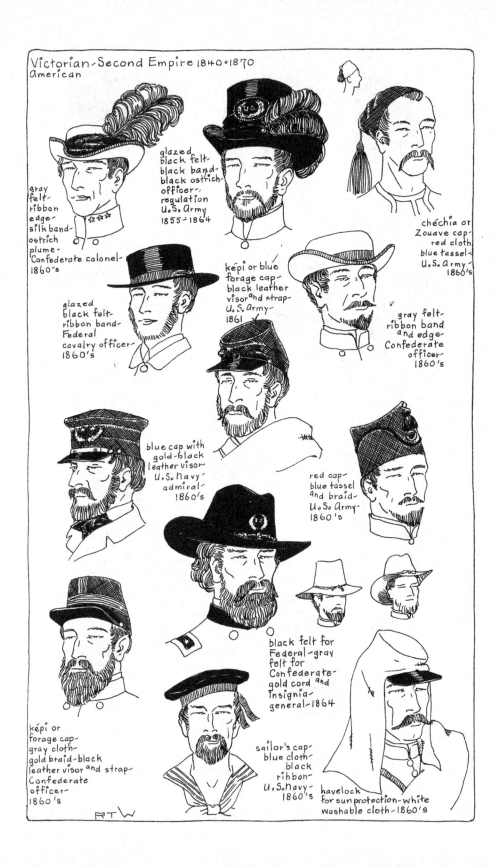

Victorian-Second Empire 1840-1870
American

gray felt-ribbon edge-silk band-ostrich plume-'Confederate colonel-1860's

glazed black felt-black band-black ostrich-officer-regulation U.S. Army 1855-1864

chéchia or Zouave cap-red cloth blue tassel-U.S. Army-1860's

glazed black felt-ribbon band-Federal cavalry officer-1860's

képi or blue forage cap-black leather visor and strap U.S. Army-1861

gray felt-ribbon band and edge-Confederate officer-1860's

blue cap with gold-black leather visor-U.S. Navy-admiral-1860's

red cap-blue tassel and braid-U.S. Army-1860's

black felt for Federal-gray felt for Confederate-gold cord and insignia-general-1864

képi or forage cap-gray cloth-gold braid-black leather visor and strap-Confederate officer-1860's

sailor's cap-blue cloth-black ribbon-U.S. Navy 1860's

havelock for sun protection-white washable cloth-1860's

RTW

Victorian-Second Empire 1840·1870

riding hat-
black silk-
green veil-
English ringlets-
French-
1842

hat all
beige-felt
with ostrich
and ribbon-
English
ringlets-
French-
1843

Queen Victoria's
military
cap of
cloth-gold
braid-black
visor-
1840

white
lawn cap-
eyelet
embroidery-
mauve
ribbons-
French-
1840

"arcade" of
white net-
Valenciennes
frills-rose-
French-
1840

evening coiffure-
loops of hair in
black velvet
ribbon cauls-
artificial
flowers-
English-1840

peacock blue silk-blue
velvet, puffing and
facing-white silk
crown and chou-
white ostrich-
English ringlets-
French-1845

bridal coiffure-pink
roses-lace net veil-
3/4 length-French-1840

"bibi" bonnet-
straw-poppy-
wisteria-leaves-
ribbon ties-
French-
1844

FTW

Victorian-Second Empire 1840·1870

Spanish headdress-black silk
lace mantilla over high
shell comb-
flower and
earrings-
1850's

Algerian
evening
headdress-
rolled
silk scarf-
tinsel
spots-
tassels-
ribbon
caul-
French-
1840's

evening coiffure-
white lace and
embroidery- pink roses-
French-
1846

evening
coiffure-
strings of
pink roses-
French-
1850

coiffure
of "chaste
bands"
French-
1850

"drawn bonnet" in bibi shape-
brown silk-beige ribbon ties-
beige and brown uncurled ostrich-
French-1847

evening coiffure-
braids, anemone
and leaves-
earrings-
French-
1851

cap of white
dotted Swiss-
blue satin
rosettes-
French-
1848

headdress of gray
pleated ribbon-
red roses-
English ringlets-
French-1840's

braids wound
over the ears-
French-
1850

RTW

Victorian-Second Empire 1840-1870

evening headdress- narrow ribbon loops-pink and white- French- 1852

a "flat"- riding hat- natural leghorn- ribbon band- French- 1852

beginning of waved coiffure- white organdy housecap with lace and lappets- French- 1852

"fanchon" bonnet with bavolet or curtain- silk with ruching of lace and flowers- bead fringe- French- 1857

riding hat of beaver- ostrich- ribbon bow- French- 1853

evening coiffure dressed over false hair- rolled ribbon- flowers- French- 1855

dark blue felt- ostrich and satin ribbon- rolled brim- hair in cadogan- French-1856

riding hat- black straw- black ostrich tips- mauve veil- French-1857

a "flat"- straw hat faced with silk- satin ribbons- French- 1856

RTW

Victorian - Second Empire 1840-1870

Empress hat-
brown felt or
velvet-yellow
and brown
paradise-brown
satin ribbon-
French-
1859

leghorn
hat-
black lace-
white ostrich-
violet ribbon-
French-
1857

cap of
embroidered yellow silk-
white lace ruching-
lace edged net veil-
French-
1861

net of
chenille-
edged bias silk
fold-French-
1861

street wear-
calotte of
shirred pale
blue silk-
jet embroidery-
pink ribbon-
French-
1861

bonnet of
brown velvet
and beige
silk-brown
bird-
ecru
veil-
French-
1862

the
waterfall
coiffure-
tiny hat of
rose taffeta-
French-
early
1860's

"fanchon" bonnet-
eyelet embroidery-
ostrich tips-
single rose-
clustered pansies-
ruching at sides-
ribbon ties-
French-
1863

RTW

Victorian-Second Empire 1840-1870

the
Windsor cap-
straw-
ostrich tips-
velvet ribbon-
hair in
cadogan-
French-
1864

white
eyelet
embroidered lawn-
blue ribbon-flowers-
wheat stalks-veil-
hair in cadogan-
French-
1863

"pork pie
hat" of velvet-
ostrich plume-
aigrette-
cadogan in
chenille net-
French-
1863

tiny lace
edged
cap
with
"flirtation
ribbons"
roses-French-
1867

toque of velvet, silk,
felt or straw-
ribbon-ostrich-
hair in cadogan-
English-
1864

"pork pie hat"
velvet with satin-
ostrich plumes-
netted cadogan-
English-
1864

"fanchon" bonnet-
brown velvet-brown
lace-bronze beads-
cream lace ruching-
cream ribbons-
cadogan-
French-
1865

straw or silk-
"flirtation ribbons"-
back hair in
English ringlets-
garnet earrings-
French-
1865

RTW

Victorian-Second Empire 1840●1870

pork pie hat-
velvet with veil-
garden flowers-
English-
1868

rolled
coiffure
with curls-
red rose-
French-
1868

small
silk pill
box-roses
and ribbon-
French-
1866

heavy looped
braids-
single
curl-French-
1869

satin crown and
bowknot-felt brim-
lace fan-
aigrette-
English-
1868

evening coiffure-
puffs and pale blue
ribbon-red poppy-
green leaves-daisy-
black eyed susan-
French-1868

Watteau or
shepherdess hat-
of straw or silk-
violets and leaves-
lace fan-
coiffure in ringlets-
French-
1869

evening coiffure-
looped braids and ringlets-
pink and yellow roses-veil-
French-1869

swirled coiffure
with single
curl hanging
from left side-
French-
1869

RTW

Victorian-Second Empire 1840•1870
French-English-American

little girl-"flat" of beaver-
satin ribbon-hair up
in bun-1859

straw
bonnet
with
black
velvet-
1843

small boy's
cap-striped
cloth
pompon-
ribbon
bowknot-
18"3

hair
dressed in
rolled coils-
springs
covered
with blue
velvet ribbon-
1855

little girl-
straw hat-
white ostrich-
and ribbon-
1855

center part-
two braids
wrapped
round head-
1848

boy's cap-
dark red
velveteen-
black leather
visor-
1854

boy's stiff
straw sailor-
black ribbon
bowknot on
left side-
1854

boy's
gray
cloth cap-
dark blue
band, tassels
and button-
1859

girl's hat-
white felt
and dark
blue velvet-
blue
pompons-
1860

black silk
top hat-
1860

braids tied with
black ribbon-
hair held
by round comb-
1868

small boy-
straw toque-
red braid
trimming-
1868

small
girl wearing
the "Empress" hat-straw and
ostrich-1860

R T W

1870-1880

CHAPTER SIXTEEN

THOUGH WHISKERS CONTINUED to adorn the masculine face into the 'eighties, the trend was toward the shaven-face with mustache. The short trimmed hair generally worn, had come to stay.

Hat styles were varied, ranging from cap, soft felt and straw to the hard felt and the topper. The dress hat was the tall black silk plush. The same shape in cloth, pearl gray, fawn or white was the proper thing for afternoon calling, the races and coaching parties. The top hat for general wear was retained by older professional men who refused to give up the believed-in dignity of that headpiece. The bowler or derby in black, brown or tan was slowly but surely establishing itself for informal wear and the preference appears to have been for light color with black band.

Travel and sports, ever on the increase, made for the popularity of the soft felt or "slouch." The fad of "mountaineering" in the Alps had much to do with the later general acceptance of the Alpine or Tyrolese hat. The felt hat with crown dented in the middle was occasionally seen in the 'seventies but it awaited the adoption by the Prince of Wales in the 1890's to make it smart.

The wide-brimmed felt became especially identified with our American

"Wild West" as the cowboy or ten-gallon hat. It was in the second half of the nineteenth century that the cowboy came to the fore with his picturesque but truly functional clothes. A great protection against the hot sun and the clouds of dust, was his large felt hat. It also served to turn the cattle when, swinging the hat in mid-air, he sung out his wild whoopee. Another name for the head-piece was the "Buffalo Bill" after the famous American guide, scout and show-man William F. Cody (1846–1917) who was always pictured wearing the wide-brimmed picturesque hat. Another popular shape in felt or straw had a low flat crown and a rolling brim.

Following an invention in 1870 of a machine for sewing straw, the sailor, boater or sennit straw coated with shellac from India became very popular. Englishmen wore it "a-punting on the Thames." As already noted in the late eighteenth century, the name sennit straw owes its origin to the nautical language of the sailor, "seven-knit," a method of braiding rope.

The soft cap with visor, made from the cloth of the jacket, was taken up by the man of fashion for sportswear, a favorite which the Englishman has never relinquished. The montero cap of knitted wool or fur continued to be worn by woodsmen and was especially favored by the American Westerner. The refugee Empress Eugénie in London at the time of the English arctic exploration, presented the sailors with knitted montero caps which they called "Eugenie's wigs."

Colored satin linings were a feature of the masculine hat. A white satin lining was very often "hand-painted" with landscape or sporting scene, some-times with ballet girls and even nudes, the fad lasting to the 'nineties.

The fashionable man continued to wear the monocle, especially the Eng-lishman, who acquired quite a manner in his use of the glass.

There was nothing new in military headgear in this decade. The forage cap or kepi was the headcovering in the Franco-Prussian War and the topee or pith helmet was for tropical use.

The prevailing feminine coiffure of the 'seventies was the waterfall which savored quite a bit of the pre-Revolution headdress of a century earlier. The waterfall with its back of cascading curls, rolls or thick loose braids in cadogan fashion made use of false hair over horsehair cushions for greater bulk. Never before was false hair so generally worn.

The front was often cut into bangs, straight or crimped, "piccadilly fringe" the English name. Another amusing but inelegant name was that given the little ringlets on either side of the forehead, "spit-curls." Ears were uncovered and toward the end of the period, the vogue of false hair diminished with the appearance of a simpler hairdo.

Ribbon bows at the back of the head were "cadogan bows." The "gondolier net" was a wide meshed net of black silk braid which encased the back half of the hair with cadogan bow in back and sometimes in front. A scarlet net was worn in the evening.

The evening coiffure was built up in back in waterfall fashion topped by flowers, feathers and aigrettes. Steel, jet and bronze bead ornaments, especially buckles, were a new note in hair decoration. In England, the coiffure of the 1850's with hair parted in the middle and drawn low over the ears to a chignon in back remained in fashion to the 'eighties.

Tumbling curls, large cadogans, flowers and plumes of hair and hat repeated the silhouette of the dress with draperies caught up in back over a bustle. "Tied-back time" is the English name for the period.

Very tiny hats were perched on the top of the head, tipped forward or back, often set higher by means of a bandeau of covered buckram concealed by flowers and ribbon.

The lingerie cap now worn with teagown and in the boudoir, was a very small bit of lace, frills and ribbons. For evening or the promenade, it was a shirred disc of satin, lace or velvet with ornamental strings hanging in front or lace-edged lappets floating in back. Hats were often worn with evening dress at formal dinners.

Hats and bonnets were elaborate affairs, often overdone, in combinations of several different fabrics and kinds of ornamentation. Velvet, silk, felt, kid, horsehair, taffeta, organdie, straw, flowers, lace, feathers and beads of steel, bronze and jet, all combined to make the coquettish headcovering. Steel buckles were a feature and jet beads and lace of jet beads were very smart indeed; in fact, there was a bonnet made entirely of jet beads and named "chevalier."

Sometimes bonnet ties were simply ornamental instead of functional and were fashioned of shirred narrow lace, chenille, plaited ribbon, strings of tiny flowers and even strips of fur. As often, the small hat and bonnet were pinned to the hair by a long jeweled hatpin topped with gold, jet or pearl head.

Bonnets were a feminine privilege not permitted to the young lady till she made her début in society or married. Until this event, she wore a hat. The widow in mourning replaced her hat with a bonnet which was of black crêpe with a bit of white ruching near the face. A long heavy black crêpe veil was draped over it.

Each style had its precise name. The "Swedish bonnet" was of black kid and had an amber-headed pin placed in a tuft of feathers on a velvet bow. The white bonnet returned to the mode to be worn with the calling costume and a special model, "Estelle" was of stiffened white tulle or white felt edged with white jet. The loss of Alsace and Lorraine in the Franco-Prussian War was noted in Paris by large Alsatian bows placed in front of the hat. A traveling hat in straw, forerunner of the popular feminine sailor and called the "midshipman," had a double or triple Alsatian bow in front. One could go on indefinitely with hats and their names.

The perennial postilion shape which Paris designated as the Rubens and the English as the Rembrandt was revived. It is to be observed in the Van Dyck portraits and took this name also.

Occasionally seen in the 'seventies was a feminine version of the mannish Tyrolese hat of felt with ribbon band and small wings or a bird as ornamentation. It was to become a fashion of the next decade under the name of fedora.

The war between Russia and Turkey occasioned many Russian names for bonnets and hats of plush and fur, the fur of the sea otter the favorite.

The nose veil of black or white lace or tulle was tied tightly in back, forming wrinkles across the face. Inez veils worn in mantilla fashion were of Spanish blonde lace or tulle edged with lace and there were the Sita or East Indian veil and the Egyptian veil crossed in back and tied in front. The bridal coiffure was dressed with myrtle or orange blossoms and the large square of white tulle which hung to the floor was placed over all, covering the face.

The colors of the period were rich in tone such as lotus blue, copper red, Van Dyck red, otter brown, violet purple and a blue-green called Venetian heliotrope. Special combinations of colors were plum and otter and Russian green and moss. Green was the color of the day in verdigris, frog green, bottle green, canary and sage.

Earrings were generally worn, a small dainty design for the young lady and her tiny sister, and lovely long elaborate ones for the matron.

No lady used make-up or was to be suspected of such a practice, even though she might most discreetly employ a dash of powder and rouge. Beautifying methods consisted of steaming and lathering the face to thoroughly cleanse the skin.

1870 to 1880

black silk
top hat-
French-
1875

fawn, gray
or white
cloth
top hat-
black
silk band-
English

center part-
mustache
and whiskers-
monocle-
English

gray felt
bowler with
black band-
American-
1879

soft felt-
ribbon
band-
French

straw
sailor-
ribbon band-
English

black or
brown felt
bowler-
American-
1879

the
"fore-and-aft" cap
for traveling
and sports-
plaid woolen
with earflaps-
English

light colored
soft felt
with black
ribbon band-
French

fawn or gray
cloth- black
grosgrain
band-
American-
1876

brown felt
"melon"-
French-
1870

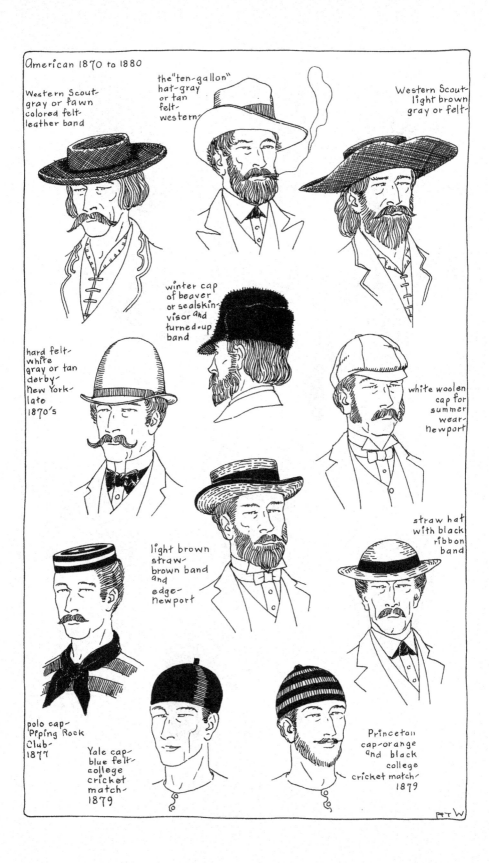

American 1870 to 1880

Western Scout-
gray or fawn
colored felt-
leather band

the "ten-gallon"
hat-gray
or tan
felt-
western

Western Scout-
light brown
gray or felt-

winter cap
of beaver
or sealskin-
visor and
turned-up
band

hard felt-
white
gray or tan
derby-
New York-
late
1870's

white woolen
cap for
summer
wear-
newport

light brown
straw-
brown band
and
edge-
newport

straw hat
with black
ribbon
band

polo cap-
Piping Rock
Club-
1877

Yale cap-
blue felt-
college
cricket
match-
1879

Princeton
cap-orange
and black
college
cricket match-
1879

1870 to 1880

puffs over padding-fringe over forehead-French-1871

cadogan dressed over horsehair cushion-straw hat-flowers-aigrette-English-1870

"gondolier net" black silk braid-shirred ribbon edge-"cadogan bow" French-1870

straw bonnet-velvet ribbon-daisies-tied spotted veil-English

yellow straw-black velvet ribbon rosettes and ruching-French-1871

gray felt-black velvet edge-mauve taffeta ribbon-gray tulle veil-French-1871

"toilette de promenade" rose satin crown and bowknot-white velvet edge-white ostrich-shirred white lace strings-French-1870

small "Rubens" hat-grosgrain ribbon and feathers-New York-1870

hat worn with bathing suit-straw with shirred silk-silk caul-French-1870

RTW

1870 to 1880

white felt—white
lace frilling—
narrow black
velvet ribbon—
pink roses in
chou of spotted
blue tulle—
rose and sky
satin ribbon—
French—
1873

yellow straw—
white lace
ruching-bandeau
with yellow ribbon—
sky blue ostrich
and bow knot—
pink roses—
French—
187

draped
black satin hat—
black paradise—
golden brown feathers
and satin rosette
at hair—
French—
1873

black silk riding hat—
green
veil
English
1873

natural
straw-beige
ribbon—
red poppy—
blue grapes—
daisies—
French-1874

toque—black
jet lace—
black velvet crown
and ribbon-peacock
blue ostrich—gold
colored rose—
French-1873

evening coiffure—
gold diadem
black
enamel—
pearls—
French—
1873

evening
cap-net with lace—
French-1872

bridal
veil—tulle
over myrtle
vine—
French-1874

RTW

1870 to 1880

green velvet
tam-o'-shanter·
green satin chou·
green feathers-
French-
1875

"Alsatian
bow"- beige
ribbon and
ostrich-
brown velvet
sewn with
bronze beads
French-
1875

natural
straw-red
ribbon lined
with yellow-
hanging
cherries-
French-
1875

white
velvet
"calling
hat"-
tan satin ribbon-
red roses-
French-
1875

black velvet bonnet-
shirred brim-
pink rosebuds
in chou of
black tulle-
black velvet
tabs and
ties-French-
1878

evening
coiffure
dressed
over horsehair
cushions-
aigrette and
ostrich-
French-
1875

skating
cap of
sealskin-
crushed velvet crown-
English-
1876

evening
coiffure-
puffs and
cadogan-
French-
1877

evening coiffure-
cabochon of
forget-me-nots-
French-1876

RTW

1870 to 1880
English-French-American

boy-
Scotch
bonnet
Balmoral-
blue cloth-
red and
white diced band

little girl-
white felt-
ostrich-
ribbon band

felt hat-
velvet edge-
ostrich-
satin ribbon

straw sailor
with
velvet
ribbon

hair
tied
with
ribbon

black velvet-
garden flowers
and
bird

felt hat
with velvet
band and
bird - small girl

hat of
taffeta-
accordion
pleated frills-
contrasting
color band
and chou

boy
wearing
straw
sailor

boy
wearing
sailor's cap-
blue cloth-
white band-
red pompon

boy wearing
Scotch bonnet
Glengarry-
blue cloth-
black ribbon-
white feathers

RTW

1880-1890

CHAPTER SEVENTEEN

IN THIS DECADE, fashionable men gradually gave up wearing a beard, that face adornment being retained only by older and professional men. The mustache was universally worn.

The black silk top hat held its position as the dress hat. The derby gained in popularity, filling the need for something between formal and casual hats. The hard straw or boater also took hold and the growth of interest in sports created comfortable soft hats of varied style.

The puggaree or puggree appeared, a scarf of white cotton or silk wrapped round the crown of the straw hat. It originated in India, where it is used as a protection against the sun and the name is "pagri," a form of turban.

The soft felt of Tyrolese origin later called the Homburg, after the place of its manufacture, was being worn more universally. Other names for the hat were the Alpine and the fedora, the latter the name of the heroine "Fedora" in Sardou's drama produced in Paris in 1882.

A white linen cap with visor was worn for bicycling, baseball and polo.

The feminine coiffure was now in a simpler mood, dressed close to the head and up in back with the bun usually on top. The silhouette was softened by a mass of curled fringe over the forehead and tiny ringlets on the nape and to the front of the ears. The front view of massed curls over the forehead, topped by the small bonnet, resembled that towering headdress of the seventeenth century, the fontange.

The bun on top of the head was held secure by a comb of ivory, tortoise shell or amber, headed by a plain band or a row of knobs. Often, a small bow of satin or velvet nestled in the hair but that was all, as elaboration in ornament was confined to the costume.

Bowknots were worn with the evening coiffure, a rosette of fine lace sometimes added. A favorite and formal ornament was a cluster of three ostrich tips with an aigrette. A costly decoration was the diamond-encrusted star worn singly or in pairs.

In the 'eighties, one notes the increased appearance of even rows of waves around the head done with the curling iron. There was also the "Lily Langtry wave," a curled coiffure with crimped bangs and low chignon worn by the English actress (1852–1929) famed as the most beautiful woman in the world. She was born on the Island of Jersey, thus her title, the Jersey Lily. Her first appearance in America was in 1882.

Her rival was our own Lillian Russell (1851–1922) whose first appearance was in vaudeville in 1881. Both women were blondes, which was responsible for the vogue of blond hair lasting to the end of the century. Many women, especially of the theater, resorted to bleaching, the term "peroxide blonde" denoting the artificially acquired golden color.

Hats and bonnets were built up high with standing ornamentation in wings, aigrettes, tightly curled ostrich, stuffed birds, wired ribbon loops of taffeta, satin and velvet. Bonnets were held to the head by short ribbon ties or pinned on with jeweled hatpins. The capote or carriage bonnet was cut away in back very much like the hood of a cabriolet, hence the name. The postilion shape continued in fashion, known by the names of the seventeenth-century portrait painters Van Dyck, Rubens and Rembrandt.

While light colors were seen in summer, the tone of the period was dark in muted shades of green, red, plum, dark blue and the staples black and gray. Brown was the dominant color.

In straw, the midshipman or sailor hat was popular, also the Breton sailor with upturned brim. The female of the species adopted the masculine fedora and the derby for sports wear, especially for hunting, "cycling," archery and "mountaineering." Such hats were finished with a ribbon band, a pair of wings or a stuffed bird. The tam-o'-shanter is often seen in contemporary pictures, ladies wearing the "tam" for "lawn tennis" and bowling. For yachting there was the masculine white cap with visor, and ladies also liked the man's hunting cap, the fore-and-aft cap of tweed.

Many ladies preferred the cambric sunbonnet for tennis worn with the day dress of the prevailing mode. The cap was known here and in France as the Charlotte Corday, in England retaining its old name, the Ranelagh mob.

Cut steel, jet and bronze beads in pins and buckles were employed as ornamentation. The craze for stuffed birds, even small seagulls, was the beginning of the devastating toll of bird life.

Mourning was rigidly observed with much dull black crêpe on dress and hat. The widow's small black crêpe bonnet lightened by a bit of white ruching near the face was heavily draped with a long crêpe veil.

The bridal costume was now invariably all-white with a long veil of lace or tulle and orange blossoms or myrtle in the hair.

In this period of no cosmetics, the complexion was, however, well protected with shade hats and parasols in the summer and gauze veils in the winter.

In 1886 appeared the book *Little Lord Fauntleroy* written by the English-American novelist Mrs. Frances Hodgson Burnett (1849–1924), a book responsible for a tremendous vogue of boys' clothes in the style worn by the young hero. They were the creation of Reginald Birch, the artist who illustrated the story and many a youngster secretly hated him for being compelled to wear long hair, a picturesque plumed hat together with a velvet suit and lace collar.

Earrings were very small, usually a gem set in a tiny gold and enameled flower or a single stone such as a diamond of modest size studding the lobe of the ear. A fashion note of October 1886 mentions the return of the eyeglass with the long handle, "the rage in Paris and seen in the hands of elegant ladies." It further states that for general use the frame is of light or dark tortoise shell and for the theater, enameled gold set with colored stones.

Viewed in the light of later times, the following note is interesting. In 1854, the American Commodore Perry succeeded in opening the door of Japan to Western civilization. The Japanese were quick to take up the modern ways of the Occident and in 1886, the Empress decreed that the ladies of the court adopt the European costume of the mode and the American headdress.

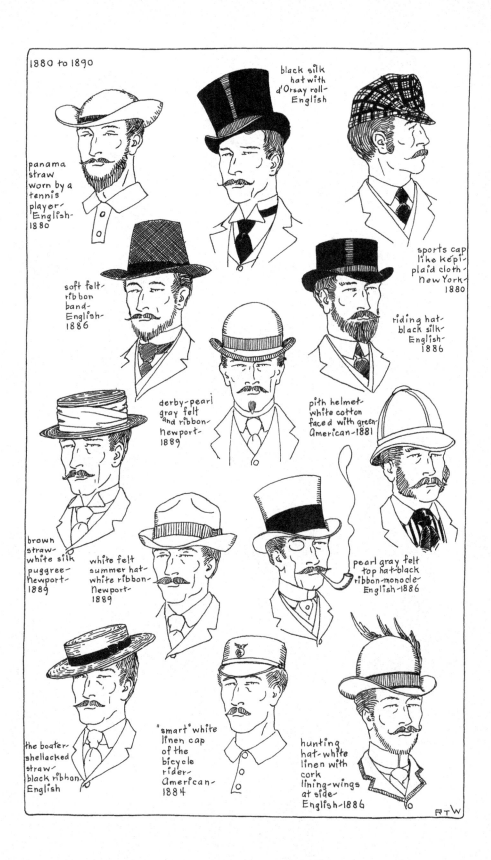

1880 to 1890

black silk hat with d'Orsay roll- English

panama straw worn by a tennis player- English- 1880

sports cap like kepi- plaid cloth- New York- 1880

soft felt- ribbon band- English- 1886

riding hat- black silk- English- 1886

derby-pearl gray felt and ribbon- Newport- 1889

pith helmet- white cotton faced with green- American-1881

brown straw- white silk puggree- Newport- 1889

white felt summer hat- white ribbon- Newport- 1889

pearl gray felt top hat-black ribbon-monocle- English-1886

the boater- shellacked straw- black ribbon- English

"smart" white linen cap of the bicycle rider- American- 1884

hunting hat-white linen with cork lining-wings at side- English-1886

RTW

1880 to 1890

fringe-
puffs and
chou of
curls held
by barettes-
English
1885

court
headdress-
three white
ostrich tips-
floating
tulle veil-
diamond stars-
English

evening coiffure-
center part-
fringe-
gardenias
and leaves-
French-
1885

evenly
waved hair-
shell comb
with knobs-
English
1886

evening
coiffure in
pompadour-
pink rosebuds-
lace fan-
French-
1889

crimped
bangs-hair
rolled up
into topknot-
English-
1885

hair dressed
in loops-
English-
1886

evening
coiffure
up in
back-fringe
over forehead-
English-
1884

evening
coiffure-
yellow satin
and white
lace-
English-
1887

front half
of hair
fringed and
crimped-black
moiré ribbon-
English-
1886

bridal headdress-
lace rosette-orange
blossoms-long tulle veil-
American-1889

RTW

1880 to 1890

opera bonnet of lace-pink satin bow-pink rose-English-1886

brown taffeta-pink lace frills-pink picot edged ribbon-French-1885

black lace bonnet edged with jet beads-black velvet bow-pansies-French-1884

black satin bonnet-white lace fan and border-yellow grosgrain ribbon bow and ties-beaded wired black lace sprays-French-1886

navy blue taffeta-red ribbon-yellow feathered cockscomb-French-1887

house cap-pleated white lace-old blue velvet ribbon-English-1884

black satin capote-black lace-straw braid-black jet beads-white ostrich and aigrette-French-1886

widow's bonnet-long veil pleated crêpe-silk crêpe band with white crêpe-French-1885

pink felt, ribbon and gardenias-ivory lace-gray ostrich-French-1885

full mourning-long crêpe veil pinned over bonnet-French-1885

RTW

1880 to 1890

gray felt~gray
plumes tightly
curled~blue
and yellow
striped ribbon~
French~
1888

brown
velvet~
ivory
lace~pink
ostrich and
ribbon~
English~
1887

gray felt
with
black velvet~
gray bird
French~
1884

hat of
Persian
lamb~bird
of paradise~
French~
1886

summer bonnet~
pale blue
taffeta and
variegated
petunias~
English~
1885

Tyrolese hat
of brown felt
or straw with
wide grosgrain
ribbon~
French~
1884

brown
straw~pale
blue figured
gauze~yellow
roses~
English~
1884

bonnet of
turquoise blue
velvet~red bird~
French~
1885

beaver and
brown
satin~
English~
1885

red velvet~
three gray
birds~
French~
1886

RTW

1880 to 1990

navy
blue
velvet-
gray satin
ribbon-
blue ostrich-
English-
1886

poke bonnet-dusty
yellow taffeta-
yellow velvet
band-yellow
plumes-
French-
1883

plum
colored
velvet and
silk-white
ostrich-
English-
1884

black beaver-
black satin
ribbon-shaded
rose and
brown plume-
French-
1886

bonnet of
brown lace with
gold thread
stitching-chou
of brown
satin sewn
with bronze
spangles-beige
colored bird-
English-
1885

brown lace
and dark
red velvet
ribbon-
English-
1884

yellow straw-
royal blue velvet
ribbon-garden
flowers-
French-
1883

embroidered yellow taffeta-
high crown black satin
folds-black ostrich-
French-1887

sage green bonnet-
taffeta crown-
straw brim-
violet velvet ribbon-
French-
1885

RTW

1880 to 1890 - Sports

gray felt riding hat with gray veil - English - 1886

small felt fedora - silk band bird - archery tournament - New York - 1880

riding hat - black felt derby - English - 1884

"midshipman" or straw sailor - striped ribbon - English - 1884

attired for tennis - sun bonnet - yellow cambric - English - 1886

"fore-and-aft" hunting cap woolen cloth - tied up side flaps - French - 1885

riding hat - black silk - English - 1883

white felt - brown velvet - yellow bird - French - 1885

straw sailor - yellow with blue and purple band - French - 1884

"yachting cap" white cloth or linen - white leather visor - French - 1886

Breton sailor - navy or black straw - American - early 1880's

white woolen tam-o'-shanter worn for tennis - English - 1881

RTW

1880 to 1890
English • French • American

riding
hat-
black felt
derby-
hair tied
black ribbon-
1885

all white-
beaver hat-
silk band-
ostrich-
gauze
veil
crossed in
back-tied
in front-
1886

felt hat
with
velvet
ribbon and
ostrich-
1884

dark
red
velvet-
gray bird-
1886

boy wearing
"Little Lord
Fauntleroy"
hat-felt
or straw
with ostrich-
1886

black felt
derby-
early
1880's

small girl
with
ribbon-tied
hair-
1885

straw hat-
satin ribbon-
satin facing-
1884

tam-o'-shanter-
velveteen with
ribbon stripes-
1883

tam-o'-shanter of
velveteen-silk pompon-
1886

brown
straw
sailor
hat-
brown
ribbon-
newport-
1889

boy's
"Turkish cap"
red cloth
with
woolen
tassel-
1885

RTW

1890-1900

CHAPTER EIGHTEEN

IN THIS LAST DECADE of the century, the "fin de siècle" or "Gilded Age" as we Americans say, the clean-shaven face and the mustache-adorned visage vied with each other in popularity. The small waxed mustache and the monocle were the signs of the "dude," the fastidious dresser of the period. He was the incroyable or dandy of this age. The trim Van Dyck beard was favored by the professional man. The fashionable young man parted his hair in the middle or slightly to one side with locks perfectly straight, curls having entirely disappeared. The "Cholly Knickerbocker" or "football haircut" were names for the style.

In headgear, the many different styles that had become part of the well-dressed man's wardrobe over the nineteenth century were here to stay, varying slightly from season to season. The black silk topper remained the dress hat while the derby in black, brown or English tan was generally worn.

By the 'nineties, the fedora had acquired British styling and royal prestige in being worn by the Prince of Wales, later Edward VII of England, from

1901 to 1910. Photographs show him wearing the hat at Bad Homburg. The hat was manufactured at Homburg, hence its name. In one picture, he wears a white felt with white ribbon and ribbon-bound edge.

The boater or hard straw became the generally worn summer hat. The loss of it by sudden gusts of wind was prevented by a black silk cord or elastic worn round the crown with an end attached to the wearer's coat lapel.

To the Orient moved a great part of the Italian and English straw hat business. The volcanic content of the soil, especially that of Japan, produced a superior wheat straw to which were added low labor cost and Oriental dexterity in providing new weaves.

The vogue of the panama as a smart summer hat had its beginning in this decade. It was in 1895 that American sailors bought bales of unblocked, unlined panamas and sold them here in the streets of American ports. The panama had been worn for a long time by the British in the tropics and in our South where it was known as the "planter's hat."

The panama had been made for nearly three centuries in Ecuador but takes its name from Panama where it was marketed. The finest hats are made in Monte Cristi and known by that name. Several months are required for the making of a high-grade hat while one of ordinary quality can be completed in a week. The splitting of carefully selected young leaves of the jipijapa is done by hand in an exceedingly moist atmosphere to prevent the straw becoming brittle. From this fact arises the fallacy that the weaving is done under water. The only time the hat is immersed in water is when the completed job is washed. Some hats are so finely plaited that the texture resembles closely woven linen and the value varies, according to quality and weave, from twenty to two hundred dollars.

American soldiers returned to the cocked hat of a century earlier, in the large felt of the Spanish-American War of 1898–1899. But this time it was in khaki, the crown creased and the brim cocked on one side only. It came to be known as the "rough rider hat" after Colonel Theodore Roosevelt's troop of Rough Riders.

The experience of the British Army in India brought into effect the beginning of camouflage in warfare and Great Britain adopted khaki and olive drab for the army uniform, which we followed.

A dandy of the 'nineties was E. Berry Wall, New Yorker. At first a businessman, he became a leader of fashion, enjoying the title "the best-dressed man in America." He went to Paris to live in 1912 where he carried on the traditions of his position in "le beau monde." He attempted without success to revive in 1930 the top hat for general wear, but that fashion, except for dress, had definitely passed.

The feminine coiffure was simple, dressed up in back in a topknot, a Psyche knot or low into a chignon or "figure eight" and usually off the ears. The manner of twisting or rolling the hair over in back of the head was the French roll or twist. New was the dipping of a curl over the forehead in center front and "spit curls" at the temples were effected. The size of the head tended to increase from the middle of the decade, the hair brushed over a pad. The side part was occasionally seen.

The arrangement of the evening coiffure was the same as for day. To the topknot was often added a small ribbon bowknot or a cluster of tiny ostrich tips from which protruded the smallest of aigrettes. There were small ornamental combs in Spanish style of tortoise shell with rhinestones or pairs of side combs.

A Parisian coiffeur named Marcel was most expert in the use of his curling irons in dressing the hair into carefully arranged waves around the head and by the turn of the century, the "marcel wave" was very fashionable.

There were few good hairdressers outside of Paris. New York could boast of only two or three.

About this time, the bent hairpins of iron and brass wire were superseded by pins of tempered steel wire which were lacquered black or bronze.

The use of cosmetics was still frowned upon and make-up was confined to an almost imperceptible touch of rouge and only a "dash" of powder on the nose. The Spanish papers of the seventeenth century were still in use but of French manufacture, small books of thin paper covered with white or rose powder to be rubbed on the face, really the first compacts. Cold cream as a facial beautifier appeared, applied usually upon retiring for the night. Powdered talc or talcum powder, an American contribution, was placed on the market about 1890.

Hats which perched straight and high upon the head were both large and small with trimming standing upright. Ostrich plumes, paradise feathers, aigrettes, heron, goura, wings, stuffed birds and wired bowknots of ribbon, velvet and lace, all rose upward. Feather quills were a new decoration. Steel, bronze and jet buckles were the vogue, and in flowers, violets, roses and garden species were favored. The slaughter of bird life for millinery purposes reached such proportions that public opinion began to take a hand in preventing it.

Hats were made of felt, straw and varied fabrics according to the season. For sports, the fedora or felt, the woolen tam-o'-shanter and the straw sailor were the proper hats. There was no definite sports costume yet, and as to headgear, an English fashion journal recommends that "the hat should not be large and ostrich feathers to be avoided."

In 1897, during the international matches of ladies' hockey, the English contestants wore a cap resembling the masculine cricket cap. Their opponents wore no headcovering, of which one writer approved with the following statement that a hat, "in a game in which hatpins are disbarred as dangerous, is apt to be a source of embarrassment."

The short length or nose veil was fashionable and veils of embroidered net or spotted chiffon were tied in back, hanging loosely in front or drawn tight to the chin.

Children kept their hats on the head by means of an elastic band which passed under the chin. While fond mothers were dressing their small boys like Little Lord Fauntleroy, they were also dressing their little girls in the long frocks and the frilly bonnets created by Kate Greenaway, an English artist (1846–1901) who published a series of "Almanacs" from 1883 to 1897 in which she clothed her child characters in quaint versions of the First Empire fashion.

The 'nineties witnessed the birth of the Gibson girl, a charming American type and the handsome square-jawed Gibson man, the creations of the artist Charles Dana Gibson (1867–1944).

1890 to 1900

black silk top hat- French 1897

pearl gray felt-gray ribbon-worn by the Prince of Wales, later Edward VII at Bad Homburg- 1896

monocle- straw boater- silk band- English 1898

Tyrolese felt hat- silk cord and tassel- feathers- German

panama- black ribbon- Newport

derby-black or brown felt- American- 1890

khaki felt- cord-gilt insignia- American soldier

cap of plaid cloth- American

gray or tan felt-four dents- ribbon band- southern planter- American

center part- monocle- English

panama with ribbon band- American

"football" haircut- American

RTW

1890 to 1900

toque-gray felt
and Persian
lamb-black
velvet bow-
yellow
paradise-
French-
1892

sailor of yellow
felt-orange
velvet
ribbon-
black
ostrich-
gilt buckle-
French-
1892

vanilla
straw-
peacock
blue
velvet-
black
wings-pink rose-
spotted black veil-
French-1892

yachting costume-
blue straw
hat-white
ribbon-
white
quills-white
gauze veil-
French-
1892

sailor of
white straw-pale blue
ribbon-white wings-
French-1892

evening coiffure-
marcel wave-
topknot-silver
ribbon bow-pale
blue ostrich-
French-
1892

evening coiffure-
side part-
rose velvet
bow knot-
French-
1892

saucer hat
of white felt-
black satin
bows-black feathers-
French-
1892

bonnet of pleated
black lace-
beige ribbon-
pink flowers
in crown-
French-
1892

RTW

1890 to 1900

"saucer bonnet" gray felt gray satin ribbon - red roses and buds - American 1891

taupe gray felt and satin ribbon - French - 1891

"Spanish toque" pale blue velvet - blue ostrich - pink satin roses - silver band - French - 1891

evening hat - all yellow - felt - satin ribbon and ostrich - French - 1891

yellow straw - pink satin ribbon - pink ostrich - 1892

tricorne - navy blue felt, grosgrain ribbon, pompons - black paradise - hair in cadogan - black taffeta ribbon - American - 1891

evening coiffure - pompadour - twist and figure eight - ostrich tips - aigrette - American 1892

natural straw - white petunias - green foliage - French - 1891

French roll in back - topknot and puffs - French - 1890

RTW

1890 to 1900

velvet hat
with
paradise-
satin
chou-
New York

riding
hat-
black silk-
New York-
1896

brown felt
fedora or
Alpine hat-
wings-
spotted
veil-worn
"cycling"-
Newport

tam-o'-shanter
for "cycling"-
plaid woolen-steel
buckle-black quills-
black taffeta
bow in hair-
American-
1895

evening coiffure-
side part-
figure eight in
back-ostrich tip-
French-
1893

brown
velvet-
turned-up
brim-
brown and
white
ostrich-
French-
1894

beige straw
faced with
black velvet-
black wings-green
ribbon bow knots-
New York-
1895

black velvet with
black and royal
blue ostrich plumes-
spotted veil-
French 1893

sailor hat
for yachting-
white straw
with blue and
white ribbon-
French-
1893

RTW

1890 to 1900

yachting cap - white linen -
black leather band and visor -
New York -
1895

small
toque -
violet velvet -
gray ostrich
and goura -
New York -
1895

white woolen
tam-o'-shanter -
red pompon -
hair in
marcel wave -
French -
1896

bridal
headdress -
marcel wave -
topknot -
long white
tulle veil over
cluster of
orange blossoms -
French -
1897

sailor hat
for yachting -
black
straw
white
ribbon -
white spotted
veil -
New York -
1898

felt fedora -
crushed silk
band with
jeweled
brooch -
Newport -
1896

black straw -
red and white
geranium blossoms -
red taffeta loops -
New York -
1894

toque of
shirred velvet
frills with
paradise -
French -
1898

evening coiffure
with
black wings -
French -
1895

RTW

1890 to 1900
English-French-American

felt hat-
ribbon
band
and
feathers

bonnet of
frilled
taffeta-
ribbon
ties

white
woolen
tam-o'-shanter

velvet hat-
ribbon
band and
loops

natural straw-
navy blue
ribbon

hat of
white
horsehair
with pansies

"Kate Greenaway"
bonnet
(mobcap)
white
lawn-
ribbon-
rose

boy's
straw
sailor-
navy blue
band

shirred
taffeta
bonnet

straw
bonnet-
shirred silk
facing-lace frill-
satin ribbon loops

boy's
checked
woolen
cap

straw hat-
garden flowers-
velvet ribbon

RTW

1900-1910

CHAPTER NINETEEN

THE TWENTIETH CENTURY found Paris firmly established as dictator of fashion in the feminine world and London, the arbiter of men's apparel.

The masculine haircut parted in the middle was seen until 1905, replaced then by the side "part." The clean-shaven face predominated but there was also the occasional small waxed mustache of the dude, the Van Dyck of the professional man and the rare side whiskers of elderly gentlemen.

All the hats and caps of the preceding century had become the staples of this new period. The silk hat, the centenary of which was celebrated in Paris in 1905, remained the dress hat worn evenings but more especially to afternoon receptions and Sunday church. The more practical gibus or collapsible opera hat of grosgrain silk was rediscovered and worn with the tail coat and the black Homburg or derby with the dinner coat. The opera hat had almost disappeared in the latter part of the nineteenth century. The gray top hat worn by Englishmen, especially to the races, is rarely seen in the States.

The principal day hats were the derby and the fedora or Homburg. Black was the general color of the derby with brown the choice of the "fancy dresser." City men wore the black Homburg, changing to gray in summer but the fastidious man changed to his straw hat, the boater or the panama, definitely in the month of May.

From the Philippines, China and Japan came the many fine and fancy straws employed in the making of both men's and women's summer hats.

More and more men took to wearing the expensive panama hat. Both panama and hard straw carried a ribbon band of college or club stripes. The visored cloth cap was decidedly popular for sports, travel and motoring and polo players adopted the pith helmet. The aviator's helmet of this period resembled that of the football player, a padded leather cap with flaps which fastened under the chin.

A Frenchman, M. André de Fouquières of Paris, typified the beau or dandy of the new century. He was a society man and an authority upon style in men's clothes, often invited to lecture thereon at important gatherings.

The feminine coiffure was dressed in pompadour fashion, but the twentieth century version of the headdress of the Marquise de Pompadour, the favorite of Louis XV was greatly exaggerated in silhouette. The front hair, either straight or waved, was drawn over a "rat" or pad of false hair or a finely meshed wire roll. Many women roughed the under hair with a comb, forming a matted foundation over which the outside hair was dressed. Combings for the purpose were saved in an ornamental container kept on the dressing table.

Topknot, chignon, coronet, braids, switches and clusters of curls were all in fashion but the fluffy coiffure came to an end with the appearance of the carefully arranged undulations of the marcel wave. The side part became popular.

The marcel wave was all the vogue and no doubt inspired the invention of the "permanent wave." That momentous event occurred in London in 1906 and was the creation of Charles Nestlé, a well-known fashionable coiffeur. In the first year, only eighteen women were brave enough to endure the eight to twelve hours necessary for the operation, or rich enough to afford the fee of one thousand dollars.

The craze for blond hair died out with auburn color taking its place and many women making use of henna dye to acquire the reddish hue. Henna, of which the colorful leaves produce the dye, is a small bush which grows in moist localities in Northern Africa and the Orient. It is also called Egyptian privet. That the fashionable world was becoming more tolerant of beautifying aids was apparent. Where the bleached blond hair of the earlier period had met with universal disapproval, the henna-dyed locks were now accepted in "genteel society."

Hair ornaments were small ribbon bowknots, tulle rosettes or a single fresh flower tucked into the chignon behind the ear. The evening coiffure in the second half of the decade was enhanced by the luxurious bunch of bird-of-paradise plumage. For horseback, the hair was usually dressed into a low tight chignon and finished with a large black taffeta ribbon bow. The last year of the period witnessed a complete change in the silhouette with the hair wrapped or swirled round the head and covering the ears, the beginning of the mode of the small head and paving the way to the bob.

Ornamental combs in pairs and threes held the hair in place for both day and evening dress. Fashionable was the large single comb of tortoise shell or amber decorated with gold filigree, baroque pearls and colored stones.

The bent hairpins were two to four inches long, lacquered black or bronze and new, was the "invisible hairpin" of very fine wire of a shorter length. There were also hairpins of varying shape, size and color fashioned of shell, amber, bone, hard rubber, horn and celluloid.

Until the latter years of the period, the feminine hat in general flared up and off the face, a bandeau setting it still higher on the head. Many long hatpins, usually jeweled, held the hat securely in place. Larger and larger grew the hat, by 1907 attaining an incredible size. In this period the theater ruling arose, compelling a woman to remove her hat during the performance.

The picturesque large velvet hat, the Gainsborough or Marlborough of the eighteenth century, was revived. In tailored hats, sailors and tricornes of mannish felts were smart, also fur toques for winter. In 1903 appeared the cartwheel type of sailor of straw for summer wear and named the "Merry Widow" after the popular operetta by the Viennese composer, Franz Lehar. This extremely large sailor was also worn with the riding habit.

Huge quantities of paradise, ostrich, aigrettes covered the hat in place of the former flowers and ribbon. The pleureuse or weeping willow ostrich plume with flues lengthened by additional tied ones, was extremely popular, and long quills were "chic."

The vast destruction of bird life brought about the organization in the United States in 1905 of the National Audubon Society which was responsible for the Audubon Plumage Law preventing the slaughter of native birds and the importation or merchandising of paradise or aigrettes in this country. Artistic substitutes were created of goose and chicken feathers, beautifully dyed and fashioned into wings and cockades.

In the early twentieth century, the street costume was still an elaborate affair judged by today's clothes and the dressy hat was worn at all hours of the day, accompanying a train on suit or dress. It was customary for the modish woman to wear her new spring hat on Easter Sunday, especially to church.

About 1907, the large brim turned down; next, the bandeau was eliminated, permitting the hat to settle down on the head, forced to a more secure position by the open motor car. A wide chiffon veil, two or three yards in length, enveloped head and hat and was tied under the chin when "automobiling." Bonnets of silk were especially designed for motoring and called "automobile bonnets." Goggles were a very necessary protection for the eyes from the dust of the poor roads.

The tam, fedora and a panama resembling the man's hat, were worn for sports, the linen cap with leather visor for yachting and the silk top hat and derby for horseback.

The vogue of the face veil continued unabated, tied tightly under the chin or hanging loosely from the hat. There were lace and colored chiffon veils, also coarse filet meshes spotted with chenille or velvet dots. Sometimes veils were lace-edged. Bright green was the favored color of the "automobile veil," considered the most effective protection for the complexion.

The twentieth century found women becoming "make-up conscious." Tiny powder boxes of gold or silver were carried in the handbag. Compact powders appeared in white, flesh, rachel and rouge and a novelty was vanishing cream. The delicately scented toilet waters were being replaced by rare and costly perfumes. But any of these beautifiers were still applied discreetly and in the privacy of a "lady's boudoir." The first beauty shop outside of Paris was opened in London by an English woman and followed in the same decade by a branch in New York. A few hairdressing establishments were in existence but this is the first instance of the beauty shop for face treatments presided over by a "specialist."

The fashionable woman preferred the simple pearl ball earring. Until this period, the pierced lobe of the ear held the pendant or screw earring but now, a new form of screw on the earring eliminated piercing the ear. The large round lens was used in gold and silver lorgnettes and spectacle frames fashioned of tortoise shell were very smart.

1900 to 1910

leather hood over padded helmet worn by an "aeroplane or airship driver" English-1910

gibus or opera hat-black grosgrain silk

pearl gray felt Homburg-ribbon edge and band

black felt derby

gray beaver hat worn by a Western senator

panama in "pork pie" fashion

side part-prevailing coiffure

cap of herring bone tweed

straw boater with college band

black silk topper-broadcloth band

"pork pie" felt with college band

RTW

1900 to 1910

evening
coiffure-
pompadour-
braid-
figure eight-
pink rose-
American-
1902

evening
coiffure-
top knot-
pompadour-
tortoise
shell comb-
French-
1901

toque of
pleated
magenta
chiffon-
pink rose-
French-
1901

pleated chiffon
over wire frame-
roses and
ribbon bowknots-
French-
1903

yellow straw
sailor hat-
black velvet
band-
French-
1902

evening coiffure-
pompadour
in marcel wave-
puffs in back-
French-
1903

black silk
riding hat-
broadcloth
band-
English-
1903

the ends of
the hair
twisted into
a puff on
top-
French-
1904

coral satin
hat-green
weeping
ostrich
plumes-
French-
1904

RTW

1900 to 1910

the "Merry Widow" straw sailor - black, white or natural - New York - 1904

white felt faced with black velvet - black and yellow paradise - French - 1906

white straw faced with black taffeta - bright green bird - French - 1905

white straw with pink roses - white aigrette - French - 1905

beige felt - violets draped with beige chiffon veil - French - 1906

day or evening coiffure - side part - figure eight in back - French - 1907

riding hat black felt derby - taffeta ribbon bow - New York - 1904

evening coiffure - tea roses - brown and yellow paradise - French - 1907

RTW

1900 to 1910

"burnt orange"
straw-emerald
green velvet band-
green wings-
amber ball
pin-
English-
1907

black velvet-
weeping ostrich plumes
shaded blue and cerise-
French-
1908

the
marcel
wave with
puffs-
French-
1907

black straw-
Venice lace
round crown-
white ostrich-
black veil-
French-1909

white straw-
white tulle
and white
paradise-
French-
1909

black velvet-
black paradise-
hair wrapped
close to head-
French-
1909

hair brushed
to top of
head-ends
held by shell
comb with
knobs-
French-
1909

RTW

1900 to 1910

Eton cap with visor- woolen cloth- 1907

felt faced with lace- taffeta- folds and loops-1902

side part and ribbons- 1902

velvet, silk or lingerie fabric- satin ribbon- c. 1903

tan felt "pork pie"- striped band- 1905

little girl- "Dutch haircut"-white felt hat-white satin rosettes and chinstrap- 1909

pink taffeta hat-white taffeta sash- c. 1905

pompadour- braids and large black taffeta bows

little girl- navy blue beaver with grosgrain band- c.1908

boy- blue cloth sailor cap- black ribbon band

leghorn hat-roses and foliage- satin ribbon-1906

boy with "Dutch haircut"

HTW

1910-1920

CHAPTER TWENTY

THE CLEAN-SHAVEN FACE and the small mustache were both popular in this decade and headgear varied slightly.

An influence of World War I was the general adoption for sports wear by men and women, of that very smart dark blue cap worn by the French Alpine troops, the age-old Basque beret. The Basques, whose origin is not quite clear, are a people living on the French and Spanish sides of the Pyrénées. Two hundred years ago, most of the Basques were sailors and many were great fishermen, a fact which might explain the appearance of the same cap in Scotland. The Scotch bonnet and the beret are the same cap woven in one piece without seam or binding. The Basque beret is either blue or red but the real Scotch bonnet has never been other than blue, and called the "blue bonnet."

The barracks cap of the soldier, the round cap with visor, was replaced by a new forage cap, the "overseas cap" we call it. It resembles the Scotch bonnet, the Glengarry. In World War I, it first appeared on the heads of the soldiers of the Belgian Army but as far back as the American Civil War, a Pennsylvania regiment of Zouaves wore such a cap and, like the Belgian cap, it had a tassel in front. French, English and Americans also adopted the comfortable cap. It was constructed like a helmet, the upturned flap let down and fastened under the chin in inclement weather.

Early in the war, American soldiers wore the broad-brimmed felt campaign hat encircled by a cord. The "Anzacs" or Australians and New Zealanders wore a like hat but with puggree band round the crown. They wear the same hat today and the brim then as now, is often worn cocked on one side.

Modern mechanical warfare revived the need of the "iron hat" of the seventeenth century in the "tin hat" or helmet of steel, worn over a padded leather lining like that of the football player. Modern warfare at the same time created an entirely new and strange-looking headpiece in the gas-mask.

In the feminine world, the tendency was to dress the hair close to the head with the side hair brought forward over ears and cheeks. The use of false hair in braids and postiches was gradually dispensed with. A skillfully and lightly made caplike wig now called a transformation, was often worn by fashionable women when in need of a hairdresser.

In the last years of the decade, the side hair was often cut short and brushed over the cheeks, forerunner of the bob. Some of the mannequins of Paul Poiret (1880's–1944) that great artist couturier of the first quarter of the century, wore bobbed hair cut in Dutch fashion as did some of the youthful dancers of Isadora Duncan's troupe. A few brave women bobbed their hair but shorn locks were not the fashion till the 'twenties. The permanent wave reached America about 1915, being constantly improved and lowered in cost. It was indulged in by practically all fashionable women with straight hair. The vogue for auburn hair prompted many to dye their hair with henna.

The change from the fluffy head to the trim coiffure made for the popularity of the almost invisible net of human hair, especially for day and sports wear. No machinery can make the fragile net which is hand-tied by Chinese women. The latter possess the skill, patience and too, a low cost of living, necessary to the production of the article.

Ornaments in the hair were very popular and worn both day and evening. Such gew-gaws were usually of imitation amber or shell in the form of brooches or Chinese hairpins and worn in pairs. The long pins protruded from topknot or chignon at any odd angle. Large combs with rows of knobs were smart and those encrusted with rhinestones were for evening wear. The fillet or circlet of narrow ribbon or a band of rhinestones reappeared. Upstanding paradise and aigrettes waved from the evening coiffure. Poiret loved to tie a wide crushed band of metal tissue or brilliantly colored silk round the feminine head to accompany his beautiful gowns. He was responsible for the Russian and Oriental influence in headdress and costume in this and the following decades.

The dominant feature of the Russian costume was the elaborate pearl headdress of great value treasured by aristocrat and peasant alike. Among the peasants, the pearl cap usually represented at least half the wearer's fortune. It was worn all day, every day, even in the kitchen, and at night guarded in a casket under her pillow.

Of Byzantine origin was the jeweled headpiece embroidered with gold and silver thread. There are many versions of the gorgeous headdress, the foundation of which was damask, velvet or cloth of gold sewn with priceless pearls, rubies, emeralds or even mother-of-pearl and colored glass. Outdoors, the headdress was always covered with a veil which might be of white muslin, linen, taffeta or heavy silk. The muslin and linen veils were embroidered in colored silk, gold and silver thread and the silk veils likewise embroidered were also fringed with gold and silver.

Many caps were ornamented with brides of pearls or precious stones, a style which appealed to the Western world for evening wear. The headdress of the Russian married woman always covered the top of the head and the open diadem was a sign of maidenhood.

In 1919, after the war and the lifting of the ban on evening dress in the Paris theater, evening headdress reappeared in extravagant fashion in turbans of gold and silver tissue, jewels, feathers, flowers, tulle, jet and pearl tassels and tiaras set with pearls, diamonds or rhinestones.

Hats were both small and large with roomy crowns worn well down on the head, usually to the eyes. Ornamentation flared out or upward. The newer shapes were founded upon all that had gone before: the turban, toque, beret, tricorne, top hat, postilion, sailor and pillbox, made of felt, straw and fabric of every kind.

A new, distinctive and exceedingly smart hat of the last years of the period was the silk hat, a sailor of black silk plush with grosgrain ribbon band. The beehive-shaped crown of many hats was the forecast of the popular cloche of the 'twenties.

Of the mode were aigrettes, paradise, ostrich, wings and wired velvet and silk loops. Here in America, cleverly manufactured substitutes replaced such feathers, as the Audubon Law forbade the importation or sale of osprey, paradise, aigrettes or native wild bird plumage which Paris continued to wear.

After the war, the trend in hat and costume was toward utter simplicity and black. The black cloche, relieved by a jewel, became the classic of the next decade. With the hat hugging the head, hatpins lost their use and instead, became purely ornamental with tortoise shell, amber, pearl or jeweled beads.

Veils, about to disappear with the coming vogue of bobbed hair, were draped over the hat or tied tightly in back. They were of lace, plain and spotted nets and often bordered with wide chiffon bands. A novelty was the harem veil which covered the face from the nose down.

The boudoir cap reappeared but instead of the sheer white lacey lingerie affair of old, it was made of any rich colorful fabric and oftener than not, finished with gold or silver tissue flowers and lace. The boudoir cap accompanied a costly and gorgeous negligee or perhaps a costume composed of Oriental trousers and coat.

In this period of exotic influence in dress, it followed that earrings were popular, ranging from the pearl button to the very long jeweled designs.

The bride wore the traditional white with orange blossoms and tulle or lace veil, but newer was the tiara of stiffened lace or pearls in Russian miter shape.

The use of cosmetics was growing, rouge quite generally worn and powder in light tints. Make-up here in America was tempered to a certain extent by artful application but not so in Paris where cosmetics were frankly applied for effect. The average woman now added lipstick and eyebrow pencil to her beauty aids. The beauty mask treatment became popular, the application of an earth pack over the face, left to harden and kept on for twenty or thirty minutes. There are various kinds of such plaster-like preparations each containing properties considered beneficial to the skin. Masks or packs that could be applied at home, followed on the market, meeting with decided success.

The end of this decade saw "beauty parlors" or "beauty shops" spring into existence even in small towns with service at a price all could afford. The large city department stores gave over a special section to the cult and beauty treatments by specialists became available to women in all walks of life, not only to queens as in bygone days.

1910 to 1920

panama
with
black
ribbon
1911

checked
cloth
cap
1913

black
felt derby-
ribbon band and
edge-eyelets-
anchor cord
round crown
for riding
1910

checked
cloth
pork pie-
machine
stitched
brim-
1912

pith helmet-
white cloth-
green lining-
worn by polo
player

gray cloth
topper-
black ribbon
band-
English-
1914

sports hat-
white or
natural linen-
ribbon band-
stitched brim-
1912

black
silk
topper-
broadcloth
band-
1918

boater or
hard straw-
college or
club band-
1913

tan or gray
Hamburg-
striped
silk
puggree-
1918

riding hat-
felt pork pie-
ribbon band-
1914

RTW

1914 to 1918 – World War I

cloth cap with tassel – Belgian soldier

khaki cloth cap – leather chinstrap – British Army Officer

greenish gray felt – green feather – Italian Alpine soldier

blue woolen béret – French Alpine soldier

khaki cloth – British aviator

padded steel helmet – German

Glengarry bonnet – blue woolen – red and white diced band – black ribbon cockade and strings – Scotch soldier

padded steel helmet – French and Belgian

khaki cover over turban East Indian

padded steel helmet Canadian soldier

"blue cap" black ribbon band – sailor U. S. Navy

"white hat" machine stitched linen – sailor U. S. Navy

British

U. S.

blue cloth cap – earflaps – black leather visor – cockade – black cock feather – Austrian Tyrolese soldier

"overseas cap" khaki cloth – officer U. S. Army

khaki cloth cap – leather chinstrap – Russian soldier

khaki felt puggree of lighter shade – Australian soldier

RTW

1910 to 1920

natural
straw-moss
green velvet
band-wired
ecru lace
bowknot-
New York-
1910

white beaver-
black
aigrette-
black satin
bowknot-
French-1912

riding
hat-
black felt
derby-
black
taffeta
bowknot-
Baltimore-
1910

black velvet-
black aigrette-
black ribbon
rosette-
French-1912

toque of
chinchilla-
white
aigrettes-
French-
1912

felt
hat-silk
band with
pleated
edge-
willow
plume-
French-
1912

evening
coiffure-
diamond
tiara and
paradise-
French-
1913

riding hat-
gray felt-
black ribbon-
Piping Rock-
1913

hair wrapped
round head-held by
circle barettes-French-1914

ATW

1910 to 1920

classic
evening
headdress
of lamé-
jewel over
forehead-
French-
1913

black velvet
cloche-
wired black
satin loops-
French-
1914

evening
headdress-
Russian
tiara of
pearls
and jewels-
1913

black taffeta
hat with
black
feathers-
French-
1914

evening
headdress-
hair in
French roll-
black
aigrettes-
French-
1914

sports hat-
panama-
ribbon band-
New York-
1915

straw hat
with wings-
French-
1916

wired organdy-
ribbon band-
dagger shell
hairpins-
New York-
1915

bathing
headdress-
rubberized satin
black and white
striped kerchief
tied over
rubber cap-
New York-
1915

RTW

1910 to 1920

evening coiffure-
rhinestone fillet-
jeweled disc-
black enameled
wire and rhinestones-
French-
1916

riding hat-
black silk
topper-
broadcloth
band-
English-
1916

sealskin
shako
faced with
amber velvet-
amber pin-
French-
1916

navy blue
beaver, wings
and satin
fold-
New York-
1918

white
straw-
wired
velvet loops-
pearl headed
pins-
French-
1916

evening coiffure-
rose silk
turban-
French-
1918

black straw
sailor-white
silk puggree-
harem veil-net
with chiffon border-
New York-1918

draped
silk
turban-
French-
1918

side part,
French roll,
bangs and
top knot-
French-
1918

draped
black taffeta
toque
with black
feathers-
French-
1918

RTW

1910 to 1920

Red Cross Service—
square of
cotton
cloth
pinned
round
head—
1918

navy blue
beaver
or felt
for winter—
navy blue
straw sailor
for summer—
Navy or
Army nurse—
U.S.
1918

overseas
cap like
British
aviator—
khaki
cloth—
Motor Corps—
U.S. 1918

steel helmet—
London
ambulance
driver—
1918

slate gray
felt hat—
overseas
American
Red Cross—
1918

the
bobbed
coiffure—
1919

beaver hat—
white cock
feathers—
French—
1919

long square
bridal veil—
lace edged
tulle—orange
blossoms—
pearl tiara—
Worth—
1919

black felt
faced with
shirred
cerise velvet—
French—
1920

turban of
draped
beige silk
crêpe—
black plumage—
French—
1919

RTW

1910 to 1920

linen or pongee hat - machine stitched brim - 1911

small girl's hat - straw with shirred chiffon - silk roses and leaves - 1910

cap of green tweed - 1911

girl's hat of plush - feathers and cockade - 1912

small girl's hat - gray velvet - gray ostrich - pink roses - 1912

boy's hat - straw with ribbon band - 1910

knitted silk stocking cap with tassel - 1912

little girl - silk crown - straw brim - spotted ribbon - 1918

sailor cap - blue serge - black ribbon name band - 1919

boy's knitted yarn stocking cap - 1912

boy's hat of linen or pongee - machine stitched brim - 1920

felt hat faced with taffeta - velvet ribbon - wings - 1918

soft felt - grosgrain ribbon band - 1918

girl's hat - velvet with corded silk - silk flowers - 1918

RTW

1920-1930

CHAPTER TWENTY-ONE

ALL THE MASCULINE HATS of the previous period continued in fashion. The sports cap, however, though still worn by the British gentleman, gave way here in the States to the soft felt hat with snap brim for golf, country and sea-shore wear. The "handkerchief felt" it was called, made lightweight and paper-thin, its great advantage being that it could be rolled and packed in a suitcase. It was worn in light shades of pinkish brown, also green, but beige was the favored color. Very popular was the dark blue woolen Basque beret for sports and especially for riding in the revived open motorcar.

Both the beret and the snap brim felt hat were sponsored by that beau of the twentieth century, the Prince of Wales, later for such a short time King Edward VIII of England and now the Duke of Windsor.

In America, Western ranch life lured Easterners to spending their vacations on "dude ranches." Life on a ranch calls for the very large picturesque felt hat, the "ten-gallon hat" or sombrero. Popular too, is the Mexican sombrero of straw, though originally the straw hat was the headpiece of the peasant and the costly felt was worn by the gentleman.

The late 'twenties saw the beginning of the hatless mode, a fashion which originated at the resorts of Southern France and Palm Beach. It lasted through the 'thirties, becoming a real menace to the hat trade.

The bobbed head, occasionally observed in the latter half of the preceding period, was now definitely adopted by the woman of fashion. First appeared the Dutch cut, a length just covering the ears and straight round the head. In 1923, fruitless attempts to revive long hair only succeeded in more firmly establishing the short coiffure in the "boyish bob" or "shingle," very short in back, trimmed to a V at the nape. The popular "wind-blown bob" was a revival of the Titus coiffure of the Directoire period.

Many women, not caring for the bob, found that shoulder-length locks permitted a change in the arrangement of the coiffure besides comfort, at the same time retaining the small head. Other women kept their hair short for convenience but added a postiche to create a dressier hairdo. Transformations, skillfully made and very light, defying detection, were often resorted to for a fashionable head.

Of short duration was an evening fashion of the colored transformation in orange, red, green or mauve. And the eighteenth century practice of tinting the hair returned but it was not done with powder. Instead, smart women with whitening locks, kept their gray hair but used a blue or violet rinse after the shampoo which produced a most flattering effect upon the complexion, a procedure indulged in today.

All women patronized beauty shops to have their hair trimmed, shampooed and set into shape or waves with a plastic lotion while still moist. The permanent wave was so perfected and its cost so reduced that every woman desiring wavy hair could have her wish. The Paris hairdresser Antoine acquired a vast reputation with his individual cut and arrangement of the bobbed head.

With the general adoption of short hair, tiaras, fillets, combs and pins all disappeared, elaborate long earrings making up for the loss. For the first time in centuries, hairpins changed their shape, a smaller pin that would "stay put" being required. The cotter pin of machinery furnished the idea in a pin of flat wire with the ends sprung tightly together. This new gadget is the "bobby pin." Bobby pins and the tiny invisible wire pins were all that was necessary to keep the head trim looking.

After the first World War, hats lost their extravagant and costly ornamentation. The large crown prevailed in toque, turban, tricorne and sailor with narrow or wide brim. Satin, duvetyn, velvet or hatter's plush fashioned winter hats. Summer hats, usually large-brimmed, were of all kinds of fine straws such as hemp, picot, Milan, tagál, transparent horsehair and Neapolitan straw. The summer shade hat was often of linen or chintz and embroidered with brightly colored wools and beads in peasant style. Trimming was confined to feathers of which there were glycerined ostrich, cock feathers, aigrettes made of monkey fur and cockades of tiny feathers or ribbon.

The Oriental turban of plain or richly brocaded metal tissue was a favored evening headdress but, as often, the shingled head unadorned save for long earrings was the general fashion.

A revolution occurred in the millinery world with the appearance of the small untrimmed felt cloche or mushroom shape which hailed from the ateliers of Maison Reboux. It became the rage about 1923, lasting throughout the period. A hood of "chiffon or handkerchief" felt, usually black, brown or beige, was placed on the lady's head and fashioned into shape by cutting and manipulating the felt, a few tucks and stitches completing the operation. A grosgrained ribbon or a handsome jeweled brooch or sometimes both finished the tiny hat.

The cloche did away with the age-old silk lining which was replaced by a grosgrain ribbon band. Fancy hatpins were merely ornaments. The little felt hat fitted skull-tight and was worn winter and summer, accompanying all costumes whether dress or sports, even in the evening. Short hair and tight hat eliminated the veil. By 1927, the uniform shape began to take more individuality in design and color. Flaps resembling the helmet of the ancient Roman warrior came down over the cheeks.

Another well-liked fashion was the turban of tricot fabric draped tightly round the head, a creation of Agnés. And by way of repetition, nothing dimmed the popularity of the Basque beret for sports.

For horseback, correct hats, then as today, were required to resemble as nearly as possible those of the men. The proper riding hats were the black silk topper for dress, the derby and soft felt for winter and the stiff straw or sailor and panama for summer. When hunting, the English woman wore a woolen lace veil tied tightly over her derby while across the Channel her French neighbor wore the traditional black felt tricorne edged with gold galloon.

By this age, every woman, rich or poor, lady of leisure or businesswoman, availed herself of the many fine beauty aids on the market. The application in her boudoir of a make-up base over which she applied rouge and powder and then "glamorized" her eyes with eyebrow pencil, mascara and eye shadow, was no longer a feminine secret. Every handbag had in it a vanity case of artistic design, not necessarily of great cost, which contained powder, rouge and lipstick, all of which she calmly applied in public if repairs were found necessary. Unlike olden times, the contents of all cosmetics were regulated by law to insure that the ingredients were harmless.

The cinema, especially Hollywood, had its effect upon make-up. The Medieval fashion of plucking the eyebrows into a thin line was revived but in this day the eyebrow was reshaped to an arched line with an eyebrow pencil. Since eyebrows naturally grow along the edge of the socket, the operation produced an unpleasant artificial effect. The fashion lasted several years after being carried to an absurd extreme.

Late in the 1920's the smart world went in for lounging on the beach, men and women both acquiring a very brown complexion and immediately, many kinds of oils and lotions appeared to hasten a "sun-tan" or to protect a delicate skin during the process. Brownish face powders for women became the vogue and if one's skin were not of the type to take on a fashionable tan then one painted the flesh the desired color.

We find the American man's prejudice against the use of scent disappearing as he took to toilet water. But it must be noted that his toilet water was definitely prepared for him, of a perfume to suit the masculine taste.

The small square-framed lorgnettes of past days were carried again and in this period we see women for the first time, frankly wearing spectacles when necessary, generally in shell frames, these aids made imperative by motor-car driving.

1920 to 1930

Basque béret worn by the Prince of Wales

the "ten-gallon" hat of the range and dude ranch- pale tan felt-tan ribbon band- American

straw sombrero- colored cord chinstrap with beads- Mexican

black felt derby- ribbon band- English- 1922

panama- black ribbon- worn by the Prince of Wales- 1924

polo helmet with visor- white cotton reinforced throughout- English- 1922

formal hunt cap- black velvet- reinforced crown- black ribbon bow denotes gentleman rider- 1925

checked cloth cap- "Beatty Tilt"- worn by the Prince of Wales- 1922

light colored snapbrim felt-ribbon band-worn by the Prince of Wales

the "very smart" battered soft felt of the American college man- 1926

skullcap of the American college man- 1926

sports hat- machine stitched pongee-pinked bow in back- 1926

leghorn hat- ribbon band- 1927

RTW

1920 to 1930
French

tricorne of beaver
felt with silk
cockade-
1920

lace veil
tied over
draped velvet
toque-
1920

boudoir
cap-lace-
chiffon-
silk roses
and foliage-
1920

bobbed
coiffure
with side
part-
1921

evening
coiffure-
hair
cut shoulder
length-small
chignon-
1921

bridal coiffure-
pearl and
diamond tiara-
tulle veil-
1923

wind-blown
bob-
1922

black satin
turban-
black ostrich-
gold brooch-
Alex-
1921

beige felt hat-
bright colored
wool
embroidery-
1921

beige satin hat
with padded
rolls-
1922

RTW

1920 to 1930
French

day or evening
coiffure-
shingle cut-
1923

formal hat-
black velvet-
black uncurled
ostrich-
Maria Guy-
1923

day or
evening
coiffure-
shingle
cut-
side
part-
1923

white felt
for summer-
felt band-
Reboux
1924

evening
headdress-
colored bead
embroidery on
silver lamé-
pearl strings
1923

straw
cloche
with velvet-
1923

cloche of
brown picot
straw-shaded
brown birds-
Maria Guy-
1924

toque of black
cock
plumage-
Agnès-
1924

"bonnet
Phrygien"-
cobalt blue
felt-ring of
brilliants-
Agnès-
1927

soft beige
felt-tucked
crown-beige
grosgrain
ribbon-
Gaby mono-
1927

dark blue
felt with
felt
wings-
Agnès-
1927

1920 to 1930
Sports

formal hunt hat-black
felt-gold
galloon-
hunt
button-
chignon
with
black
ribbon-
French

riding hat-
black felt
derby-
English

informal
riding
hat of
felt, panama
or leghorn-
American
1925

formal
riding hat-
black silk
topper-
broadcloth
band-
American

polo
helmet-
reinforced-
white cotton-
puggree band-
American

the
"ten-gallon
hat" for
ranch and
western
riding-
beige felt-
American

tied silk
turban band
for
tennis

the
dark blue
Basque
béret

the woolen
tam with
pompon-
1922

the
black silk
sailor-
grosgrain
band-
American-
1921

RTW

1920 to 1930

boy in white linen hat-machine stitched brim

knitted woolen stocking cap-bright green with tan pompon

small girl in red felt tricorne-black ribbon edge

tan felt with brown ribbon band

black velvet riding cap with visor-ribbon bow

girl or boy's white woolen tam

brown velvet hat with dyed brown squirrel-velvet tie round crown

white piqué headband fastened in back-tiny bows

bonnet of white Swiss dotted with red-flower embroidered banding

small girl's cloche of felt or straw-ribbon band

the dark blue Basque béret worn by boy and girl

boy's light brown tweed hat

RTW

1930-1940

CHAPTER TWENTY-TWO

THERE WAS NO CHANGE in the grooming of the masculine head and slight variation of silhouette but a wider choice of color and texture marked the basic mode of men's headgear. In America, the casual soft felt hat was universally adopted for informal wear but the Britisher adhered to his bowler in black or gray. The bowler, Homburg and soft felt were correct for winter wear in town, the silk top hat for formal day or evening and the collapsible opera hat for formal evening dress.

The classic boater or sennit straw continued smart for summer town wear but its popularity was definitely overshadowed by the newcomer of the mid-thirties, the planter's hat. By the last years of the decade, the hatless summer fashion lost its novelty and the lightweight, soft-brimmed, loosely woven straw became very popular. The planter's hat of a variety of palm straw weaves worn by the sugar planters of Jamaica was introduced by way of Nassau, the fashionable winter resort.

To note some of the weaves, there was the mesh weave panama, hanokai, baku, hemp, leghorn, coarsely braided water silk palm, jipijapa and multi-colored raffia. The planter's hat, ranging in color from light to dark brown or mahogany, was encircled by the puggree band of cotton or silk, plain or figured or club stripe. When worn with the summer dinner coat, the puggree was of plain white Indian madras.

Another summer straw hailing from Jamaica was the Spanish style Montego hat, wide-brimmed with flat crown and narrow cord of straw or leather tied at one side.

While the Englishman remained faithful to his woolen cloth "flat cap" for general sportswear on golf course or campus, the brimmed hat of felt, tweed or cotton was preferred in the States.

The simply dressed feminine coiffure of the early 1930's was lacquered into shape, either a slightly longer shingle diagonally swirled across the back of the head or shoulder-length locks done into a horizontal roll or tiny chignon. In 1933 an upward trend became perceptible, the hair brushed away from the temples, off the ears and up in back and by 1937, the coiffure of the 'nineties had returned. The chou of curled bangs reappeared and in 1938, the lacquered pompadour.

Also in the picture were straight bangs and puffs, the loose chignon and that Victorian fashion, the large roll framing the back of the head and called a cadogan. Young women favored the Medieval page boy bob, straight flowing shoulder-length hair with the ends artistically turned under, a style which took hold in 1937. The hatless fashion permitted the dressy hairdo day or evening and though some coiffures were elaborate, the contour of the head was never marred. In place of a hat, many young women wore a bowknot in the hair, velvet ribbon attached to a small comb.

All the feminine world adopted shoulder-length hair, making it simple with the aid of a setting-lotion to arrange the hair in any fashion without adding false pieces. The practice of giving the whole head a permanent wave had passed, only the ends now curled. The vogue of the soignée headdress prompted many older women to take advantage of the wig or half-wig which the hair-dressers had long been making for the movies. Skillfully and beautifully made, the wig was also very costly.

A fad for "platinum blond hair" followed the appearance of an American star of the cinema, Jean Harlow (1911–1937), a silvery blond type, which gave rise to the term "platinum blonde." Some women among the very young bleached their locks to the new color.

This was the beginning of the present vogue of lightening, brightening or changing the color of the hair especially among the younger generation of women. The stigma attached to "dyed hair" disappeared. Hundreds of rinses, tints, bleaches and dyes were put on the market for professional use or to be applied by milady herself at home.

A vast improvement was made in the dyeing agents and in the United States, all cosmetics are made of colorings certified by the Food and Drug Administration. A Federal law requires a "patch test" made twenty-four hours before the actual application to ascertain the reaction, if any, of the individual's skin to the dye.

In headgear, the deep crown disappeared, replaced by a very shallow version. Noteworthy in 1931 was the revival and rage of the Empress or Eugénie hat worn to one side of the head with ostrich feathers. Its vogue was short but it was the beginning of all styles of headtire from a bunch of flowers on a ribbon band to the gigantic cartwheel or no hat at all.

Of the early 'thirties was Schiaparelli's "doll's hat," a small headdress composed of flowers or ostrich tips attached to a crushed headband of silk or velvet or held on by a black silk elastic round the back of the head. Important, too, was the pompadour hat designed for the Duchess of Windsor by J. Suzanne Talbot, a calotte of felt ornamented with flowers or ribbon.

Small birds and wings were again in the mode but the importation of feathers into this country was prohibited. Plumage consisted of ostrich, eagle, pheasant or barnyard fowl fashioned into cleverly made ornaments. Every conceivable fabric was employed for the frivolous headpieces, even cellophane, that most modern of fabrics was utilized. It was a period of deep brilliant color in red, purple, orange and yellow with a predominance of black. A startling new color was Schiaparelli's "parlor pink" or "shocking pink," a purplish rose shade. The small fur toque was modish in mink, Persian lamb, nutria, sheared beaver, leopard and fox.

The sensation of the period and still with us in the 'forties, was the artistic and ancient caul, "net" in the Victorian era and now incorrectly termed a "snood." Snood originally signified the narrow ribbon round the head of the

Scotch or Irish maiden which she exchanged after marriage for a linen kerchief tied under the chin. But snood it is!

Some accredited the launching of the snood to Schiaparelli in 1935 in a tiny fur toque attached to a chenille net but others say that Suzy, famous for her berets and her absurd little sailor hats, is responsible for the craze. The style caught like wildfire, women of all ages with long or short hair wearing the snood for sports, day or evening. To it was attached a ridiculously small hat, flowers or ribbon or it was worn plain. And the chincloth or wimple of the Middle Ages came into fashion, of chiffon or velvet with the small toque on top of the head.

The diagonally folded gay headkerchief tied under the chin in peasant fashion appeared upon the heads of young women for sportswear, a head-covering particularly suitable for riding in the open car. In line with this, the hood attached to the wrap returned and, sometimes of fur or fur-lined, graced smart heads in the evening. The parka, an outer woolen shirt with a hood, was taken up for sports. The original parka is of Siberian or Alaskan origin and made of fur skins.

Casual headpieces were bandeaux and caps, crocheted or knitted. The turban was a classic for day, sports or evening, the fabric varying according to the occasion. By 1937, it was no longer a sewn affair but a prepared piece of fabric which the wearer tied into shape round her head. For sports there was also the Tyrolese felt hat with gay feather in a ribbon band and the ever-popular Basque beret.

Black or colored velvet bowknots adorned the evening coiffure, also small feather and spangled fantasies, jeweled clips, Juliet caps and of course, the chenille or ribbon snood and the small lace mantilla. Most favored of all were the beautiful artificial flowers.

The short veil invariably finished the diminutive hat. Of fine or very coarse mesh, in black or color, it covered the face or just the nose or perhaps was nothing more than a frill over the eyes. By way of change the bridal veil was more often short than long.

Women, young and old and of every station made use of cosmetics. The schoolgirl now used lipstick. Make-up consisted of a powder base, rouge, eye shadow, eyebrow pencil and lipstick. There were helpful creams and lotions, brilliantine was applied to the hair, cream on the eyelids and the vivid-colored lipstick matched the lacquered finger and toe nails. A cyclamen shade of lipstick and lacquer was to be had, to accompany the fashionable new color of shocking pink. Gray hair was tinted with a flattering mauve or blue rinse. The exaggerated sun-tan craze of the previous years declined.

An influence of Hollywood make-up was the large full mouth, a most surprising idea. Never before had woman deliberately enlarged the size of her mouth. The desired shape has always been small, a cupid's bow or rosebud mouth as the pictures and sculpture of the ages testify. The lips were outlined with a tiny brush of rouge and then covered with the red pomade, usually of an indelible nature.

Earrings were fashioned after the designs of all periods, with both clip and screw back and particular emphasis was given to the large jeweled button type in beautiful antique and modern styles. Like the jeweled clip brooch and the clip watch, earrings too, were made with clips for fasteners in place of screws.

1930 to 1940

gibus, opera, or collapsible evening hat-black grosgrain or merino cloth-formal

black silk top hat-formal day or evening

polo cap-white cotton covered-reinforced

gray derby worn to the races-British

black silk hunting hat with guard

stitched tweed hat for country wear

black Homburg-business or semi-formal evening

felt riding hat-colored cord-Mexican

gray felt topper worn with cutaway coat-British

tweed grouse shooting hat

black felt derby for day wear in town

dark gray pork pie felt

montego hat-vegetable fiber-for resort wear

snap brim-brown felt with feather

black hunting derby-reinforced

"ten-gallon hat" pale tan felt-ranch or range

tweed cap for sports

black velvet hunt cap-reinforced-worn with pink coat

straw with dark red cotton puggree band

two-tone straw-spotted silk puggree band

brown leghorn-white shantung puggree band

panama with black grosgrain band

for duck shooting-tan gabardine-corduroy flaps

boater of sennit straw-silk club band

pith helmet for tropics-tan gabardine

ski cap-dark blue gabardine-flaps inside-black ribbon

Basque béret-dark blue woolen woven in one piece

black felt Tyrolese hat-cord band-feathers

yachting cap-navy blue-gold insignia

deer shooting-bright red cloth-leather visor

RTW

1930 to 1940

short hair
curled in
back~
Antoine~
1933

side part
with roll
round
back
1930

curled
bangs
and
chignon~
1935

short hair
dressed in
"up hair•do"~
curled ends~
1938

heart•shaped
coiffure~
short and
rolled~
1938

modern
"snood" of
cord, ribbon,
or chenille~
day or
evening~
1938

"page•boy
bob"
with
rolled
pompadour~
1937

"infanta
coiffure"~
satin loops~
Balenciaga~
1939

short hair
parted
and
rolled~
1939

short
coiffure
parted
and rolled~
1939

short
coiffure
with
pompadour
and puffs~
1939

"page•boy
bob"~
ends rolled
under~
1939

RTW

1930 to 1940

draped turban in two colors- jersey or crêpe de chine- Reboux- 1930

black knitted skullcap- flaring top- Schiaparelli- 1932

"Eugénie hat" of black velvet with rolled brim- black ostrich- 1931

shallow-crowned felt sailor- pearl pin- Marie Christiane- 1932

cap of mink and black mesh net- Schiaparelli- 1935

evening hood and short cape- black tulle- black satin ribbon- Mainbocher- 1935

black felt béret attached to mesh stocking cap with tassel- Schiaparelli- 1936

black velvet toque attached to black chenille snood- Schiaparelli- 1935

country hat- soft gray felt- dark red flower fashioned of small feathers- 1936

black felt bowler worn with tailored costume- coarse black mesh veil- Schiaparelli- 1936

RTW

1930 to 1940

bridal headdress-
short circular veil-
pale smoke-blue
tulle and birds-
Mainbocher-
1937

toque of
Persian lamb-
black georgette
wimple-
1938

"burnt-
toast"
straw sailor-silk
scarf red, white
and blue-
Bruyère-
1939

"doll's hat"
black ostrich-
pink cabbage
rose-black
velvet ribbon-
Schiaparelli-
1938

Cossack
cap of
black Persian
lamb with
gold bead
necklace-
Rose Valois-
1939

stiff red
felt-black
grosgrain
ribbon-
Rose Valois-
1939

red plush
toque-black
silk cords
and tassels-
black
quill-
Suzy-
1939

black velvet
shako-black
cock feathers-
Patou-
1939

self-tied
turban-
silk or
wool-
1937

modern "snood"
red velvet-
day or evening-
Suzy-
1939

RTW

1930 to 1940
Sports

natural
straw with red and
white printed cotton-
for beach wear-
1931

rubber bathing cap-
all colors and white-
worn by men
and women
from the
1920's

calotte-dark
blue
wool-
1932

sun shield
for tennis-
stiffened white
cotton faced
with green-
1930

beach
hat of
brown
linen-
1932

western
riding hat
for range
and ranch-
black felt-
colored cord
with beads

printed
cotton
handkerchief-
1938

conventional
Mexican
riding hat-gray
felt-black or gray
ribbon

sun glasses-
winter and
summer
sports-
men and
women-frames and lenses
all
colors

formal
black silk
hunting
hat-chenille
veil

ski cap-
wine colored
gabardine-
stitched
visor-
Patou

beach hat of
coarsely
woven
straw-
1939

black felt
hunting bowler-
silk cord guard-
chenille veil

RTW

1930 to 1940

cap of white
corduroy
velvet-
French

black silk
top hat-
unique
feature of
Eton
College-
England

blue cloth
cap of
Eton
College-
England

dark blue
felt and
grosgrain
ribbon

cap to
match
coat-
hunter green
tweed-beaver
pompons-
stitched
brim

felt
bonnet-
wine or
teal brown-
ostrich tips-
grosgrain
ribbon

Tyrolese
hat-brown
or green
felt-
cord and
feather

Tyrolese
hat-rust
cloth with
tan
cording

Eton cap with
earlaps-
of tweed

calotte
of bright
colored
wool
felt

tweed cap-stitched
brim-English

storm
helmet-
rubberized
yellow
fabric

felt hat
with
cord and
feather

toque of
silk or
wool
jersey-
embroidered
motif

tweed
bonnet
matching
coat-stitched
brim-wool flower

RTW

1940-1944

CHAPTER TWENTY-THREE

THESE WERE the grim and tragic years of the Second World War with France fallen and shut off from the outside world. Heroic London was turning out a limited amount of designing, and New York, more fortunately situated, carried on in costume design and did very well at it.

The masculine mode of the times was military but with many innovations brought about by modern warfare. Today's warriors are equipped for fighting in every climate, in the sky and under water, camouflaged for the jungles, the desert sands, the plains, the mountains and northern ice and snow. Ancient, yet modern was the new "battle dress." The padded helmet was again important and high-altitude flying necessitated an oxygen mask. The "centuries-old" Monmouth and montero caps were in use and still worn was the dress uniform which entailed such traditional accessories as the plumed helmet and cocked hat, laced with gold and silver.

The universally worn masculine coif of the Medieval and Renaissance Periods returned. Now as then, it tied under the chin like an infant's cap. It covers the heads of the ground personnel of the United States Air Force and its color denotes the specific service of the wearer, in green, blue, yellow, red or white. White is for the pharmacist's mates, who give first aid in emergency.

A picturesque headpiece was the béret of General Sir Bernard L. Montgomery, British Commander. The cap inspired a new vogue of the béret in the feminine world. The General liked hats and often wore the broad-brimmed Australian felt but he appeared to prefer the béret of the British Tank Corps. The Corps adopted the blue béret when the French Alpine soldiers, so the story goes, presented their caps to the Britishers in World War I, as a token of gratitude for aid in battle.

The feminine fashion for short hair continued if only by reason of its great practicability in those busy war-working times. In general, the hairdo was sleek and glossy with undulating wave whether brushed up from the nape, down in chignon or long bob. Despite curls, rolls, pompadours, chignons, cadogans and page boy bobs, the coiffure resolved itself into a more or less clean-cut silhouette. Very popular was the net, fine or coarse, which invariably encased chignon, cadogan or long bob in snood fashion.

The "feather cut" was new in the manner of irregular cutting, the hair trimmed so as to produce loose curls over the head.

The war curtailment of the manufacture of bobby pins of high carbon steel was a contributing factor toward keeping short hair in the mode, as only the making of low carbon steel was permitted and such pins had not enough spring to hold long hair in place.

New York became the home of several French master wigmakers who produced tiny cap-like transformations, some dressed with flowers and ribbon bows, also fringes, circlets, chignons and cadogans. These false pieces defied detection even in the parting which was accomplished by crocheting strands of hair to a fine net foundation. The hair brushed back from the temples actually appeared to grow from the wearer's head. Many busy older women with the means to possess them resorted to the use of the half-wig.

The permanent wave, formerly applied by an electrical heat machine was now given without heat, a cold chemical permanent wave, it was called. The advantage came in being able to curl the hair right to the head, lack of heat obviating the need of the thick protective pads. The hair dressed with a chemical was wound on small wooden rods, then covered with small wooden clips, the whole operation consuming much less time than the machine method.

Tinting gray hair with a mauve or blue rinse continued, also the general use of cosmetics. In fact with so many women in service and war-work, more thought than ever was concentrated upon the manufacture of beauty aids. The wearing of a uniform did not discourage the practice and warplants definitely encouraged the care of the face and the hands. Despite the many necessary wartime restrictions, cosmetics in plastic containers instead of metal were plentiful and designed for the hair, face, skin and fingertips.

A telling note from war-controlled Paris of 1940 under German domination stated that make-up and dyed hair were frowned upon and that the mode was being "purified."

The prized feminine treasure "the Paris bonnet" disappeared with the fall of France. Wartime priorities curbed fabric, color and yardage but, of course, something chic in headgear could always be evolved by the clever designer from "almost nothing." And often the restrictions themselves made for a simple, clever style.

From London in the spring of 1944 came word that turbans and knitted scarfs of the early years of the war were being replaced by new spring hats, and that the new creations, "as charming as any presented in peacetime years, are made of ends of curtain fabrics, floor felting, fringe and ribbon but the prices are exorbitant." Though American designers produced most worthy models we were still in a French cycle of the mode.

All the styles of the nineteen-thirties were with us, the snood, calotte, béret, turban, cartwheel, sailor, tricorne, toque, pompadour hat, doll's hat, fedora, postilion and bonnet. The small black bowler launched by Schiaparelli in 1936 was seen with the street suit on many young women. The tiny hats dispensed with the elastic because small pins, invisible hat grips or small combs sewn inside the crown held the hat to the head.

The young woman liked the kerchief style of headcovering tied under the chin, revived under the Victorian name of capote or fascinator or called by the Russian name of "babushka." Frivolous bits of head gear termed half-hats, chaplets or curvettes became the vogue, worn at any hour, ornamented with flowers, ribbons, sequins and whatnot! The snood, plain or festooned with bowknots and flowers, was popular. Velvet bowknots and artificial flowers adorned the coiffure, day or evening and the most diminutive bit of headtire was finished with a gay little veil. That precious hat ornament of the Renaissance, the jeweled necklace or the brooch decorated the simple béret or sailor.

By the end of this period news of very large hats by Balenciaga reached us, said to be worn in Madrid and Paris. Like models were displayed by a few New York milliners, all the styles reminiscent of the early twentieth century.

In 1941 in New York, a new agreement was reached between the National Audubon Society and the Feathers Industries of America, Inc., whereby the use of wild bird plumage for millinery and decorative purposes ceased. At the end of a six-year period, any remaining stocks of paradise, egret, golden or bald eagle were to be turned over to the State Department and the agreement was to be countrywide.

War work in the factory created a new line of costume including protective helmets, caps and snoods and in 1943, the Brooklyn Museum exhibited such garments on wax mannequins.

Quite a departure in the styling of women's spectacles was the "Harlequin frame" designed by an American, Altina Sanders, in 1944. The upward tilting corners of the plastic frames proved indeed flattering to many faces and the design was intended for general use or sports with either clear or colored lenses. In jewelry, earrings were a very definite style feature of the period with design varied indeed, both modern and antique, the authentic piece more eagerly sought than any.

1940 to 1944

pompadour with puffs in back - 1940

stocking-cap dark blue silk - blue and white tassel - silver chain - Bruyère - 1940

black silk béquin with stitching - black quill - curls in snood - Talbot

pale pink flowers - green foliage - pink veil - Suzy 1940

mushroom-brim hat - old rose suède - greenish bronze - veil - Suzy - 1940

short hair with lacquered curls on top of head - 1940

upstanding béret - beige felt - flat brown grosgrain bow at back - Molyneux - 1940

long bob with ends turned under - 1941

blue woolen hood with ribbon ties - Bruyère - 1940

heart-shaped coiffure dressed over rolls - ribbon bow - 1940

coiffure dressed over pompadour roll - 1940

"Harlequin" frames - general or sports wear - 1940

RTW

1940 to 1944
New York

pillbox
of green
taffeta-
jewel at
one side-
Henri Bendel-
1940

large felt
hat-black
chenille
snood-
Valentina-
1940

fringed turban-
mixed black
and navy
blue
cashmere-
Lilly Daché-
1940

turban of
draped red
fabric-
Walter Florell-
1940

dark blue
béret with
veil-
Bergdorf Goodman-
1940

snood for
day wear-
silk morning
glories-
blue velvet
ribbon-
Lilly Daché-
1940

"pancake"
béret of
felt-
New York-
1940

Breton
sailor-dark
blue felt-
grosgrain
ribbon-
New York-
1940

turban of
elephant gray
jersey-blue
fox head-
Nettie Rosenstein-
1940

"snood-turban"-
wool jersey-braided
border figured
jersey-jewel-sewn-
Lilly Daché-
1941

pillbox of
black velvet-
rhinestone buckle-
black silk fringe-
Hattie Carnegie-1941

RTW

1940 to 1944
New York

hand-crocheted
hat-black wool
with yellow-
John-Frederics-
1941

red felt with
black coq
plumage-
Lilly Dache-
1941

babushka-
black velvet-
gold colored
braid-
John-Frederics-
1941

open-worked
straw-sulphur
yellow headband-
new York-
1941

capote of
mink and black
broadcloth-
Lilly Dache-
1941

brown felt
bonnet-
brown
grosgrain
ribbon-
brown tulle-
John-Frederics-
1941

black velvet
hat-black
grosgrain
ribbon-
Lilly Dache
1941

hood-beret of
brown felt with
crocheted yarn-
John Frederics-
1941

Spanish
sailor-
velvet
band and
binding-
Bergdorf Goodman-
1941

black fox
beret-purple
and black velvet ribbon-
du Plessix-
1942

RTW

1940 to 1944
New York

black grosgrain
faced with
black velvet—
black ostrich—
John•Frederics—
1942

bridal headdress—
cap of Alençon
lace—hair
in cadogan
dressed
over roll—
Bergdorf
Goodman—
1942

mauve felt
and ribbon—
red roses—
blue green
foliage—
Lilly Daché—
1942

fedora—
red felt and
ribbon—
tan veiling—
Sally Victor
1942

béret of
black
Persian
lamb—
Lilly Daché—
1942

fez of
deep pink
felt with
rope tassel—
Lilly Daché—
1942

black felt—
chou of
satin ribbon—
Reine—
1943

black Milan straw
cartwheel—black
satin bows—black
chiffon edge—
Florence Reichman—
1943

"snood•hood"—
black net
with
layers of
Mexican pink grosgrain ribbon—
Sally Victor—1943

"Montgomery
béret"—
dark blue
felt—
simulated
insignia—
Florence Reichman—
1943

jeweled Renaissance béret—
black felt with crystals—
net•covered bobbed hair—
John•Frederics—1943

RTW

Spring 1944

turban of
pale gray satin-
Balenciaga-
Madrid

sports hat-
felt with
grosgrain
ribbon-
Sally Victor-

white lissé straw-
black wings-
white veil-
Mainbocher

gray
taffeta
folds in
clover leaf
shape- and
gray
white wings-
Suzanne et Roger

milan
straw-velvet
band-
Knox

small white straw
with yellow
chiffon puffings-
yellow milliner's
rose-green foliage-
Walter Florell

"sable cut"
short coiffure-
with
velvet bowknots-
Antoine

"sable cut"
short coiffure-
curls held
in place by
side combs-
Antoine

false chignon
with barette-
Elizabeth Arden

false padded
cadogan
with short
coiffure

RTW

1940 to 1944
New York

olive green felt with
black grosgrain ribbon-
Mme Pauline-
1943

RTW

yellow
plush
felt-gray
grosgrain
ribbon-
pleated
ribbon
"bongrace"
hair in snood-
Bergdorf Goodman-1943

summer hat of
yellow felt-
yellow cloth border-
John-Frederics-
1943

"widow's coif"-black
felt edged black satin-
Bergdorf Goodman-1943

"chaplet,
curvette or half
hat" wool and
jewel embroidery
on printed challis-
hair in snood-
Sally Victor-1943

black felt
sailor-
jeweled
band-
John-Frederics-
1943

short hair
dressed in
pompadour
and roll-
1944

helmet-
dark blue felt-
feather coxcomb
of lighter shade-
Hattie Carnegie-
1944

bridal
headdress-
white satin
fillet-
Flemish
lace fan-
jeweled
brooch-
Hattie Carnegie-
1944

one-sided hat-
black satin-
Hattie Carnegie-
1944

Holbein
hat-
black
straw and
ricrac braid-
Josephi-
1944

curls with velvet
bow for nape

wig
snood to
match owner's
hair-bows and flowers

cadogan-all
hair pieces-
Antoine-1944

1940 to 1944
United States

"Anywhere-
Anytime-
Anyhow-
Bar Nothing"
padded
steel
helmet

parka-
white twill
lined with
bear fur-colored goggles-
whistle on cord

bombardier wearing
khaki garrison cap

helmet of
navy air
ground force-
yellow, blue,
green or red-
color denotes
special function
of wearer

tropical helmet-
khaki fiber
reinforced-
leather chinstrap-
officer Marine Corps

winter cap-
cloth with
lamb's
wool flaps

helmet and
improved
gas mask-
canister
of
protective
chemicals
attached to
facepiece,
eliminates
former hose

crash helmet-
tank corps-
steel and
leather-
goggles

heavy netting
over helmet for
sound proofing
and holding
foliage for
camouflage

reinforced
leather
helmet
of the
fighter
pilot

khaki cotton
fatigue
cap

white ski cap-
colored goggles-
mountain trooper

RTW

1940 to 1944

general's full dress cap – dark blue with gold – U.S.

the famous béret of British General Montgomery

krimmer Cossack cap – officer U.S.S.R. Army

fiber helmet – officer U.S.S.R. Army

green cloth cap with gold – black band – black visor – German Army officer

white cotton turban draped round conical skullcap – sepoy

steel helmet – black cock plummage – Italian Army officer

hood over cap – khaki with red star – U.S.S.R. Infantry

cocked hat – black beaver edged gold galloon – white ostrich – dress hat French Marshal

blue cloth – gold embroidery – black braid – black strap – Royal Canadian Air Force

full dress cocked hat – black beaver white cock plummage – British Army officer

full dress – white helmet – white, red and black cock plummage – Scottish Army officer

summer cap – white with black ribbon – British sailor

cocked hat – black beaver gold braid – black cockade – black ribbon bows – full dress – flag rank U.S. Navy

RTW

1940 to 1944
United States

Red Cross
nurses' aide-blue
and white cap

Army nurse-
padded
steel
helmet

Navy
Nurse Corps
summer cap
white with
blue and
gold—
winter
cap blue
with
gold

WAVE officer
blue and white
with gold-
stitched
brim

Army nurse
dress cap-
olive drab
with gold

WAC private-
khaki cap-
gold insignia

Navy
yeoman-
white
crown-
blue
brim-
dark
blue
ribbon

Marine
Corps
officer-
green cap-red
cord-gold insignia

WASP-
dress béret-
"San Diego
blue"
cloth

AWVS
dark blue
cap with
color of
rank

Red Cross
Motor Corps-
Oxford gray cap

Red Cross
Field
Service-
gray blue
cap

WAVE
rubberized
havelock
for
stormy
weather

metal helmet-
air Warden-
Civilian Defense

1940 to 1944

WRNS officer - navy blue hat - British

brown cap - red band - gold star - black visor and strap - sharpshooter officer - U.S.S.R.

warworker's cap - U.S.

blue cap - black strap - gold insignia - Canadian

warworker's cap - U.S.

dark green cap with red piping - U.S.S.R.

warworker - self-tied turban - U.S.

A T S - khaki cap - all cloth-stitched band, brim and flap - British

warworker's cap with protective havelock - U.S.

Princess Elizabeth's Regimental Grenadier's cap

khaki hood lined with lamb's wool - goggles - U.S. Air Force

warworker's helmet with movable transparent plastic shield - U.S.

dark blue and gold - French

RTW

1944-1959

CHAPTER TWENTY-FOUR

THE SUBJECT of modish contemporary hat fashions is almost inexhaustible what with headgear fashioned in every style, shape and size and in every possible fabric, regardless of season. Looking over the silhouette of these years one is struck by the wide range in the source of ideas of the designers. Every bygone period is represented. We have the bandeau, snood, cap, béret, hood, turban, sailor hat, picture-hat and what appears to be a revival of mannish styles, the derby, the fedora and its feminine counterpart of the 1930's, the "Garbo slouch." Hoods are simply pinched into shape, crowns are non-existing or stove-pipe high, brims wide, narrow, or none at all, some hats trimmed with every pretty, traditional ornamentation, others merely a stark shape. Ribbons, veilings, flowers and furs are rampant and feathers soar to new heights.

Fake feather ornaments are manufactured of synthetics and barnyard plumage and happily, are excellent imitations and substitutes. The Audubon ban against the killing, importation and use of feathers of fine birds to save them from extinction still holds. Stored in a vault of the Museum of Natural History in New York for thirty-two years was a package of ninety-seven fiery orange and white plumes and skins of the gorgeous bird of paradise impounded when the law went into effect. The treasure was publicized in 1956 in connection with the coronation of the king of Nepal when, upon the suggestion of an ornithologist of the museum the package, truly worth a king's ransom, was flown to Nepal as a gift to King Mahendra from the United States. Since 1924 when international traffic in plumes of all birds came to a halt, the king's courtiers, prime ministers and generals had been forced to wear their old, shabby paradise or plebeian rooster tails, save the king who uses a half dozen in his crown. So, whereas the gift involved no destruction of live birds, it made a fitting and most impressive coronation gift.

There has been a vogue of hatlessness in this era, a fad adopted even on city streets as well as in the country, seashore and suburbs.

Hatlessness, a real bugaboo, has pursued the milliners these past years. It appears to be passing, or at least the hatmakers hope so. There are many reasons for it, the very first the doll hats of the 1930's which gave women a taste of wearing a "little nothing of a hat," casual dressing during and after World War II, flight travel with curtailed luggage, avoiding disarranging a freshly-done, expensive hairdo, the freedom of the closed and heated automobile, not omitting the very car itself. The newly designed, low cars had as much to do with hatless heads by being built too low for comfort since it fairly enrages man or woman to have the hat knocked awry when climbing in or out of the vehicle.

As fashions go, the years of the feminine mode of which we write bear a close resemblance to the second half of the eighteenth century in its many foibles, but let's trust no heads will fall, for we are again indulging in all the glamorous fancies of Marie Antoinette's court and her ladies. Only, instead of messy hair powder, we now have wonderful tints and dyes plus the flowers, ribbons, feathers, laces and tulle of her day. We have wigs which far surpass those of that period not only in lightness and comfort but in a sanitary way. And today, in our democratic world, a fashionable hat, coiffure or even a wig is the prerogative of any well-groomed woman regardless of wealth or social status. Too, no longer a luxury for some few, is having the hair shampooed and dressed by a skilled hairdresser, a performance which has become a weekly rite in most women's lives.

Wigs are big news! Partial wigs or "crown falls" have always been resorted to by many men and women to conceal a deficiency of natural hair. A well-known wigmaker tells us that there are as many bald women as men but that three women to every one man take to wig-wearing when in need. So much for the necessity of a wig!

The new fashion for the wig has been built up by two Parisian hair stylists of Spanish origin, sisters Maria and Rosita Carita, who insist that a well-groomed woman needs two coiffures, her own natural hair and a dressed wig for emergency in a busy, social life. When not in use the wig is supposed to be carried in a special designed case of straw and leather, not unlike a chic summer handbag. Not since the French Revolution has the fashion created such a sensation and once again the wigmakers are reaping a fortune. The wearer matches her hair color or not, as she wishes, a well-made wig of human hair costing from $175 up to $250.

The first wigs created by the Carita sisters appeared in Paris in 1958 in the salon of De Givenchy on the heads of his mannequins and met with wild approval. The "Bubble wig" is basically strands of hair woven into a cap of elasticised net held to the head securely by a snug elastic band, needing no other device to fasten it firmly. As simple as that! No wonder its success was instant! The style resembles a huge chrysanthemum.

The craze extends to hair wigs in such hues as light green, to say nothing of shocking pink. Much further down the scale are wigs of acetate yarns in bright colors including red, green, blue and purple priced around seven dollars. One New York department store had a near riot the day these low-priced wigs were put on sale. For those who like their own tresses but like the novelty of a wig, flattering substitute is the flower wig, a cap of net or nylon covered with flowers and a headpiece which covers the head to the hairline. And there are bushy wigs of tulle sparkling with paillettes or brilliants and a bridal wig of white net done Oriental turban fashion with a veil floating in back.

Excepting the youthful, teen-age pony tail, the coiffure remains a short-cut one. Often the effect of long hair, especially for evening dress, is due to a skillful cut and set and frequently to an added false chignon. The very short poodle cut of tight curls was certainly given impetus when charming Mary Martin in "South Pacific" daily shampooed her very own hair on the stage. In 1951 appeared the Pompon cut, a creation of Michel and a startling new shape with a trend toward much less curl. It was accomplished by manipulated undercutting and puffed out over rolls, a head which paved the way to the bouffant hairdo of 1956. Next came the loose, ragged ringlets worn by the Italian movie stars, the hair dressed high over the forehead. This eased into the "pompadour" or portrait style, a coiffure which imparts a patrician look to almost any wearer.

Too, the large hats have played a part in developing a fuller, fluffier head and have made for the sudden flair of the bubble wig with its bouffant effect.

When it comes to coloring the hair of our heads, this age of synthetics is an age of marvels. Not only women but many men too, take advantage of the modern rinses, tints and dyes. One can change to the color of one's dreams in short time by having it done in the hairdresser's salon or simply, by doing the job one's self. The metamorphosis through the use of rinse or tint can be temporary, or if dyed, long-lasting. Or the hair can be lightened with a bleach. Gone is the terror of having chosen the wrong color, because tint or rinse can be washed out. And gone is the day when to change the hair color was a stigma in society. Manufacturers of the magic formulas claim that at least seventy-five per cent of the feminine world have rinsed, dyed or bleached because science has eliminated guesswork in the operation. Just about any color and its varying shades are available for a change of mood, a glamorous popular hue of the moment being tangerine, a pinkish orange.

The use of cosmetics in a woman's life has come to be a most important part of the daily regimen. Every up-to-date man expects his women folk to be in the mode and that, of course, means the proper application of beauty aids. Only a raving beauty could afford to ignore the helpful creams, lotions and powders available. This is all very different from the eighteenth century and the earliest days of our century when a dab of talcum powder on the nose and a whiff of toilet water was all a "lady" dared used to enhance her charm.

The suntan complexion has given way to a light, delicate toned skin which will be carefully protected from now on if the straw beach hats of fantastic sizes be any criterion of a new trend. The eyes are lined along the upper lids and the lower lashes slightly penciled, with perhaps some mascara on the upper lashes. False eye lashes formerly used only by the stage and Hollywood are now being bought and applied to many non-professional eyelids. A faint tone of green or blue on the lids and a light coating of rouge high on the cheeks finishes with an over-all puff of powder in a shade lighter than the natural coloring. Red and scarlet enameled fingernails are passé, a lighter color being more in keeping with the subtle, pearly quality of the facial makeup.

Lipstick, too, is very often a pink shade instead of a deep red. At the moment of writing a battle is raging between the United States Pure Food and Drug Administration and the manufacturers of lipstick. The government claims that by test, certain red, orange and yellow coal-tar dyes used in the beauty aids are injurious to animals. The manufacturers hold that the amount used is so small that it does not harm humans. And, according to those in the know, as the battle continues, women go right on buying their pet brand and color.

After World War II and by 1950, hatlessness in the masculine mode as in feminine headgear became a vital problem to the many people connected with the production of hats. In 1951 when sales fell to a new low, hatmen decided it was urgent to do everything possible to discourage men from going without or wearing a ten-year-old, beloved hat with an expensive, well-made suit, by revamping the styles, in other words as is done in women's wear, "to date the hat." With this thought in mind the popular fedora was given a narrower brim and a lowered tapered crown, a first move in the subtle propaganda to make a man hat-conscious. And surprisingly enough, the scheme worked especially among younger men; anyway they actually bought and wore the new model.

In the next move the hatters gave the new design a flat-topped crown and lo! and behold! his lordship meekly and happily wore the newest creation. The flat top was brought out in conventional felts and straws, in grays and charcoal browns for city wear. These were in turn followed by more casual felts with textured finish and fancy straws banded with flannel, silk and woven braids in rich, muted colors, often sporting the feather ornament in Tyrolean fashion, a really popular style. For the sportsman hats were made of suède, velours, tweed and other rough mixtures so that by 1956, even the traditional western and southern ten-gallon hat bore evidence of fashionable influence in an occasional flat-top crown and a narrowed brim.

Crushable summer straws arrived in 1958 available in panama, tissue Milan, split macora and raffia, this latter particularly a favorite. Even the boater was made of softer straw and with a snap brim.

The quest of greater comfort and less weight in all of men's wearing apparel has led to a lighter felt, thus producing a pliable hat body of but a few ounces that can stand crushing, folding and packing without injury. The hat follows the lines of the rakish English "trilby" which Rex Harrison wore in "My Fair Lady." Another advantage of no small value is that the crushable piece can be tucked into the pocket, thereby eliminating the parking tip in restaurants and other places.

There are signs of the return of the derby or, if you wish, the bowler or the billycock. This headpiece designed a century ago has always carried an air of elegance when worn by the well-dressed gentleman. Since 1950, an Edwardian trend in masculine dressing has been observed and the derby is in line with it or as we say "Ivy League." After World War II in London, all ex-Guards officers and Guards officers were ordered to wear bowler hats when in civilian dress and that perhaps explains the renaissance of this style. New York has taken it up and it is appearing in Washington, Philadelphia, Chicago and points west. The newest derbies are conceding much to comfort in being lighter than formerly and also being built of a soft felt which can be dented and pushed back into shape without damage. A representative men's shop tells us that the soft derby has been discovered and is being bought by some feminine wearers.

The silk top hat and the Gibus or collapsible top hat are casualties of two world wars, in fact all formal day and evening dress clothes are less frequently worn than formerly. Like the derby, the silk topper will undoubtedly make a comeback since no masculine accessory equals it in elegance. More often the black or midnight blue Homburg is the chosen dress hat. The topper alone accompanies the cutaway or morning coat whereas the Homburg is acceptable with the sack or British lounge coat while many men dispense with any hat when in evening dress.

The Homburg of the 1950's was made as soft as a sports hat but continues to be a somewhat dressy accessory. In his first inauguration in 1953, President Eisenhower chose a black Homburg in place of the traditional "stovepipe." This fact added to the prestige of the style as the elegant hat for formal wear. In 1957 he again wore a black Homburg at his second inauguration and this time the "international Homburg" as the hatters termed it, was fashioned by skilled hatters of ten countries, a process consuming three months. Italy, England, France, West Germany, Canada, Australia, Mexico, Brazil, Argentina, and the United States, all took a hand in the making. For instance, rabbit and hare skins were flown to Italy where the body was formed, then shipped to West Germany for additional shrinking and brushing. The hood was then shipped to six other countries each of which performed an operation in the finishing of the important inaugural headpiece of the president of the United States.

The current popularity of the open sports car is given credit for the return of the centuries-old flat cap which can be so conveniently slipped into the pocket. Peaked caps are being worn in plaids, tweeds and solid colors and in both woolen and cotton fabrics.

Of the sportswear family and in 1954, the British helmet also came under modern re-styling. Suitable alike to spectator and participant, it fills a definite need in shading eyes and the back of the neck. Made of lightweight felt, the hat stands rolling and tucking away without marring the headpiece.

As to masculine coiffure though the hair be cropped very short there are many variations "on the theme." The "crew cut" appears to be the favored silhouette of the period and originated among the varsity crews to differentiate those gentlemen from other undergraduates, thus its name, "varsity cut." At first a collegiate fashion, it also became known as the G.I. cut and the Prussian bob in World War II. When the top is slightly longer and a bit touseled, it becomes a "feather crew" or more recently the "Ivy League."

The very opposite in grooming is the well-established English or Continental cut of London origin and belatedly reaching New York. In what the uninitiated would suppose to be "in need of a haircut" the locks are long enough in back to edge over the collar, a help to the older man with thinning hair, or so he thinks. And right here we shall hold forth on "natural appearing headpieces" which are bought and worn in the United States by an estimated 350,000 males both young and old. Such pieces can be had in the close-cropped styles to the very long English cut or in the luxurious Hollywood toupee. A considerable size of business is carried on through the mails by means of catalogue and a carefully detailed questionnaire to be filled out. A survey of the largest wigmakers reveals an annual business in millions of dollars. On the other hand it is not unusual for the young man with a good head of hair to undergo a permanent in order to acquire a wave or two in a pompadour hairdo. Such masculine wiles are not essentially of today but date back several thousands of years.

Along with the foregoing vanities the well-groomed man has acquired a liking for scented soap, talcum powder, after-shaving lotion and toilet water for his handkerchief, in fact most manufacturers of cosmetics now include these masculine toiletries in their list of products.

1944 to 1946

dinner hat of red plush and pink satin - Suzanne et Roger - 1944

turban of taffeta and velvet - Suzanne et Roger - 1944

coiffure with coronet braid - Paris - 1944

black velvet toque - black plumage - Henri Bendel - 1944

hair in a snood - hand-crocheted bag with velvet bow knots - Bonwit Teller - 1944

toque of velours with feather trim - Hattie Carnegie - 1945

ermine bowler - black velvet brim - Sally Victor - 1945

satin hat - soft, padded bèret crown - Lilly Daché - 1945

the page-boy bcb - 1946

bonnet of deep-piled velours - Bonwit Teller - 1945

the horsewoman's derby - hair in a net 1946

straw beach hat - 1945

RTW

1946 to 1949

woolen Breton
sailor worn over
woolen hood·
1946

draped felt
and velvet·
Henri Bendel·
1947

pillbox of
bright·colored
velvet·
Mainbocher·
1948

hair
dressed to one side·
green velours béret·
hatpin·   Dior·1947

peaked plateau·
bright green
faille · black
wings·
Balenciaga·
1948

toque of stiff
taffeta· high
flame·colored
plumage·
1948

hair
brushed from
crown center·
Empire coiffure·
Michel·
1948

short·haired
coiffure·bangs
and side rolls·
Antoine·
1949

fluted
poke bonnet
of taffeta·
Hattie Carnegie·
1948

straw bonnet
faced with
velvet·
Otto Lucas·
1949

black felt derby·
brown veil tied
with red silk scarf·
Mr. John·
1949

coiffure with
center part·
one side curled·
one side smooth·
Antoine·
1949

black
melusine
cloche with
black jet
earlaps·
velvet ties·
Irene·
1949

RTW

1950 to 1951

the poodle coiffure- Caruso- 1950

dinner cap of black ostrich curls- Lilly Daché- 1950

bicorne- black velvet- gold kid edging- Castillo- 1950

tambourine style toque- orange velvet- black ball fringe- Braagaard- 1950

black felt toque- cabbage rose- Balenciaga- 1951

all-white winged veil cage- Lilly Daché- 1950

plateau or skimmer in brown velvet- Saks F.A.- 1951

cushion-like beret- bright-colored fabric- Balenciaga- 1950

bouffant coiffure- Michel- 1951

béret of bronze-green velours- coq feathers and jewel- Maud et Nano- 1951

hat and bowknot of deep pink felt- Braagaard- 1951

the pony tail coiffure- from 1948 on

mushroom shape of black velvet- Balenciaga- 1951

pagoda shape of black felt- Balenciaga- 1951

red velvet pillbox pinned to a chignon- Dior- 1951

RTW

1952 and 1953

capeline of black bengal and black velvet- Claude St. Cyr- 1952

circlet with narrow brim turned up front and back- Saks F. Ar 1952

short bridal veil floating from a mushroom- shaped toque- Balenciaga- 1952

cocktail hat- white feathers on a navy blue faille calotte- Maud et Nano- 1952

Watteau hat - green velvet with back filled in with roses and daisies- Braagaard- 1952

Chinese toque- black velvet- velvet folds of cerise topped by dove gray- Legroux- 1953

bicorne of black baku with black pompons- black velvet band- Albouy- 1952

the fad of the artificial blond or white streak- 1952

"portrait coiffure" short hair dressed into pompadour- Michel- 1952

shaggy coiffure of Italian movie stars- Marcel- 1953

elaborately draped turban of brown chiffon- Jacques Fath- 1953

Renaissance headdress- embroidered béret worn over wool jersey hood- Sally Victor- 1952

RTW

1954 to 1956

tiny tricorne - black
suède - diamond horseshoe -
Dior -
1954

knitted
wind - sock
sports cap -
Sidney Wragge -
1954

sailor hat in
gondolier
style - natural
colored straw -
black velvet -
John Fredericks -
1954

waved wings
brushed back -
chignon of
curls -
Claude -
1955

revival of the
medieval coif
in all fabrics -
Emme -
1955

béret of
black velvet -
wired wings -
Galanos -
1956

monkey hat
for evening fun -
black velvet
and jet -
pink feathers -
Balenciaga -
1955

hat of brushed
yellow beaver
felt - satin
bowknot -
Emme -
1955

short hair
dressed in a
French roll -
Jean de Chant -
1956

"Garbo" fedora -
Glen Urquhart
plaid worsted -
velvet band -
Galanos -
1956

turban of
satin - emerald stripes on
gray ground -
Mr. John - 1956

coiffure
fashioned of
hair four
inches long -
Bergdorf Goodman -
1956

large draped
béret of
Dior blue
velveteen -
Paulette -
1956

RTW

1957 to 1959

leopard béret with black velvet bowknot-Svend-1957

white organdie hat-wide brim turned up in front-dark green satin bowknot-Dior-1957

shaped béret of brown suède gathered to a knob-Irene-1957

black suède shell-black plumage-black satin bowknot-Henri Bendel-1957

white coq feathers on a velvet cap-jeweled buckle-Paulette-1958

turban of pleated floral-printed challis with band of mink-Tatiana-1958

skimmer of black velvet-bias folds of white organdie-John Fredericks-1958

oversized, velvet crown and straw brim-Walter Florell-1959

bell bonnet of velvet-Lilly Daché-1959

crushable, packable cloche-citron yellow velveteen-Emme-1959

cap of starched, white, embroidered organdie ruffles-Cardin-1959

deep-brimmed cloche of shaded pink face veiling-Jean Barthet-1959

RTW

wigs and veiling–
1957 to 1959

bowknot of silk
point d'esprit–
John Fredericks
1957

black Chantilly lace–
white satin bowknot–
brooch of brilliants–
Adolpho
1957

evening wig
of black tulle–
chenille–dotted
Pierre–
1957

coronet of jet-
black velvet
bows–nylon net
veiling–wired edge–
Sally Victor
1957

evening hat
with false
topknot and
black velvet–
Lord and Taylor
1958

"half wig" of
hair pieces
attached to
satin covered
clip–a rose–
Joseph
Fleischer–
1958

"bubble wig"–
hair attached
to elastic net
cap–velvet
head band–
Carita
1958

day or
evening
cap of the
1950's–black
veiling with
black silk or
velvet ties

classic
Jane Austen
coiffure–
short or long
hair–false
chignon or
bunch of curls–
1959

"bubble wig"
hair attached
to elastic net
cap–ribbon
head band–
Carita–
1958

"half wig"
with bangs
and top combed
over one's own hair–
Elizabeth Arden–
1959

black silk
veiling over
blond straw
boater–red
grosgrain
ribbon with
jewel in front–
Chanda–
1959

the
touseled
coiffure–
1959

RTW

1945 to 1955

brown felt fedora with silk ribbon- 1945

black felt Homburg- black ribbon- 1947

sports cap- woven Madagascar straw- 1947

gray fedora- black silk ribbon- 1949

Tyrolese style hat-rough felt- double cord- 1950

beach hat- silver top coconut palm- blue feather lei- 1950

tan felt with narrowed brim- dark green ribbon- 1950

bowler or derby as worn by a smart Londoner- 1950

Tyrolese hat of dark green felt- braided felt band- feather panache- 1953

"Sconset Cap" denim-linen- shantung or poplin- 1951

sports helmet hat- waterproofed, pliable green felt- side vents- self band- British- 1954

"flat cap" British worsted- 1950

Tyrolese sports in straw- brilliant feather lei- 1955

silk top hat- black cloth band- 1954

RTW

1953 to 1959

the flattened crown-beige felt and band-1953

bowler or derby of rough felt-woolen braid band-British-1956

flat top-gray felt-black ribbon-1956

straw Breton sailor-blue ribbed ribbon band- 1957

flat top for casual wear-brown or green felt-ribbon band-1957

pinch top fedora-felt-ribbon band-1957

the crew or varsity haircut-1957

sports hat rough beige felt-woven woolen band-1958

flat top with telescope crease-felt with ribbon band-1957

snap-brim-sennit straw-club ribbon band-1958

bowler or derby of lighter weight, softer felt-1959

boater or skimmer of sennit straw-black and orange school band-1959

crushable black velvet with black ribbon band-1959

sports hat of checked pongee-1959

RTW

1944 to 1959

Basque béret-
dark blue
wool woven
in one piece

Eton cap
of wool
tweed-
1940's and
1950's

Breton
sailor-
natural
leghorn-
black
velvet
ribbon-
Paulette-
1949

Glengarry
bonnet
of cloth or
velvet with
white
cockade-
1946

blue or rose
tweed bonnet
with beaver
trimming-
1948

winter sports cap-
sand color twill-
alpaca lined earflaps

snap-brim
fedora-beige
felt-brown
ribbon band
1947

navy blue
straw cloche-
white frill of
pleated
organdie-
Schiaparelli-
1949

the bowler
worn by
a young
Etonian-
1950

summer helmet-
white piqué-
Schiaparelli-
1949

the
bouffant
coiffure-
1958

the
crew cut
1950's

the pony tail
hairdo-
1950's

felt or straw flat top-
cord band-
1956

chechia of
felt, straw, knit,
velvet or silk-
1958

frilled cap-
felt, straw or
fabric-
1958

Robin Hood
type hat-
felt or velours-
1958

FTW

BIBLIOGRAPHY

ITALIAN — *Habiti Antichi e Moderni*—Cesare Vecelli—2 vols.

FRENCH — *Le costume historique*—A. Racinet.

Histoire du costume en France—J. Quicherat.

Costumes français depuis Clovis—illustrations par L. Massard.

Les Arts—Moyen âge et la Renaissance—Paul Lacroix.

Vie militaire et religieuse—Moyen âge et la Renaissance—Paul Lacroix.

XVIIe siècle—Institutions, usages et costumes—Paul Lacroix.

The Eighteenth Century—Its Institutions, Customs and Costumes —Paul Lacroix.

Directoire, consulate et empire—Paul Lacroix.

Un siècle de modes feminines, 1794-1894—Charpentier et Fasquelle.

Fashions in Paris—1797-1897—Octave Uzanne.

Mesdames nos aïeules: dix siècles d'élégances—Robida.

Le costume civil en France du XIIIe au XIXe siècle—Camille Piton.

Histoire de Marlborough—Carran d'Ache.

Histoire de la dentelle—Mme. Bury Palliser.

Le costume en France—Ary Renan.

Costumes vrais—Monde féodal, Europe XVe siècle—Loredan Larchey.

Les grands maréchaux de France—Illustrations par Henri Thiriet.

Histoire de la marine française—Librairie Larousse.

Histoire de la marine—L'Illustration.

Histoire de la peinture classique—Jean De Foville.

Histoire du costume—Jacques Ruppert.

Histoire du costume—Librairie Hachette.

Le costume—Miguel Zamacoïs.

Les soiries d'art—Raymond Cox.

Cent ans de modes françaises—1800-1900—Mme. Cornil.

La mode feminine 1900-1920—Editions Nilsson.

The History of Fashion in France—M. Augustin Challamel.

GERMAN — *Die Trachten der Völker*—Albert Kretschmer.

Münchner Bilderbogen—Zur Geschichte des Kostums.

An Egyptian Princess—George Ebers.

Die Mode im Mittelalter—Max von Boehn.

Die Mode im XVI. Jahrhundert—Max von Boehn.

Die Mode im XVII. Jahrhundert—Max von Boehn.

Die Mode im XVIII. Jahrhundert—Max von Boehn.

Modes and Manners of the XIX Century—Fischel and von Boehn —4 vols.

Die Moden des XIX. Jahrhunderts—Collection Geszler.

Le costume chez les peuples anciens et moderns—Fr. Hottenroth.

Kostümkunde—Hermann Weiss.

Allgemeine Trachtenkunde—Bruno Köhler.

Das Ehrenkleid des Soldaten—Martin Lezieus.

ENGLISH —*Cyclopaedia of Costume*—James Robinson Planche—2 vols.

Costume in England—F. W. Fairholt, F.S.A.—2 vols.

London Illustrated News—1850-1859.

Manners and Customs of the English—Joseph Strutt—3 vols.

Everyday Life in Anglo-Saxon, Viking and Norman Times—M. and C. H. B. Quennell.

Everyday Life in Roman Britain—M. and C. H. B. Quennell.

History of Everyday Life in England—1066-1799—M. and C. H. B. Quennell.

Life and Work of the People of England—16th Century—Hartley and Elliot.

Life and Work of the People of England—17th Century—Hartley and Elliot.

London in the Time of the Tudors—Sir Walter Besant.

Chats on Costume—G. Wooliscroft Rhead, R.E.

The Grammar of Ornament—Owen Jones.

Historic Costume—Francis M. Kelley and Randolph Schwabe.

English Costume—Dion Clayton Calthrop.

Dress Design—Talbot Hughes.

English Costume from the 14th through the 19th Century—Brooke and Laver.

The Armies of India—Major A. C. Lovett and Major G. F. Mac-Munn, D.S.O.

A History of the Uniforms of the British Army—Cecil C. P. Lawson—2 vols.

The British Tar in Fact and Fiction—Commander Charles N. Robinson, R.N.

Male and Female Costume—Beau Brummell.

The Art of Heraldry—Arthur Charles Fox-Davies.

Knight's History of England.

Illustrated Histories of the Scottish Regiments—Groves and Payne.

Greene's History of the English People—J. R. Greene, M.A.—4 vols.

Generals of the British Army—Francis Dodd.

Wellington and Waterloo—Major Arthur Griffiths.

Parliament, Past and Present—Arnold Wright and Philip Smith

Napoleon—J. T. Herbert Baily.

AMERICAN—*Canada in Khaki*—World War I.

Historic Dress in America—Elizabeth McClellan.

Two Centuries of Costume in America—Alice Morse Earle—2 vols.

Watson's Annals of Philadelphia—2 vols.

Wimples and Crisping Pins—Theodore Child.

Arms and Armor—The Metropolitan Museum of Art—1911.

Arms and Armor—The Metropolitan Museum of Art—1915.

Arms and Armor—The Metropolitan Museum of Art—1916.

Ancient Egypt—William Stevenson Smith, Ph.D.

The National Geographic Magazine—*Egypt*—October, 1941.

The National Geographic Magazine—*Persepolis*—October, 1933.

The National Geographic Magazine—*Greece*—March, 1944.

The National Geographic Magazine—*Ecuador*—December, 1941.

Century Cyclopedia of Names.

Man's Book—Fairchild Publications, 1910.

New York Sunday Times—Roto Sections—1914 to 1918.

Adventures of America, 1857 to 1900—John A. Kouwenhoven.

Heirlooms in Miniatures—Anne Hollingsworth Wharton.

Battles and Leaders of the Civil War—Edited by Robert Underwood Johnson.

History of the United States—J. A. Spencer, D.D.—3 vols.

Art in Ancient Rome—Eugénie Strong.

Photographic History of the Civil War—Francis Trevelyan Miller—10 vols.

Uniform Regulations United States Navy—1941.

Army Regulations—War Department—1941.

Pictorial Field-Book of the War of 1812—Benson J. Lossing.

History of the United States Army—William Addleman Ganoe.

Life of Joseph Brant—Thayendanegea—William L. Stone.

Godey's Lady's Book.

The Work of Hans Holbein—Brentano's.

The Boy's Book of Famous Regiments—H. A. Ogden.

America Learns to Play—Foster Rhea Dulles.

Memories of Manhattan—Charles T. Harris.

Social New York under the Georges—Esther Singleton.

A Dictionary of Men's Wear—William Henry Baker.

History of the City of New York—Martha J. Lamb.

Accessories of Dress—Lester and Oerke.

The Psychology of Dress—Frank Alvah Parsons, B.S.

Economics of Fashion—Paul H. Nystrom, Ph.D.

The Ways of Fashion—M. D. C. Crawford.

Early American Costume—Edward Warwick and Henry Pitz.

A History of the Ancient World—George Willis Botsford, Ph.D.

Ancient Times—James Henry Breasted, Ph.D., L.L.D.

The Encyclopedia Britannica.

The Fairchild Publications.

The Language of Fashion—Mary Brooks Picken

Historic Costume for the Stage—Lucy Barton

This is Fashion—Elizabeth Burris—Meyers

The Story of Marie-Antoinette—Anna L. Bicknell

Once Over Lightly—The Story of Man and His Hair—Charles de
    Zemler

Vogue

Harper's Bazaar

Apparel Arts

Gentry

Gentlemen's Quarterly

Life

Time

The New York Times

The New York Herald Tribune

The Wall Street Journal

Swiss—*Ciba Review*